INTERNET MARKETING FOR LESS THAN $500/YEAR

Other Titles of Interest From Maximum Press

INTERNET MARKETING FOR LESS THAN $500/YEAR

Second Edition

How to attract customers and clients online without spending a fortune

Marcia Yudkin

MAXIMUM PRESS
605 Silverthorn Road
Gulf Breeze, FL 32561
(850) 934-0819
www.maxpress.com

Publisher: Jim Hoskins

Manager of Finance/Administration: Joyce Reedy

Production Manager: ReNae Grant

Cover Designer: Lauren Smith Designs

Compositor: PageCrafters Inc.

Copyeditor: Andrew Potter

Proofreader: Jacquie Wallace

Indexer: Susan Olason

Printer: P.A. Hutchison

This publication is designed to provide accurate and authoritative information in regard to the subject matter covered. It is sold with the understanding that the publisher is not engaged in rendering professional services. If legal, accounting, medical, psychological, or any other expert assistance is required, the services of a competent professional person should be sought. ADAPTED FROM A DECLARATION OF PRINCIPLES OF A JOINT COMMITTEE OF THE AMERICAN BAR ASSOCIATION AND PUBLISHERS. Copyright 2002 by Marcia Yudkin.

Recognizing the importance of preserving what has been written, it is a policy of Maximum Press to have books of enduring value published in the United States printed on acid-free paper, and we exert our best efforts to that end.

Library of Congress Cataloging-in-Publication Data

Yudkin, Marcia.

  Internet marketing for less than $500/year : how to attract customers
and clients online without spending a fortune / Marcia Yudkin.— 2nd ed.

    p. cm.

Includes index.

  ISBN 1-885068-69-7

  1. Internet marketing. I. Title.

  HF5415.1265 .Y828 2001

  658.8'4—dc21

                        2001003601

for Chen, again

"What, you want to get on the Internet — *you??!*"

You see, Readers, if I can do it, so can you.

Advance Praise for *Internet Marketing for Less Than $500/Year*

"Here's a cool thing: I send out an e-mail message and within 24 hours, I've gotten more than $200,000 worth of conference revenue. Sound too good to be true? Well, 75% of my company's revenue comes in from the Internet, using the techniques that Marcia Yudkin writes about. This book is a must-read for anyone who has good products and wants to sell them online."

Jared M. Spool, president, User Interface Engineering

"Marcia Yudkin's unique description of 'cyber-schmoozing' can help you reach people online, yet spend next to nothing. If you want to succeed online without blowing your budget, read this book!"

Peter Kent, author, *Poor Richard's Web Site*

"From schmoozing to creating linkage campaigns to e-mail marketing, Marcia Yudkin covers it all. This is a must-read for every small business owner who wants to make it online."

Stephanie Gallagher, editor, *What's Working Online*, author, *Fabulous Bargains*

"The Internet isn't just for the rich. There are hundreds of ways to do marketing online and this book shows you the least expensive and most effective. If you have the time, but not the budget, you've come to the right book."

Jim Sterne, Internet marketing strategy consultant, author, *Customer Service on the Internet* and other books

"... skips the hype and instead uses real-life examples from regular people who are profiting online without breaking the bank."

Mary Westheimer, CEO, *BookZone.com*, the Net's largest and oldest publishing community

"Packed with real-life examples, Internet Marketing for Less Than $500/Year is a fantastic tutorial for small and home-based business owners. This practical resource will help any entrepreneur establish a strong Web presence without spending a fortune."

Kathryn Tyler, co-author, *Guerrilla Saving: Secrets for Keeping Profits In Your Home-Based Business*

"Marcia Yudkin reveals sophisticated and free schmoozing strategies to help you make thousands of dollars through the Net. Every progressive entrepreneur and professional can find gems in this book."
Marilyn Ross, author, *Shameless Marketing for Brazen Hussies*, and 11 other books

"Full of tips, guidance, examples and resources, it's more than just a business book, it's a must-read for any small-business entrepreneur who wants to grow."
Ramon Ray, publisher, *Small Business Technology*

"At last! A book that understands that online marketing is NOT putting up an expensive Web site. Marcia Yudkin explains the real tactics of online marketing and how even the smallest business can do it inexpensively and effectively."
Teresa Mears, editor and publisher, *Freelance Success* newsletter

"Forget expensive banner ads and their meager click-through rates—Marcia Yudkin's book gives you under-used secrets that really work."
Bob Bly, author, *Business to Business Direct Marketing*

"Discussion lists and other online forums are often overlooked by marketers. Yudkin does a wonderful job of showing small business owners how to use these valuable tools to increase credibility and acquire new business."
Donna Stryk, moderator, Online Ads Discussion List

"A thoroughly written guide with practical, motivating information on the structure of doing business as a savvy networker—online."
Susan RoAne, author, *The Secrets of Savvy Networking*

"If you've been intimidated by online marketing—or just procrastinating— Marcia Yudkin's book will get you going. She shows you that the digital marketplace is no more exotic than a Middle Eastern bazaar. This is easily the most user-friendly book on the subject."
Barbara J. Winter, author, *Making a Living Without a Job*

"Marcia Yudkin brings practicality, insight and logic to the world of online marketing. She has a good sense of what works, what doesn't, and what readers can do to generate business in the world of online communication."
Peter Miller, creator and host, Real Estate Center, America Online

"Marcia Yudkin towed me out of the breakdown lane of the information superhighway. Her chapter on responding to authors' appeals lured me toward the high-speed lanes."
Alan Weiss, Ph.D., author, *Million Dollar Consulting*

Acknowledgements

As usual, I would like to thank my literary agent, Diana Finch, and all my interviewees, who graciously shared their experiences and insights for this book.

Disclaimer

The purchase of computer software or hardware is an important and costly business decision. While the author and publisher of this book have made reasonable efforts to ensure the accuracy and timeliness of the information contained herein, the author and publisher assume no liability with respect to loss or damage caused or alleged to be caused by reliance on any information contained herein and disclaim any and all warranties, expressed or implied, as to the accuracy or reliability of said information.

This book is not intended to replace the manufacturer's product documentation or personnel in determining the specifications and capabilities of the products mentioned in this book. The manufacturer's product documentation should always be consulted, as the specifications and capabilities of computer hardware and software products are subject to frequent modification. The reader is solely responsible for the choice of computer hardware and software. All configurations and applications of computer hardware and software should be reviewed with the manufacturer's representatives prior to choosing or using any computer hardware and software.

Trademarks

The words contained in this text which are believed to be trademarked, service marked, or otherwise to hold proprietary rights have been designated as such by use of initial capitalization. No attempt has been made to designate as trademarked or service marked any personal computer words or terms in which proprietary rights might exist. Inclusion, exclusion, or definition of a word or term is not intended to affect, or to express judgment upon, the validity of legal status of any proprietary right which may be claimed for a specific word or term.

Table of Contents

Part 1: Internet Business Fundamentals

Chapter 1:
How Getting Wired Produces Business   3

Chapter 2:
Reputation Building Online   12

Chapter 3:
The Internet Won't Bite   26

Part II: Schmoozing for Profit

Part IV: Problems and Solutions

Chapter 14:
Online Style Tips   179

Chapter 15:
Inspiring Trust   193

Chapter 16:
International Considerations   201

Chapter 17:
E-mail Etiquette   213

Chapter 18:
Handling Hotheads   221

Introduction

The days when you could make a splash on the Net with a home-made Web site are long over. Don't even think about creating a Web presence for your company for less than $20,000. People who have been online for awhile can tell the difference in an instant between an amateur effort and one powered by a reasonable budget. And if you truly want to make money online, start thinking in the millions.

Although not an exact quote, this sentiment is one you'll find expressed everywhere in the business press, in most books on marketing online, and by most people who make their living providing Internet services. If you're reading this book, however, you suspect otherwise. Or you just don't have $20,000—not even $2,000, perhaps—and pray that I can reveal another way.

Indeed I shall. So relax and stay awhile.

I've been rounding up business online since before the first business card touting "Web designer" appeared. Banner ads didn't exist yet, either. Don't worry, I'm not a primordial geek. I have trouble changing the time on my car clock and the VCR when Daylight Savings Time comes around, and I hate installing and learning new software. In 1994, however, I fell in love with cyberspace as a communication medium, a vehicle for making contact with distant business people. I stressed that aspect of marketing online in an earlier version of this book published in 1995.

Then Big Business discovered the Internet. Billions of dollars poured into the World Wide Web, and Wall Street rewarded e-commerce sites that lost money hand over fist. The paradigm of the Web as a blinking, mouse-driven amalgamation of storefronts and TV-like ads took hold. When businesses heeded the imperative to spend big to create a Web presence, however, most owners of a spanking new Web site began to wail, "What's wrong? Why isn't anyone coming?"

Partly the no-traffic syndrome comes from ignorance of effective promotional strategies, and you'll find plenty of those here. But disappointment also resulted from a misleading picture of how the world-wide network of computers is actually revolutionizing buying and selling.

FAST FACTS

The Three Biggest Obstacles for Small Businesses Online

1. Lack of knowledge of how to take their business online.

2. Mistaken belief that without a huge budget, Internet marketing is fruitless.

3. Disappointment when the mere launch of a Web site produces no results.

Recently, iconoclasts and visionaries, in tracts such as *The Cluetrain Manifesto*, have spoken out against the corporate face of most big-money Web sites and argued that conversation in a human voice represents the essential nature and greatest potential of the Internet. Exactly what I've been advocating all along! To return to the $500 a year theme, it does not require much money to use human-scale techniques to attract business online. Keeping expenses that low, you can turn a rate of profit that mega-funded sites can't begin to touch.

If you have more energy and creativity to invest than money, this book demonstrates how to collect a whopping return on your investment. Unlike most books on Internet marketing, I do not start with the assumption that of course the fundamental foray of your business online must be a Web site. Simply using e-mail (now called "the killer application" by some Internet marketing experts) effectively, you can attract business online. Astute e-mail use plus a Web site makes a powerful combination. However, a Web site alone, not backed by big advertising dollars, will not get you much.

By trying out and mastering the non-Web techniques I teach here, either before or along with creating a Web site, you will soon find your $500 a year—or less—generating a net profit while businesses that spent big on design and consultants are complaining about their lack of traffic. Then increase your spending, add improvements, and fine-tune your customer service, and leave those sites far behind, covered with dust.

But $500 a Year—Really?

Let me now get specific about how you can spend just $500 a year in Internet marketing expenses and generate a profit. Practically everyone I've run across who has questions about how to take their business online already owns and uses a computer. Practically everyone already has a modem installed in their computer, too. So I don't include the price of a computer or modem in the $500.

Similarly, existing companies that want to accept credit cards online (not a requirement to succeed) usually already have a merchant credit card account, so I haven't included any of those costs in my calculation, or other typical start-up costs like stationery and business cards.

Some readers may decide to purchase Web-authoring software, which makes it easy to design and install a Web page, but some small-business Web hosting sites make this unnecessary. Buying a program like Microsoft FrontPage or Adobe PageMill would mean a $100 additional investment the first year. I didn't have to pay this because my husband owned a copy of FrontPage and finally mentioned it one day to me when I started talking about creating a Web page. Several small-business hosting services provide their clients with whatever they need to design and launch a basic Web site. So I consider software an optional expense.

With these assumptions, then, here's how I figure you can run a professional Internet marketing program for $500 a year or less:

- $239.40 ($19.95/month) Internet access for e-mail and Web browsing (there are innumerable providers at this price)

- $35.00 fee for your own domain (that is, a special address in the form of "yourcompany.com")

- $200.00 Web hosting (fee including prepayment discount from pair.com)

- Total: $474.00 a year

Strictly speaking you don't need your own domain to have a Web site, so the $35 is an optional, though recommended, expense. You can also go with a free e-mail service and do away with the $239.40. And you might find a totally free Web hosting deal, either because you agree to run a hosting service's ads or because you are providing unique visitor value to a larger site of which you're part.

Join the $500 a Year Club!

I know there are tens of thousands of canny business owners out there who are earning money through low-cost Internet marketing. So at a companion Web site exclusively for readers of this book, I've created a $500 a Year Club, which I invite you to join by visiting the Maximum Press Web site at *http://www.maxpress.com*. Follow the links to the *Internet Marketing for Less Than $500/Year* site. To enter, you'll be prompted to use the following username and password:

- User ID: *$5002e*

- Password: *extend*

FAST FACTS

Free Web Hosting for Small Businesses

The following firms enable you to build a Web site using their online resources for free, with no monthly hosting fees at all and no need to purchase software:

- Bigstep.com (free Web hosting using their site-building tools)

- Bizland.com (free Web hosting, free e-mail, free e-commerce setup without instant credit card processing)

- GoBizGo.com (special starter membership of two Web pages, free)

- HyperMart.com (free Web hosting using their site-building tools or popular Web authoring programs like FrontPage)

The companion Web site can help you in several ways:

- If you have created a profitable Web site for $500 a year or less, then tell us your story and we may post your Web address there, along with links to the services you use to keep your expenses down.

- If you don't even have a Web site and are turning a profit online using other methods, I invite you to submit your story for posting at this special password-protected site.

- If you haven't created your Web site yet, or want some money-saving tips from shrewd online operators, come visit and learn. You'll qualify as an Honorary Member of the $500 a Year Club.

When journalists call me wanting examples of professionals and business owners who have earned membership in the $500 a Year Club, I'll provide them with the password to this special site, so that you could then find yourself featured on television, in magazines or at online news sites. Don't forget—visit *http://www.maxpress.com* to submit your story or explore real-life examples of the principles in this book.

What Lies Ahead

Throughout this book, I concentrate on strategies—what should I do to make money online?—rather than technicalities—which buttons should I press when? Even so, I've tried to explain ideas and concepts that may puzzle Internet newcomers. There's also a glossary at the end of the book for your reference.

Part I provides an overview of how online activities produce business and what you need to understand about the Internet to use it effectively for business. In Part II I describe methods of online networking that yield opportunities and sales worldwide. What I call "online schmoozing" continues to produce results for those who understand its unwritten rules. Here, as in many other aspects of business, results depend on the details, so you'll find plenty of examples to learn from and follow.

In Part III I describe how to set out information online that attracts either worldwide or local inquiries—or both—making your business life more productive and profitable. If your business is conducive to direct online sales, I describe how to arrange those cost-effectively too, on a more down-to-earth order of magnitude than the massive "dot-com" sites. Even with respect to the World Wide Web, I concentrate on personal marketing, with which you can make a large impact on a small budget, and which affords you advantages over larger companies that dump megabucks into e-commerce. When you add schmoozing to a corporate presence on the Web, an individual or small company can use expertise and personality as a powerful, 24-hour magnet for attracting customers. Part IV covers additional pointers that help you communicate well online, understand the Net's international reach, and remain safe from troublemakers.

Although cyberspace has been growing and changing month by month, the strategies I recommend in this book will not go out of date. Too many people have become accustomed to—and benefited from—interacting electronically for online communication to dwindle and die with some new technology or cultural innovation. Rather, opportunities for meeting up with potential customers online will

FAST FACTS

How to Read This Book

1. Read once with highlighter pen in hand, marking passages that contain ideas you want to remember.

2. Jot down actions you want to take in a notebook or a special computer file.

3. Explore the additional resources available at the readers-only Web site, *http://www.maxpress.com*.

4. Report back on your successes and become a member of the $500 a Year Club at *http://www.maxpress.com*.

5. Reread at intervals for fresh ideas.

simply grow as more and more people use the modems, communications software, and browsers preinstalled in new computers that they buy. Of course, some will try out the equipment and fail to have any interest in continuing to use it, while others, media hype having ratcheted their expectations to the breaking point, will quit in disillusionment.

In my opinion, bandwagon arguments like "It's the now thing to do!"; "Listen to these numbers!"; and "Don't be left behind!" constitute poor reasons to go online. If you lack patience, consistency, even-temperedness and an average ability to express yourself in words, traditional methods of marketing may pay off better for you. Indeed, even if you surpass the results of those I've profiled in the book, I recommend keeping up with time-honored marketing methods such as targeted mailings, print advertisements, attending professional meetings, and contacting the media by phone. As I'll explain, these can dovetail beautifully with your online marketing efforts.

Originally I thought I would be able to include some criteria here to help you decide whether marketing online would suit your line of business. Yet the more my research progressed, the more assumptions of mine exploded. I believed a prerequisite for taking advantage of cybermessaging was being able to serve or sell to a national, if not international, clientele. But lawyers licensed to practice only in one state told me that hanging out online brought them referrals from lawyers in other parts of the country whose clients had matters that needed to be taken care of in their territory.

Similarly, it's hard to imagine a less likely candidate for Internet marketing than take-out food, with an area of service circumscribed by the reach of a 15-minute drive. Yet when Pizza Hut in Santa Cruz, California, set up a Web site, local college students found it easier or more fun to zip an order in on their computer than to drag themselves across the room to a phone. I also thought you'd need to accept credit cards if you seriously set out to round up customers online. But out of twenty-five professionals I surveyed who had found a significant amount of work online, only ten accepted credit cards. The rest managed fine with invoices, contracts, retainers, bank transfers, purchase orders, or sending merchandise C.O.D.

In the same way I think it's important to suspend any assumptions about demographic groups that you can and can't reach online. In 1995, when 80 to 90 percent of regular modem users were male, I wondered whether a product or service aimed at women had a chance of succeeding electronically. Take quilting, for example—a craft going back hundreds of years whose enthusiasts are mainly female. Would you imagine quilters gathered online in any great numbers? In fact, they did, and do! Sharon Orella, a quilter in Wilsonville, Oregon, got the idea of selling so-called "charm packages"—assortments of 5" by 5" or 6" by 6" pieces of fabric that quilters use in their creations. Through notices on discussion areas for crafters, she asked if there was a demand for this sort of product. Enough responded with their names and addresses to enable her to get her business off to a rousing start. Bill LaSalle, owner of a Lakeland, Florida, crafts supply business called Craft King, theorized, "A lot of people involved with computers also have an interest in working with their hands—or someone else in their family does."

Not only has the online gender gap closed in 2001, you don't need to be heavily "involved" with computers these days to link up via modem with people in your target market. I myself would say I'm not even moderately adept with computers. "I operate strictly on a need-to-know basis," I explain whenever someone gets incredulous at the holes in my knowledge (about once a week). I've kept technicalities to a minimum in this book. You'll find scores of links to explore at your leisure in the special Web site for readers of this book at *http://www.maxpress.com.*

In the chapters ahead you'll learn

- How to choose the most promising online areas for your business and begin creating relationships that lead to business.

- How to make the most of your online participation by understanding the medium of electronic messaging.

- How to convey your marketing message without violating online customs and expectations.

- Ways to set out bait online and, over time, reel in clients.

- The most effective inexpensive methods of driving traffic to your Web site.

- Ethical, legal, and practical dangers you must consider.

- Why and how to set out the welcome mat for international customers.

- How to prevent your online activities from taking over your life.

- Ways to meet the press online and get invaluable offline publicity.

But before we get to strategies you need some perspective.

PART 1

Internet Business Fundamentals

1

How Getting Wired Produces Business

My sole purpose in going online was to use it as a marketing channel," says Paulette Ensign, a professional organizer in Bedford Hills, New York. Within her first three days online, she had connected with a publisher in Milan who decided to release an Italian translation of an organizing-tips booklet of hers. Within her first four months online she landed spots on several radio shows, enticed people to sign up for a seminar in Seattle, sold numerous special reports, found two producers interested in an interactive CD-ROM of her work, and got herself interviewed for this book—all direct results of dialing up the Internet from her computer and exchanging messages from her home with people located anywhere from Anaheim to Zurich.

Some Success Stories

Ensign's coups are far from a fluke. Consider the successes of these other folks:

- Through online discussion forums, Stefan Kolle of Trust Services Benelux in Amsterdam, Holland, lined up writers, producers, and sources of financing for several feature films. Signing up projects like these normally happens only at film festivals and markets such as at Cannes, Berlin, or Las Vegas, Kolle notes.

- Mike Bayer, a Laguna Hills, California, public relations consultant who specializes in working with lawyers, estimates that he does 25 to 30 half-hour introductory consultations a year for attorneys who seek him out after reading informative files he has provided online. Typically two of those prospects become clients with billings totaling more than $10,000 each. Total investment beyond his online access fees: $0.

- Christian Martin, marketing director of Rail Pass Express, Inc. in Columbus, Ohio, generated $55,000 in sales of Eurail and Britrail passes from an investment of $400 by posting travel information on America Online and answering questions from Europe-bound travelers.

- Before she even had a Web site, Jan Melnik, who runs a home-based desktop publishing business in Durham, Connecticut, received one or two credit card orders in her electronic mailbox and two or three checks in the U.S. mail every day for her books or her newsletter by advising prospective desktop publishers on how to get started. The fan mail she received online helped convince her publisher to offer her a contract for another book.

- Shortly after setting up shop on the Web, Singapore-based Asia Online began receiving inquiries from surfers all over the world who had stumbled across its site. One company wanted to find an Asian source of plastic gloves, another to sell cement mixers in Asia, reports cofounder Hoo Shao Pin. Worldwide magazine advertising can't hold a candle to the Internet's cost-effectiveness.

In the twenty-first century, electronic communication is no longer just for computer whizzes. Anyone who can click a mouse and compose a business letter can negotiate the technology necessary for online connections. And while hooking up with other computer users can be a source of fun, it has also evolved into a serious business tool. Night and day, all over the world, smart, creative business owners and professionals are swapping information and sending messages that lead to lucrative deals of almost every imaginable sort. You don't need expensive equipment. Paulette Ensign got her results with what she called an "archaic" IBM system with two floppy drives and no hard disk, the kind you might pick up at a tag sale for $50.

The Benefits of Going Online

Whatever your line of business, whether you're starting up or established in your field, you need some method of attracting new people into the orbit of being your customers or clients. Going online offers numerous advantages over other methods of marketing.

- *It gives you an enormous geographic reach.* Soon after Laura Fenamore, president of the Golden Gate International Speakers Bureau in San Rafael, California, put up her Web site (see Figure 1.1), she received inquiries from all over the world that she would have been hard put to generate through any other promotional medium. "Right now I have four orders on my desk—from South Africa, Turkey, Austria, and the Netherlands—which all developed from hits at my Web site. It's rewarding to connect with so many distant corners of the world," she said.

- *It bypasses gatekeepers and puts you directly in touch with important decision-makers.* Lawyers, business owners, and executives who are active online look around and participate in exchanges on their own, not through a subordinate. A woman who was trying to launch a newsletter for dentists bemoaned how hard it was to get her telephone calls past the receptionist or her mail onto the dentist's desk. I advised her that her problem might be solved if she sought out places where dental professionals congregated online, like the Internet Dental Forum, at *http://idf.stat.com.*

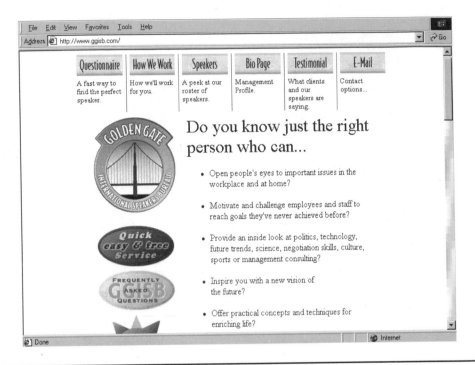

Figure 1.1. Golden Gate International Speakers Bureau home page.

- *It enables you to zero in on prospects with highly specific needs or interests.* Retired engineer and inventor Pat March's greatest expertise lies in mold making for plastic parts. "I'm good at cutting down the total number of parts and designing for low-cost production," he says. On the Hobbies Board of Prodigy, he offered suggestions to people designing and manufacturing model airplanes and has ended up being hired on a consulting basis by several.

- *It can save you gobs of money.* Barry Gainer, president of the Indian River Gift Fruit Company (see Figure 1.2), says that monthly expenses for his smallest retail store in Florida amount to more than $6,000, while his Web site costs him less than $2,000 a month to operate. The corresponding revenues are $365,000 a year for the retail store and $1.5 million for the

Figure 1.2. Indian River Gift Fruit Company home page.

online store. "Add it up," Gainer says. "How can you not justify it?"

- *Compared with face-to-face networking, it's time-effective.* Instead of having to get into the car at a specified time, drive, find a parking space, and maybe suffer inedible chicken and boring speeches, you can meet peers and prospects whenever you happen to have time and as often or seldom as you like. Online networks are available for your participation 24 hours a day. "When my kids are asleep and I don't have anything to do, I can go online and promote my book in parenting forums at 2 A.M.," says Bill Adler, author of *Tell Me a Fairy Tale* and other books.

- *Want quick results? Sales can occur in an eye blink.* While she was trying to get the shopping cart at her brand-new Web site to work properly, Suzanne Kelly wrote a few messages one evening mentioning her newsletter on retiring to Mexico at Mexico-related Web bulletin boards. The next morning she learned that overnight, six people had tried to order her newsletter. "I lost three sales because of the hassle of the shopping cart not working, but I made three sales by fax order!" she says, shocked that orders could come in so fast.

- *Because the millions of people who might come across any particular message each know hundreds of others, your reach goes far beyond the online universe.* Through participating in online forums on FoxPro and computer consulting, Christian Desbourse, a Belgian software developer, landed five months of work in Istanbul, Turkey, with a company that itself was not online. "Another consultant, who was working on site in Turkey at the time, put us together," he explains.

- *Its efficiency of communication is unparalleled.* Compare the zap, zap, zap of electronic messaging with the days it might take to end a desperate game of telephone tag or the weeks it takes for a series of letters to cross the oceans. Unlike faxes and telephone calls, you can send as detailed an electronic message as you need—even an entire software program—without inconveniencing yourself or your recipient. "You

---

FAST FACTS

Sample Return on Investment (ROI) Calculator

Christian Martin, Rail Pass Express, Inc.:

- $400 ➜ $55,000

- ROI: 136.50, or 13,650%

Barry Gainer's retail store (Indian River Gift Fruit Company):

- $72,000 ➜ $365,000

- ROI: 4.06, or 406%

Barry Gainer's online store (Indian River Gift Fruit Company):

- $24,000 ➜ $1,500,000

- ROI: 61.5, or 6,150%

You:

- $500 investment ➜ $20,000 in new business

- ROI: 39, or 3,900%

don't need to know when your correspondent is available," says Desbourse. "It's noisy receiving faxes in the middle of the night, but you can pick up e-mail any time that suits you." From his home in the woods 40 kilometers south of Brussels, it costs him only a local call to send a message to a client of his in Taiwan.

- *Compared with the telephone and in-person communication, you don't need to be quick-tongued.* "I like the fact that online I can take time to reflect on what I want to say," says Gary Ellenbogen, a computer consultant in Winooski, Vermont, who has been active online since 1993. "I always try to review my responses to people's questions before I send them off, and sometimes I'm astonished by what I see. I'll see that I didn't address the question after all, or said something that could be construed as condescending, or wrote something that now looks to me like gibberish. This way I get the chance to clarify my thinking."

- *You can quickly build a reputation.* It took just one month, says Jan Melnik, before desktop publishers-to-be began spreading the word for her that she was the expert to direct questions toward, and that her book, *How to Open and Operate a Home-based Secretarial Services Business*, was what someone wanting to get started in her business should buy. "Simply post pleasant, well-informed notes on your topic," says mystery writer Lary Crews, who quickly gathered fans first on Prodigy, then in America Online's Writer's Club, and finally on the Internet, "and pretty soon people are saying, Gee, Ostrich Man seems to know about Ostriches."

- *You can bypass prejudices that may come into play face to face.* "I'm a fat guy with a beard," says Lary Crews, "and when I meet people online there's no initial opinion about that that I have to fight against." Cathryn Conroy, a senior writer for *CompuServe Magazine*, told me an unfortunate variation on this theme: A man in the graphic arts business who had found a lot of clients online agreed to an interview with her. After his picture appeared in the magazine, however, several clients who had been working with him by phone and e-mail dropped him, sending his business into a tailspin. They had had no idea he was black.

- *It helps you find prospects you may not be able to reach through other media.* Literary agent Wendy Zhorne of Pasadena, California, was thrilled to have found in writers' discussion groups two highly qualified, prolific authors whom she took on as clients. "They don't read writers' magazines, go to writers' conferences, or know about the publishing industry directory *Literary Marketplace*, so I wouldn't otherwise have had access to them. They were impressed by the way I answered questions, so they came to me rather than asking around for some other agent," she says.

- *It keeps you in touch with the beliefs, assumptions, and preferences of your market.* Online, you can easily and quickly eavesdrop on thousands of conversations among members of the population you are attempting to serve. Helen McGrath, a literary agent in Oakland, California, says she has as many clients as she can handle. Nevertheless, she too finds writers' discussion groups useful because "it tells me how writers feel about agents—what drives them crazy, how they think, what misconceptions they have, what they really do and don't understand about the business."

- *If you travel a lot, you can stay plugged in with that line of communication.* When Nicholas Negroponte, Director of the Media Lab at MIT, flies to distant parts of the globe, he keeps up with his electronic correspondence without anyone needing to know he's left Massachusetts. "People are sending messages to me, not Tokyo," he says, adding that unstandardized plugs throughout the world—twenty different types in Europe alone—do present a challenge.

- *You can make overnight changes in your offerings.* New prices? No problem. Instead of having to toss away or add stickers to printed catalogs or brochures, online you can adjust prices as soon as you learn of changes. My Marketing Minute e-mail newsletter, described in Part III, enables me to concoct and distribute special offers any week my work flow slows down, and to run more long-range offers when I'm too busy for immediate new clients. This helps me avoid Feast-or-Famine syndrome.

Those are some of the many advantages of marketing online. Next we turn to how the process produces business results.

FAST FACTS

Advantages of Marketing Online

- Global reach
- Direct contact with decision makers
- Ease of reaching niche markets
- Big dollar savings
- Time savings
- Indirect reach to offline customers/clients
- Fast, efficient communication
- Opportunity for considered communication
- Speedy results
- Bypassing face-to-face prejudices
- Reach to some people not reachable otherwise
- Continual access to the pulse of your market
- Continuity of communication while traveling

2

Reputation Building Online

Let's say you restore pianos—you take an upright or a grand that's been knocked around and neglected and make it look and sound more wonderful than the day it first stood in the showroom. Your fundamental, never-ending challenge, as for anyone who offers a service or product, is to persuade the people with the means and motivation to buy to contact you to trade money for your goods or skills. Those who own damaged or neglected pianos or want to buy one you've refurbished need to know that you exist and need to have a positive impression of you and your competence. Much of your business comes through referrals from people you've helped in the past, but you see a lull coming up in your schedule and wonder if there's an inexpensive way you can rustle up more customers.

Print advertising, of course, is an option but requires a lot of money and a few months' lead time for the publications most likely to reach the piano owners who need you. Reaching out to the media for publicity might work, but you'd have to think of a creative angle to earn TV or newspaper coverage in the near future. Showing up at some professional and networking groups and handing out business cards might yield some leads, but the odds don't seem that promising. You decide to look into direct mail, since it allows you to target a fairly precise audience on your own schedule, and you get a quote from a local direct-mail specialist. You wonder if you should spring for a Web page. Then, almost by accident, you discover a marvelous computer-assisted marketing procedure.

Magnetic Messages in Computer Space

Your teen-aged son knows his way around the Internet, and tells you about a discussion group called rec.music.makers.piano, where people interested in pianos and piano music hang out. But today, shocked by the direct-mail quote you received, you sign on to the Net through his modem, make your way to the online group called misc.business.marketing.moderated and post this electronic message:

> *To: All*
> *From: Dianne Weinman*
> *Re: Direct Mail Costs?*
>
> *Can somebody tell me if $3900 is totally outrageous for the following or not: a mailing to 1700 music directors at American private schools and colleges? Supposedly that breaks down to $1200 for copywriting and design, $150 for list rental, $650 for printing of envelopes, so-called "lift letters," and inserts, $550 for postage, $470 for mailing house fees, and $880 for "project management," whatever that is.*
>
> *I'm in Indianapolis, by the way, and the mailing is about our reconditioned and restored pianos.*

An hour and a half later, in Ojai, California, Jerry Naylor is at his computer, modem on, scanning the headlines of new messages in business discussion groups. Noticing "Direct Mail Costs?" he reads the whole message and quickly enters the necessary command to reply publicly:

> *To: Dianne Weinman*
> *From: J. Naylor, Creative Marketing Consultants, Inc.*
> *Re: Direct Mail Costs?*

Dianne, the quote you got is not out of line for top-notch talent to create a traditional direct-mail package. But our clients have gotten excellent results with simpler, cheaper, and more eye-catching postcards. A mailing of 1700 post-cards done by us from start to finish would cost you some-thing like $1425, including list rental. Which option is better for you has to do with whether you're looking for immediate orders or, as I suspect, just promising leads. Let me know if you'd like more information. See my e-mail address above or call me at 555-505-5050.—Jerry

Because you prefer dealing with someone local, you use this mes-sage to bargain your direct-mail consultant to a more palatable price—not exactly what Jerry had in mind. Nevertheless, both you and Jerry round up new customers because of this exchange. Two days later, Mr. Ji Ling Su of Singapore comes upon your post and responds by private E-mail:

To: Dianne Weinman
From: JLS/Republic of Singapore
Re: Direct Mail Costs?

Ms. Weinman: Indianapolis is not far from the University of Purdue, is it not? If my geography is correct, would you kindly e-mail me your address, telephone, and fax number. My niece attends graduate school there and says she is very unhappy without a piano.

(Mr.) Ji Ling Su, President, JLS, Ltd.

Jerry is equally fortunate. A real estate lawyer in Hartford, Con-necticut, reads his response to Dianne and sends a public message back that she likes the idea of the postcards, and don't they take much less time to get out into the mail as well? A few more exchanges and phone calls later, the lawyer is sending a deposit check to Jerry by Express Mail to design, prepare, and send an urgent 20,000-piece mailing.

And the dance of needs and possibilities does not end there. A week later, Dianne posts a comment in response to someone else's question in the Music Roundtable and receives this private reply:

To: Dianne Weinman
From: Hank Glontlewitz
Re: business deal?

Dianne: Are you the lady who reconditions pianos? I do the
same for brass and woodwind instruments, and have a lot
of connections in elementary and junior high schools. If
you're interested in talking about how we might work
together, give me a call at 208-555-7779. (That's Idaho
Falls, Mountain Time.)

Two months later, the lawyer whom Jerry helped spots his name
in the newsgroup and decides to thank him publicly for his help,
telling him about her very gratifying 5.5 percent response. Jerry picks
up three new prospects—who do not personally know the lawyer—
as a result of her thoughtful gesture. He also receives an e-mail from
someone putting together a seminar series on cost-cutting marketing
for small businesses.

You can't *count* on these sorts of results, but they occur plenty
often, especially to those who use the techniques in this book and
who hold the attitudes described in Chapter 22. Surprisingly, though,
this electronic sashay right and allemande left among business people
works only for individuals, not for corporate entities. There lies a key
advantage for hands-on business owners and professionals in going
online to find and attract business. When an organization or company tries to do what Dianne and Jerry did, it's like an elephant trying to fit into ballet slippers.

The Personal Advantage

Soon after I first signed on to Prodigy, the online service, a response
to one of my messages in a discussion group appeared from someone
named "Home Office Computing." Although I understood it came
from some representative of the magazine by that title, I felt affronted
by not knowing who I was dealing with. My irritation grew as I received more messages from this masked entity, until I stated that I
refused to communicate any longer with someone who wouldn't identify himself or herself. This corporate entity, I eventually learned, was

both a "him" and a "her"—contributing editor Angela Gunn and researcher Charles Pappas took turns answering questions on behalf of *Home Office Computing* magazine.

"According to the terms of the contract between Prodigy and *Home Office Computing*, we had to sign off exactly as 'Home Office Computing/Prodigy Service/Home Business Expert' on three lines," Gunn recalls. "Instead of generating discussions, however, we tended to end them. And we weren't gathering any sort of a following. Finally, after we negotiated an agreement that allowed Charles and me to use our names, a lot of people who had never mentioned their discomfort with the previous arrangement commented positively on the change."

As I'd sensed almost immediately, online discussions are an intrinsically personal medium. In this they resemble letters, telephone communication, and in-person meetings. That is, when we receive an unsigned letter, or one signed only with a company name like "National Bank," we feel vaguely affronted. When we receive a phone call from a person who refuses to provide a name, we tend to feel vulnerable, angry, or frightened. If we were trying to schmooze at a professional conference with a person whose name tag read just, "Creative Marketing Consultants, Inc." and who claimed his name was irrelevant, we'd probably walk away. We're used to person-to-person communication in these situations, so being confronted with a faceless or nameless corporate presence anywhere violates our expectations in a minor to major way.

Advertising, of course, is a totally different story—we know it's never a person-to-person vehicle. Significantly, Angela Gunn points out that the only online vehicle conducive to an anonymous voice is the World Wide Web, which most resembles traditional advertising. "The bulletin board analogy is unfortunate," says Gunn. "You always need to establish that there's a human being behind a posting who's aware that other human beings will read it." Wherever dialogue gets going online, communication is always between Jerry Naylor of Creative Marketing Consultants, Inc. and Dianne Weinman of Weinman Pianos, not between Creative Marketing Consultants, Inc. and Weinman Pianos, or between Jerry Naylor and Weinman Pianos.

Even where you put yourself forward with a company identity, as when your online handle reads "DavesDeals@aol.com," people assume that whenever they interact with "DavesDeals" they are interacting with the same person, not sometimes Jerry and sometimes Jim and once in a while Alexandra. Sharing one corporate I.D. as "Home Business Expert" led Gunn and Pappas to bizarre situations, as where Pappas posted a reply to a question that Gunn didn't believe was completely accurate. "I'd have to write something like, I'm sorry, folks, I misspoke fifteen minutes ago...," says Gunn.

These contortions and the messy maneuvers necessary when someone asked a followup question that was clearly intended for just one or the other of them show why most kinds of marketing I'm focusing on in this book can't be neatly delegated or handled by a group. For that very reason, however, they offer exceptional potential for solo practitioners and those piloting the progress of a small company. Even on the Web, you can create a competitive advantage by personalizing a site and the communications around the site.

With online marketing, your personal identity becomes the instrument for building business relationships. Who you are—your skills, experience, expertise, communication ability—along with your personality traits such as generosity, patience, tolerance, and wit, and moral qualities such as integrity—all take on as much relevance as the specific services and products you have to offer prospects. Factors like your personal hygiene, accent, body language, and speaking and listening rhythms have no influence online, but everything that can come through in words does have an impact, as a way of building up a picture of who you are, what you stand for, and the value embodied in your products and services. Although the channel of information appears limited online, everything that does come through attaches to your name and influences whether or not people pursue business with you.

In part the prominence of the whole human impression accounts for this pre-Web complaint of a newsletter publisher. "No one out there with a paid staff of more than five is making money in electronic marketing," he wrote in 1994. "It doesn't 'scale upward'. That is, you should be able to make $100 a day, then double your effort or hire a couple of people and then make $200 a day and then move to $800 a day. You quickly hit a point of diminishing returns—like with your first employee. Online marketing is greatly oversold."

In my view, it's not that online marketing doesn't "scale upward," it's that it doesn't transfer from boss to employee or from one staff

FAST FACTS

What's Personal about Online Communication?

- Your personality comes across in every e-mail or publicly posted message.

- Just by having an e-mail address you imply your availability for communication.

- E-mail and message board postings connect individuals, not companies.

- Your personal qualities attract or repel business opportunities.

- Online relationships aren't automatically transferrable to others.

- Multiple people can't easily share an online identity.

- The "human touch" and responsiveness make a difference to online customers.

member to another at all. If you, Dianne, get to know Jerry Naylor, Ji Ling Su, and others online, so that they become willing to recommend you to friends who need a piano fixed up, you can't hand things over to your son George and expect him to carry on the marketing where you left off. All the momentum you built up gets lost, because it attaches to you, not to Weinman Pianos.

It's easy to miss the significance of this point because a trend in the business world called "relationship marketing" involves a very different vision of customer–company relationships. According to this perspective, if FedEx keeps track of the fact that I prefer packages delivered on the side porch and does so on future visits without being asked, the company has cemented a relationship with me. Well, perhaps I would indeed continue to choose them as my overnight courier, but that's good customer relations, not a relationship. On the other hand, I once had a relationship with a particular FedEx driver who knew I was a writer and whom I occasionally waved to a halt if I saw him on his route and had a question. I didn't know his name, but I knew his smile and his friendly, slightly pushy manner. Person to person, we knew each other at some level. When I moved, though, FedEx lost the benefit of our cordial feelings for one another.

Some observers talk as if certain leading Internet companies, such as Amazon.com, develop relationships with customers by personalizing customer–company interactions. For instance, when I revisit Amazon.com, the site greets me by name, and when I place a second or subsequent order it remembers my credit card number (see Figure 2.1). These capabilities give me warm, fuzzy feelings toward the company and make the ordering process faster and more enjoyable, but they don't compare to getting my e-mail questions answered by a real person, who signs the message. The latter happens with my Internet service provider, and when the response truly answers my question, I feel grateful to the person. Were I to correspond with the answerer regularly, it would compare with the FedEx driver, and most of the good will generated by the exchanges would evaporate when my correspondent switched jobs.

In contrast, given the intrinsically personal nature of online communication, it's tailor-made for situations where you *are* your business. There the distinction between your behavior toward customers and prospects and marketing disappears. If I come to respect your knowledge, form cordial feelings toward you, and figure that we know

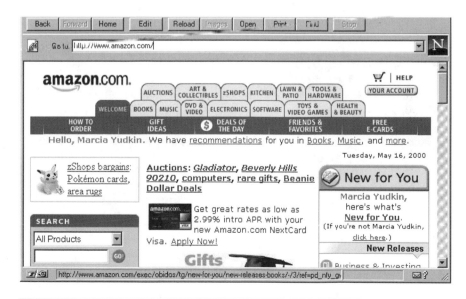

Figure 2.1. Amazon.com's home page, personalized for me.

each other, we have a relationship that inevitably feeds directly into your business. This can occur through static Web postings when it's clear the content was personally generated as well as through discussions. Time and again, well-placed business owners have contacted me with offers of work after having read my bylined material online, which I don't believe would have happened had they visited a run-of-the-mill company Web site.

Often, simply showing up in a way that announces that you're open to contact encourages the start of a conversation that leads to a purchase or a deal. "Ironically, with electronic networks we're reverting to the pattern of preindustrial times, when you bought shoes from the guy around the corner," says Wally Bock, publisher of the newsletter "Cyberpower Alert!" "There's a lot of sharing on the side of the seller before the sale. For instance, on the Internet people can get information about my newsletter from the autoresponder that robotically sends back information to them. Yet most of those who end up buying ask me a question by e-mail to which I respond, and then they order. The questions are legitimate, but they're also a way of 'sniffing me out' and starting a relationship. It wasn't obvious to me when I started that the way to tell a good subscriber was that they ask me questions."

FAST FACTS

A Personal Touch for a Company

If you belong to a small company or professional firm, here are some ways to convey that you're real people:

- Use personal names instead of departments or functions for contact addresses (ron@ourcompany.com instead of sales@ourcompany.com).

- Employ a friendly, conversational tone instead of "companyspeak" or promotional hype.

- Sign customer correspondence with full names and direct phone numbers rather than the company identity and main number.

According to Angela Gunn, this dynamic did not play out successfully with *Home Office Computing's* presence on Prodigy. "Conversation" with an organization does not have the effect that it does with an individual. "When a large organization tries to become your friend it often comes across as phony or Big Brother-ish," says new business development consultant Jennifer Starr. "But where a person is concerned, if you feel you've gotten to know the person, you're more likely to buy."

Remember too that most of the online conversations we've been considering occur in public, readable by onlookers. If you're trying to build a reputation, no medium can match the power, speed, and accessibility of online participation. Here's how and why.

Visibility + Competence + Word of Mouth = Reputation

Advertisers and marketers of all sorts have proven that the sheer number of times someone runs across your name or the name of your product has an enormous impact on their likelihood of doing business with you. When your name turns up on someone's desk or computer screen once, that is rarely enough to make that person remember you. But appear before the right audience at least seven times within 18 months, says Jeffrey Lant, author of *The Unabashed Self-promoter's Guide*, and you'll find yourself on the other side of the familiarity barrier.

Richard Ott, author of *Creating Demand*, adds that because of the familiarity factor, a greater number of small impressions adds up to a larger effect than a smaller number of bigger impressions. In other words, five one-paragraph notes have a greater impact than one five-paragraph note, just as your material on five unrelated Web sites will probably produce more responses than an equivalent quantity of content on just one. Wally Bock confirms this with his observation that when he participates frequently in an online discussion group, the number of newsletter inquiries traceable to any one appearance there goes up. In Chapter 4 I discuss choosing the right places to put out your name online, but here the important point is a rider to Woody Allen's remark that "Eighty percent of success is showing up." Online, don't show up once—do so again and again and again and again and again and again and again.

Frequency is only one factor in business visibility. The value of the medium in which your name appears—the *Boston Globe* versus your high school reunion booklet—has an influence, as does the reach of the medium—the number and characteristics of the people exposed to the message. Being quoted in the *Boston Globe* might appear to have greater value than posting your own online message in a "Creative Management" discussion group, but there's a trade off. With the newspaper article you receive a valuable implicit endorsement from having been chosen to be quoted. However, the press filters your message for its own agenda and may not present your comments in the context that you would.

When you go online, you not only have complete control over your own content, its timing, and its placement, you'll find yourself in an environment that encourages responses. I've had photo features about my work in the Sunday *Boston Globe* three times and know indirectly that they've helped my local credibility and reputation, but few readers of that medium trouble to track down my phone number and give me a call—much fewer than I hear from online. News reports online with a live link to the Web site of the individual or company written about produce exponentially more results than the same article in print. Clicking is an almost effortless way to satisfy curiosity. In addition, while the Sunday *Boston Globe* may have more readers than a "Solo Professionals" discussion group on the Internet, the latter contains exactly the people I wish to be visible *to*.

Getting your name out often to the right people builds name recognition, but for that to bolster your *reputation*, your name needs to be linked to some evidence of your competence. The newspaper article can satisfy that requirement by citing your position and accomplishments and quoting your comments. Online it's awkward for Dianne, Jerry, or you to go into as much horn-tooting detail as an article about you might, but you have a powerful ongoing opportunity to demonstrate your competence. Instead of telling about your competence, you can show it, by giving precise, up-to-date answers to others' questions, offering hard-to-find resources, and making nonobvious distinctions—rather than always being corrected by folks who appear to know better. "It's deadly to give out bogus information," says Christian Martin, who answers questions online about travel to Britain for Rail Pass Express, Inc. "If you say, 'Do such-and-such in London', and that's inaccurate, someone will turn up who's from London and set you straight. On the Internet, someone will *always* one-up you if they can."

Dan Kohane, a trial lawyer in Buffalo, New York, who was active in CompuServe's Lawsig forum for years, says, "If you're well-spoken and informed on your subject, people start to call on you for advice in that area. If there's an insurance question in the forum, for instance, people say, 'Ask Kohane, he's the insurance guru'." That third-party word of mouth is the final ingredient that cements a reputation. Ideally word of mouth builds on both visibility and competence. "If other people your prospect knows say they know you, or even better, say good things about you, she's more likely to buy from you," Jennifer Starr says.

Indeed, a study by the Canadian Congress of Advertising showed that two thirds of the adults surveyed relied for product information on "talking to friends/family/colleagues." Far below that was newspaper advertising, key information for just 44 percent, trailed by flyers, magazine ads, TV commercials, radio spots, and direct mail. In Chapter 5 I talk about online word of mouth as the "fan club" phenomenon, explaining how it's possible to gather a group of champions in as little time as one month.

If you want to play the fame game, keep in mind that success takes on momentum over time, and that there may be a threshold before which it looks like nothing is working. That's the worst time to give up! As Richmond, Virginia, marketer Richard Ott explains it, "The cumulative weight of a number of persuasive impressions can cause the brain to kick into decision-making mode. Like the drops of water that accumulate in a precariously balanced bucket, one more drop and the entire bucket tips over. The latest direct mail campaign, the latest billboard campaign (or the latest electronic message) may very well be the drop of water that causes the entire bucket to tip. You've kicked many people into decision-making mode at once, and your sales gush forth. This happens quite often to marketers that maintain a healthy dose of marketing activity on a regular basis. They have enough people with full buckets out there who only need one more drop to kick into decision-making mode."

Another reason to persist is that your prospects have their own timeline of need and their own decision-making process that necessarily remain a mystery to you. Susan RoAne (see Figure 2.2), a professional speaker and author of *The Secrets of Savvy Networking* and *How to Work a Room*, says she has come to believe in a "Go

Figure 2.2. Susan RoAne's home page.

Know!" theory of marketing: "I can be doing everything right with no effect, and then one day my Aunt Yetta is standing next to someone somewhere who just happens to…, which leads to…."

For instance, RoAne was quoted in *Newsweek* and the *New York Times* in connection with her menopause support group, the Red Hot Mamas, which, she says, triggered bookings for speeches that her book-related publicity had not yielded. Another time a meeting planner who booked her mentioned that it was the smile in her picture by which he remembered her two years after she got in touch. The unpredictability doesn't mean you throw up your hands, only that you pursue every means of staying memorable and visible. "Be patient—eventually they'll call and say, 'We read your book, we read about you in the *Wall Street Journal*, you sent us an article, and we just saw you online'."

As RoAne suggests, whatever you do online meshes with other marketing methods such as playing golf with prospects, publishing articles, placing ads, appearing on radio programs, and presenting your product at trade shows. With all that overlap, it might be hard to pin down how much effect your online activity had in that mix. The results might show up offline, so to speak, because word of mouth can migrate anywhere. Skip tracer Gerry Gollwitzer of Menomonee Falls, Wisconsin, received a call from a fellow in Las Vegas who wanted help finding his buddies from the Vietnam War. "I found 12 out of 14 people for him," says Gollwitzer, "and then I learned that he'd gotten my name and number from someone who saw it online. He himself didn't even own a computer."

Just a few people mentioned in this book market *only* online. But almost everyone finds their online efforts better than painless—downright enjoyable. You can't overlook the agreeability factor when you're in a position where your personal efforts make or break your firm. And online worlds are exceptionally focused. Let's turn now to a fear-free tour of the Internet.

FAST FACTS

The Visibility Formula

Frequency + Prestige of Venue = Positive Name Recognition

3

The Internet Won't Bite

When my older sister learned to drive, she had to master the bone-jarring difficulty of changing gears by working a clutch. Four years later, when I got my learner's permit, the family cars had automatic transmission. I never came face to face with a clutch or a choke until I later graduated to Volkswagens and Volvos. The technical concepts my father drilled into me were few: the safe braking distance to the car ahead, the need to check the oil level and tire pressure once in a while, and the imperative to pull over *immediately* if the oil light went on. Once I knew how to merge, parallel park, and avoid spinning out of control on snowy New England roads, I could concentrate on the main purpose of driving: going places. No orientation was necessary on where to go.

The computer world has now evolved to the point where you can go online with the equivalent of automatic transmission software. You still need a little pertinent know-how, like what to do when you crank the starter, so to speak, and the engine doesn't roar on, so I'll give a few pointers to help you solve problems getting connected. But mostly you business folks need an orientation to the kinds of destinations available to you online and their advantages and disadvantages when it comes to rounding up customers. Unlike the earth geography we know way before we climb into the driver's seat, few of us have the opportunity to cruise around cyberspace as passengers. What's out there, then? Hang on for a quick tour of options, just as soon as I brief you on the essential technical stuff.

The Mysterious Modem

If you were to open your computer and peer inside, your modem wouldn't look much different from the rest of its innards: colored knobs, beads, and boxes soldered onto a board printed with mazelike numbers and lines. A modem enables your computer to communicate with distant computers through ordinary telephone lines. It does this through two steps of translation: Since computer data exists in digital form and telephone transmission occurs in analog sound waves, a modem makes computer-to-computer exchange possible by changing digital signals into analog signals and then back again. (A "digital" format portrays information as a collection of separate, either-or 0s and 1s, while "analog" data exists in a continuous flow of qualitative information.) "Modem," in fact, stands for "*mo*dulator–*dem*odulator," where "modulate" means the digital-to-analog part of the transmission and "demodulate" means the analog-to-digital transformation.

FAST FACTS

Modem Upgrades

Interested in and able to afford higher-speed or from-anywhere Internet access? These three sites provide information on, respectively, high-speed modems, cable modems and wireless modems:

- Everything DSL

  http://www.everythingdsl.com/

- Cable Modem Information Center

  http://www.cabledatacomnews.com/cmic

- The Wireless Modem Product Directory

  http://hydra.carleton.ca/info/wlan.html

Got that? If not, don't worry. You really only need to know that a modem doesn't accomplish this double conversion on its own. It needs the aid of communications software, which tells the modem to do things in a certain order, like wait for a dial tone, put the speaker on, dial a number in tone or pulse mode, say "Hello, how do you work?" in &#@*ese to the computer on the other end, and so on. Whether your communications software is proprietary (specific to a service provider) or generic (allowing you to dial up anyone in modem-land), usually these modem commands are the gremlins in getting connected online. You may never come into contact with them directly, but if you continually fail to connect properly with your destination, they may be the cause. Don't assume that you have to somehow decipher the technical manual that came with your modem in order to solve the problem. Call the technical support department of your service provider and describe the symptoms, and they will usually cheerfully and patiently talk you through to a solution.

Besides encouraging you to feel free to ask for help, I'd like to add just a few technical tips:

- Invest in a good surge protector to guard your computer and modem against lightning and electrical power fluctuations.

- Either put your modem on a telephone line without call waiting or find out from your service provider how to automatically turn off call waiting signals whenever you go online.

- When buying a new modem, get the fastest you can afford. It will save you money and frustration as you cruise around online. So-called cable modems shorten the wait time on the World Wide Web better than almost any modem for a phone line.

What Is the Internet, Anyway?

Trying to define the Internet reminds me of the ancient story of the blind men groping at the elephant and taking one part for the whole. One person says, "The Internet is a place where you can find out practically anything you want to know and present your wares to millions of people around the world," and we'll have to agree. Another person says, "The Internet is the grand collection of networked computers throughout the world," and she is pretty accurate too. Someone else says, "The Internet is a collection of miscellaneous tools for accessing and exchanging information worldwide," and he is also right. Unlike the elephant, however, which was conceived and born *as* an elephant, the Internet has changed purposes and form as it has grown. So a quick historical overview provides helpful perspective.

In the late 1960s, the U.S. Department of Defense decided to develop a way to link up military computers so that if a nuclear attack knocked out a few sites or connections, the others would still be able to communicate with each other. ARPAnet, the resulting decentralized governmental network of networks, spawned other networks for nonmilitary and research purposes that eventually merged and spread into an international amalgam of networks using the same communication protocols. Since the U.S. government had directly or indirectly created and maintained the structure for research and defense purposes, commercial traffic was prohibited on the Internet until 1991, when a consortium of independent Internet access providers established new network backbones that bypassed those banning for-profit messages.

The anticommercial traditions of certain sectors of the Internet stem from the days when only academics, government employees, and corporate researchers were allowed to use the network. Right now, however, no one owns or controls the Internet, although it reaches practically every country in the world, plus Antarctica. It works through cooperation on a global scale and evolves through the widespread adoption of individual and group innovations. For example, Usenet, an electronic system for publicly exchanging ideas that predates the Web, was developed for work purposes by a group of Unix programmers, but once the system was up and running, they and others soon expanded it to cover other interests such as computer games, Eastern religions, and fine wines.

Similarly, a convenient nested-menu-based method of archiving and retrieving files called Gopher originated at the University of Minnesota, where it was named after the school mascot, and propagated quickly throughout the world. Not long afterward, a high-energy physicist proposed a system for even easier worldwide access to information that materialized in the browsing tools called Mosaic and Cello in 1993, for a new multimedia, linked-by-a-click sector of the Internet called the World Wide Web, now the most popular and fastest growing part of cyberspace. No one knows what exciting new tools are being conceived and constructed as you read!

Who else is out there on the Internet? Unfortunately, no one has a precise count of exactly how many million people use the Internet, who they are, or how much disposable income they have. According to NUA Internet Surveys (see Figure 3.1), in March 2000, 304.36 million people worldwide were using the Internet, with more than half of those outside the United States and Canada. However, estimates differ.

Just as you can't receive phone calls without an account with a phone company, to connect to the Internet you need an account with an Internet service provider. This account furnishes you with a private e-mail address that resembles *you@domain.com*. To keep your costs under control, you'll choose your Internet service provider according

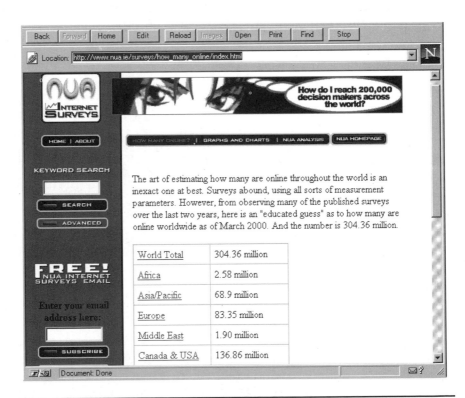

Figure 3.1. Find current Internet demographics at NUA Internet Surveys.

to what's available through a local phone call. Then, once you're equipped with a special piece of software called a browser (Netscape and Internet Explorer are the two most common), you can surf the fun and business offerings of the Web. Addresses of Web sites take the form *http://www.somedomain.com* or just *www.somedomain.com*.

If you'd like to construct your own Web site, you may need either design help (as with a brochure) or Web design software as well as a place to park the site. Unless you're working on a large scale with a big budget, you rent space for your site on a computer server owned by a Web hosting company. Sometimes your Web hosting company and Internet service provider are one and the same, but not necessarily, since once you're on the global network through your local Internet access provider, every computer in the world connected to the Net becomes almost equally close.

Put another way, the Internet includes a vast collection of resources, functions, and features that your service provider has not itself created or collected, including

- **E-mail:** Unlimited one-to-one electronic communication with anyone else connected to the Internet, as well as participation

FAST FACTS

Domain Options

Lots of people ask me how I got an address ending in *yudkin.com*. It's simple. First I checked its availability at *http://www.internic.net/whois.html*. Then I registered it through my Internet service provider. Currently Network Solutions charges $35/year to reserve exclusive use of ("register") your own domain. Some domain registrars charge less, such as Nameboy for only $19/year. You may be able to avoid that expense by using a subdirectory of your Web hosting service, like this: *www.bigspring.com/yourname*. Or, you may get free use of a subdomain, looking like this: *www.yourname.bigspring.com*.

However, the consensus of serious users of the Internet for business is that it's hard to take seriously a business that won't spring for the small annual fee for its own domain. It's a tiny price to pay for credibility.

in any of tens of thousands of professional or hobby-oriented discussion groups whose posts arrive by e-mail.

- **Usenet**: A decentralized network of more than 50,000 discussion groups ("newsgroups"), some moderated, with a tilt in topics toward computers, recreation, and culture.

- **World Wide Web**: An easy-to-navigate, multimedia system of linked pages sponsored by companies, organizations, and individuals.

- **Telnet**: A way to link up with and use the capabilities of a remote computer by typing on your own.

These (and a few others) are the features referred to collectively under the rubric of "the Internet." The scale is numbingly huge, and the scope of interests represented ranges from aquarium building to forensic economics to sadomasochism to mine clearing. Once you get linked up, you connect with the Internet community at large, not necessarily with fellow patrons of your service provider.

Since I got my start online with the commercial online services and still feel a fondness for them, let me add a note here about them. These services, with members in the millions, offer news and weather, business, consumer, and reference information, shopping, and chat and discussion areas—as well as Internet access—to members who pay a monthly fee. The world's two largest online services, now owned by the same company, are CompuServe and America Online. Prodigy and the Microsoft Network trail far behind in members. Until recently, the online services had the highest-quality discussion groups anywhere in cyberspace. As one fellow member of CompuServe's Journalism Forum once said about the comparison between the level of professional discourse there and in Internet newsgroups, "Newsgroups? Read them and weep!"

However, many specialized Web-based forums—structured as bulletin boards—offer sophisticated topical exchanges of ideas. Sometimes they're limited to members, through subscriptions. Other times they attract mostly devotees just by virtue of being hosted at a particular specialty site. E-mail discussion lists also enable you to trade insights and opinions with movers and shakers in the business world or enthusiastic amateurs, depending on your marketing goals.

Go-See vs. Build vs. Participation Options

If someone were to take you on a Grand Tour of the Internet, you wouldn't really see or experience its potential to generate business. Unlike, say, a megaplex movie theater with a parking lot crammed beyond capacity and crowds of people milling about before and after seeing the latest hits, on the Web you can't usually tell whether a site is popular beyond the creator's wildest dreams or hardly ever visited. "Surfing" is a good way to get ideas for promoting your business, to locate vendors and possible business partners and to find educational resources that can help you reach your business goals. But to receive the full benefit of this global computer network, you need to either build something to which others can come or participate in something someone else has built.

Build what? The most obvious and strongly promoted option for building something online is a Web site, a collection of image and text pages where you can tell your company's story, offer useful information, and sell your wares. Yet "Build It and They Will Come" does not accurately describe what happens for the typical business that takes that route. As you'll learn in Chapters 10 and 11, after building a Web site you'll need to take additional steps to drive traffic there so that it has its full effect. You get the best results if you view your Web site as just one component of an overall, multifaceted marketing effort and not some miraculous kind of customer magnet.

Besides or in addition to a Web site, you can build an electronic medium which allows people interested in your topic of expertise to exchange ideas—a discussion forum, hosted at a Web site or on an online service, or an e-mail discussion list, through which subscribers exchange ideas entirely by e-mail. As I'll describe in Chapter 12, you can also build a one-way e-mail newsletter or e-zine that communicates with subscribers on a regular schedule, cements your influence with that group, and increases the likelihood of their doing business with you.

For me, the most enjoyable and productive option online has always been participation. By joining discussions of likeminded, active people you can build a reputation, attract new customers or clients, materialize business opportunities, and spread your influence widely. These discussions occur in Web forums, Usenet newsgroups, CompuServe and America Online forums, and e-mail discussion lists. With its emphasis on the more glamorous World Wide Web, the mainstream business press fosters the impression that participatory vehicles for spreading the word about what you do are outmoded or puny in the results they produce. Nothing could be further from the truth. The other individuals with whom you're interacting include some of the most influential individuals on the planet.

Which Fears Do You Share?

If you haven't yet gone online, or haven't ventured far in online marketing, some fears are probably holding you back. I had plenty of these once myself and have heard many others. I've done my best to respond to them, and added suggestions for overcoming general technical intimidation. Do you recognize these worries?

- *I'm a technoklutz.* "I'm computer-illiterate," said one consultant to explain why she hadn't yet gone online. Since she has sent me papers of hers she's word-processed, I know that reflects her self-image more than her actual knowledge or aptitude. If you identify with her, find a teenager who can hook your computer up to the Net for you and demonstrate the basics for you. Perhaps someone you know who's retired and communicated with children and grandchildren by e-mail and checks stock prices online would have the patience to explain e-mail and Web browsing to you.

- *I'll spend a fortune before I realize it.* Then sign up with a provider that offers either unlimited monthly access or a flat fee for at least 50 hours per month (more than one hour per day). To learn cheaply on the Internet, you can also get a free e-mail account. There are two kinds of these: free e-mail addresses designed for those who already have Internet access through, say, their employer, and free e-mail access for those who have a computer and modem but no Internet access yet. You'll eventually want your own paid e-mail address, since the free services carry a faint stigma in business circles.

- *I have to buy a new computer first.* Not so fast! The computer press gives the impression that if you don't have Windows 98, a Pentium machine, and a humongous hard disk, you're out of luck. Not true. Older Internet service providers enable you to connect without installing any software besides the communications program that probably came along with your modem. My husband and I set my mother up with an old non-Windows computer system on which she can handle e-mail perfectly well and even surf the Web in text-only mode.

- *Don't you need a credit card for an online account?* No. Many service providers offer direct debit from United States checking accounts or payment by check or money order after receiving an invoice. Ask around in your family to see if someone has online access and never bothered to mention it to you. Only after I inquired did I learn in the early 1990s that my husband had a computer account, including unlimited Internet access, at the university where he was taking graduate courses. Employers and universities don't allow outside for-profit use of their resources, but you can get your feet wet this way.

- *I'll make a fool of myself without realizing it.* Well, you may make a few mistakes you'll regret. One woman pressed the button that meant "send to all" instead of the one for "send privately," and her passionate love letter was broadcast far and wide. Even a forum host with years of experience on CompuServe once made this kind of a mistake and had to post a public apology for something either nasty or just private he'd said about another individual. He had deleted the errant message, but after it had been up for three hours. These kinds of bloopers can happen with traditional media too, as when you put letters in the wrong envelopes.

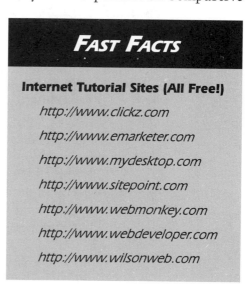

FAST FACTS

Internet Tutorial Sites (All Free!)

http://www.clickz.com

http://www.emarketer.com

http://www.mydesktop.com

http://www.sitepoint.com

http://www.webmonkey.com

http://www.webdeveloper.com

http://www.wilsonweb.com

- *I already spend enough—or too much—time at my computer.* I gave this as my major reason for not going online the year before I took the plunge. After four or five hours a day writing in front of a computer screen, I believed I needed a change. In fact, however, I'm not sure my online activities have changed the total time at my desk, because with e-mail I spend considerably less time writing formal letters than I used to. Although many effective online networkers I spoke with said they spent an hour or so a day keeping up, a few spent as little as twenty minutes a day responding to and placing messages. But since they enjoyed what they were doing and knew the payoff was worth it, even those who spent two hours a day communicating online didn't regret it.

- *I already spend too much time alone.* Then spending a little more time alone at your computer can help you feel less lonely. Nadine Keilholz, a newsletter publisher in Lakeland, Florida, called her time online, "my recreation and contact with humanity. I've always been an outgoing person, but in the last few years I've needed to stay at home most of the time to take care of my father. This way I can be at home and have all the social contact I used to." Often online cliques develop that lead to grand in-person get-togethers. Attorney Harry Dreier attends an annual lunch in the New York City area along with about 25 other attorneys from a forum for lawyers. "It's fun! I like being able to put faces to the names," he says. "It's actually easier for a person who isn't comfortable in social situations to establish a relationship online. That trepidation you experience when you meet a new person face to face isn't present keyboard to keyboard." Or you might become friendly with a distant colleague you can have dinner with when you travel.

- *I'm too late—competitors have probably sewn up the market.* It doesn't usually work that way. An analogy: After moving to a new city, you begin attending Chamber of Commerce functions. Although several other chiropractors have long been active in the organization, that doesn't affect your ability to impress and later get referrals from the banker and hair-salon owner you're eating breakfast with. Much the same is true for electronic networking, where personality, communication ability, professional competence, and availability have a great influence. The online arenas I've frequented recognize that even the three-hundredth Internet expert to show up can have valuable insights, questions, and objections to contribute.

- *Give me a break—I'm too old.* "I have all the technology in my home-business life that I need or want," wrote home-business expert Barbara Brabec in her newsletter in the mid-1990s. "I can see sixty from here, and I have no interest in networking with millions of people on the Internet, wasting time browsing computer bulletin boards, or learning new software programs." A few years later I received a personal note from her saying she had relented and even had a Web page. "Too old" is no more valid an excuse than any other. Ask around and you'll find folks in their eighties nearly as comfortable online as their grandchildren.

- *I can't type.* So? When he was governor of Massachusetts, William Weld had an account on America Online, but his staffers printed out his e-mail for him on paper, Weld handwrote replies, and they typed the responses back into the system for him. If you lack a secretary and don't relish the prospect of flailing about at the keyboard, you can learn to type, regardless of your age. The two-fingered method gets the job done.

- *I'm too shy!* This one floored me when I heard it because I'd always thought of typing onto a screen as the perfect medium of communication for bashful, retiring folks. But apparently there are species of shyness. When I asked Laura Fillmore, President of Open Book Systems (see Figure 3.2), how often she posts to discussion lists, she replied, "Not enough. I get trepidatious putting my thoughts out in front of hundreds of thousands of people." Actually, though, you can benefit from going online just by getting in touch privately with people who do bring themselves to put up public messages.

- *Wouldn't I be making my computer vulnerable to hackers?* Hardly ever. Computer viruses pose a greater threat. Even so, there's little danger of getting infected with a disruptive or

Figure 3.2. Open Book Systems home page.

destructive rogue program if you merely read and respond to e-mail and discussion postings and surf the Web.

- *Yeah, but I'd have to invest in a second telephone line.* Given that you can't use call-waiting on a line when you're communicating by modem, I used to think this was a reasonable conclusion. For a home business that needed people to be able to call in, where the owner was planning to spend more than a half hour at a time online, it seemed best to install a second line. I have my modem hooked up on the same line as my standalone fax machine, which is separate from my phone line. But I've learned of a good one-line solution: In many areas your telephone company offers voice mail for less than one third of the cost of a second line. With this setup, if you have just one line and you're on it when someone calls you, they get your voice mail, not a busy signal.

- *I'm not sure it would be beneficial to my business.* Louise Kursmark, owner of a desktop publishing service in Reading,

Massachusetts, used e-mail to stay in touch with far-flung colleagues. Beyond that she pointed out that unlike her friend Jan Melnik (see Chapter 1), "I don't have a product to sell." If Kursmark's business weren't keeping her busy enough, she could seek out locales where prospects like accountants or lawyers who wanted to start a newsletter hang out. And through a Web site she could provide samples of her work, viewable 24 hours a day. Like many service providers, she would probably discover that snagging even one new year-after-year client online more than pays for the expense and effort.

How To Splash On In

If you're game to get started with your online marketing adventures, here are some ways to reduce frustration and shorten your learning period:

- *Take a class.* Check out the low-cost adult education programs in your community. If they don't offer a class in getting online, call them to suggest one. If they do list such a class, make sure you'll have the chance to watch the instructor go online, or better yet, do it yourself. Otherwise the class is no improvement over the next option.

- *Get a book.* Before buying one at a physical bookstore, either check the back of the book to confirm that it's recommended for beginners or open it up and make sure you can follow its explanations. At the online bookstores, reader comments will reveal what level of knowledge a book is pitched for. Many public libraries do their best to stay up to date with computer books or offer regional interlibrary loan programs that widen your access to books.

- *Find a coach.* The old barter system comes in handy here—show me how to get online and I'll give you one of my paintings or repair your back stairs. When I began wading in, I found live demonstrations from two acquaintances of what they did online mighty helpful.

- *Find a public terminal.* "Internet cafes," where you can drink cappuccino and go online by the minute or hour, exist in many cities. Look for a friendly someone who doesn't mind you sitting alongside and watching him or her cruise cyberspace. In many areas, public libraries have free Internet terminals available for sign-up.

- *Blunder on in.* Just try dialing up, signing on, and following the menu options. Some people learn fine this way—but they probably wouldn't be reading a chapter called "The Internet Won't Bite." Compared to, say, learning to pilot a plane or invest in the stock market, the risks of making a mistake are quite small!

PART II

Schmoozing for Profit

4

Choosing Your Pond and Personality

My father, a pianist, used to hang out at the musicians' union building and get hired for gigs that way," says New York City new-venture consultant and dealmaker Lee Kaplan, whose projects for his company Genesis Venture Development have included electronically originated ones in Las Vegas, Albany, Boston, and San Francisco. "When I use the Internet as a meeting ground, it's similar. I try to figure out the best place to go to get good exposure, and then always keep in mind that there are live people on the other end reading my messages."

Hanging around a certain place online doesn't lead to business unless those are the appropriate people with whom to hang out. "When you have so much access to situations and people that you don't normally have, it's tempting to scan the whole universe for things to pursue," Kaplan says. "For instance, I kept seeing all kinds of international trade forum deals and spent time looking into them. But sugar, oil, coffee beans—that's a different world of business from what I know. I realized it's better to stick to your niche." Kaplan didn't want to tell me exactly where he found the best opportunities, because it took a lot of searching to find his hangouts. I do know that for him, the right group wouldn't be skateboarders, police officers, weather experts, or soap opera fans.

Like Kaplan, you will probably need to wander here and there for a while until you find the best ponds in which to fish. Here are some criteria to think about as you explore, and some guidelines to help you make a good business impression when you cast your fly there.

Is It a Puddle or a Well-Stocked Lake?

The top question to think about as you tour cyberspace is "Who goes there?" Are those posting messages mainly veterans in their area of interest or looking to get started? Do they appear willing to spend money, or are they complaining about prices and looking for freebies and bargains? Do the same names appear again and again, so that it appears to be like a club? Or do names never reappear, so that it's merely a message board, not a community? Do people stay focused on the subject matter or flit from politics to personal chitchat to car problems, as at a cocktail party? It's hard to pin down such factors as age, disposable income, and how much people spend per year on office equipment, but you should be able to find clues if you examine a large enough message base.

Remember, though, that no matter how hard and long you look at messages, you'll never be able to spot the "lurkers"—people who read and may respond privately or pass information on to colleagues but never themselves post. Experienced online marketers estimate lurkers at anywhere from equal to double or more the number of those who actively take part. People may lurk out of bashfulness, because they're intimidated by the expertise or articulateness of the participants, because they're more interested in learning than offering opinions, because they feel they're too important or famous to go public, or because they prefer making behind-the-scenes connections.

Normally it's best to try to find out where your prospects congregate online, not where your compatriots go for shoptalk on professional matters. Suppose, for instance, you're an accountant looking for chaotic companies to straighten out. The best pond for business might not be one with the word "accounting" in its title, but one focused on management issues. If you sell skis by mail, you want to network with skiers, not other ski suppliers.

But "Head toward your prospects, not your peers" isn't a hard and fast rule. Harry Dreier, a lawyer in Bridgewater, New Jersey, estimates that from 60 to 75 percent of those participating in

CompuServe's Lawsig forum are lawyers, the remainder being people either generally interested in legal issues or coming in search of information on a specific legal problem. After a year of participating in the Lawsig, business began trickling in to him from other lawyers, not from the nonlawyers looking for help. "Referrals came from lawyers outside of New Jersey whose clients had matters that needed to be taken care of in my state," he says. "I never went looking for this kind of thing, but other lawyers got to know me, and it happened."

Online guide and enthusiast Mike Holman of Queens, New York, gravitated to the areas where he felt he could make the greatest contribution. Before the Web grew popular, he offered help and advice on the online world within the topic Black Enterprise on Prodigy's Black Experience Bulletin Board, in the Afro forum on CompuServe, and in the Usenet newsgroup soc.culture.african.american. For you a more operative question might be places you can frequent that enable you to bypass your competition. For instance, if you're a Novell network consultant, you'll be one of many cruising barracudas in a pond devoted to Novell software or network problems. But if you regularly visit someplace focused on desktop publishing or one on viruses and security, you might be the only save-the-day consultant within hailing distance when problems arise concerning desktop publishing over networks or viruses on networks.

When exploring different online environments, take note of traffic patterns as well as who hangs out where. Messages are always dated, so you should easily be able to tell whether an area is buzzing with constant activity or rarely visited at all. You may also have a preference for whether the information comes to you or you go to it. Subscribe to Internet mailing lists and postings pile up in your mailbox without you having to go look around anywhere. I prefer the "go-looking" mode, however, of forums, bulletin boards, and newsgroups.

Also listen in on the tone to determine if it's a group you'll feel comfortable joining. I quit one group because it seemed populated by pros who seemed quick to criticize and find fault. Other places I seldom visit because the meaty requests and discussions are sandwiched here and there among seemingly endless small talk. Electronic enclaves change. One small-business community hopped with energy largely because of what one highly experienced, charismatic business owner stirred up. When she left, this spot lost its verve.

Of course, since your purpose is promotional, notice how far each environment lets people go in describing what they sell. Bill LaSalle,

FAST FACTS

Searching for Your Comfortable Pond

Try these three methods of searching for an online community that's fruitful for you:

1. *Specialized topical directories.* Instead of slogging through general search engine results, start with a directory devoted entirely to, say, fishing or computer networks. You can find a directory of such directories at *http://www.searchiq.com/subjects* or at *http://www.virtualfreesites.com/search.html.*

2. *Trade associations.* Many of these offer a collection of resources and recommended sites for their industry. Start this search at *http://dir.yahoo.com/Business_and_Economy/Organizations/Trade_Associations/.* (See Figure 4.1.)

3. *Guide sites.* These have hundreds of topical subsites run by a real person who points visitors toward the best of the best in that topic. Highly recommended: *http://www.about.com, http://www.suite101.com,* and *http://www.wz.com.*

owner of Craft King in Lakeland, Florida, found significant differences in crafts groups on the online services and on the Internet. "The Prodigy Crafts Bulletin Board had a sales and services section where I could leave an offer for a free catalog of craft supplies. They also allowed me to answer a question and add that I'd be glad to send along a free catalog. The CompuServe Crafts forum wouldn't let anyone present their business like that. I could offer advice, but then I could only refer people to a file in the forum library where they could find information about our catalog. It was circuitous."

The Influence of Personality

Years ago, a fellow National Writers Union member called me at a busy moment and asked me if I had the address for *Cosmopolitan*

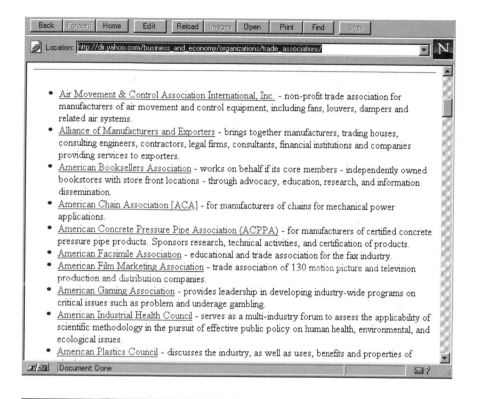

Figure 4.1. The beginning of Yahoo's list of trade associations.

magazine, which I had written for. I set the phone down on its side and sounded off out loud about how stupid and annoying I thought the question was. "Geez, if you're not #%&*!@ smart enough to find their address, you shouldn't be #%&*!@ writing for them! Here, here it is!" I'm still embarrassed that I let myself go like that, especially since I could not afterward recall the name of the person at the other end of the phone. Somewhere, someone has the ability to tarnish on my otherwise sterling local reputation.

Do something like that online and thousands of people might remember—to your detriment, since in the world of electronic communication, business opportunities blossom or wilt because of the imprint in readers' minds left behind by words on a screen. Sales and marketing consultant Ralph Katz of Newton, Massachusetts, remembers a time when he was about to explore business opportunities with another consultant when that person's conduct stopped him short. "Someone had asked that consultant a straightforward question like 'What do you recommend?' and what came back was a totally unprovoked slam at the person who had asked the question. I was aghast and completely lost interest in any sort of communication with him."

"From what people say and how they express themselves, you can get a good feel for their personality," reflects Paula Berinstein, an independent researcher in Los Angeles. "People who get really sarcastic, for instance, and don't seem to care what their audience thinks are probably hard to deal with. Other people seem to become argumentative for no reason. And I don't like to see people putting others down. Once a writer wanted to fire his agent and asked seemingly endless questions after getting some advice. The other person came back on and said, 'Look, I was just giving you a suggestion. Take it or leave it.' I didn't think that was called for." On the other hand, Berinstein gets a positive impression of people who contribute witty, eloquent, or insightful comments on an issue. Even typing style can have an influence, she says—to her, typos show carelessness.

To understand how the way you express yourself and interact with people affects your business prospects, consider this data from a survey taken by public relations consultant Mike Bayer. Of 71 business owners with revenues of $1 million or more a year, 93 percent identified their main reason for hiring a particular lawyer as their "inner feeling about the attorney"; 91 percent said that how well the attorney showed an understanding of their problem was a "major factor" in their hiring decision. "The overwhelming conclusion is that business owners do not hire attorneys that they don't feel good about," Bayer wrote.

Another indication of the pertinence of personality comes from a very different realm of business: software. With "shareware," software authors distribute copies of a program as widely as they can and request that satisfied users send in a stated registration fee. Several surveys have showed that a measurable number of those who register do so because they "like the author." Unless users call the shareware author by phone with a question, their impression of the author's personality derives completely from their writing voice in the instructions for the program, in the trust they've shown by releasing it as shareware, and in the wording of the invitation to register the product.

"It's comparable to the reason my wife shops at the supermarket where she does," explains Bob Schenot, author of *How to Sell Your Software*, "because the store is active in the community, hires disabled workers, and has a reputation for being generally nice people. With a shareware product, this kind of likability is terribly important because you're asking people to send you money when they've already received most of the value they'll receive." Dallas investment banker Fred Richards told me about an agricultural

FAST FACTS

Have a Clue!

1. Markets are conversations.

2. Markets consist of human beings, not demographic sectors.

3. Conversations among human beings sound human. They are conducted in a human voice.

4. Whether delivering information, opinions, perspectives, dissenting arguments, or humorous asides, the human voice is typically open, natural, and uncontrived.

5. People recognize each other as such from the sound of this voice.

Read the rest of the 95 Theses for Communication in the Internet Age at *http:// www.cluetrain.com* or in the book *The Cluetrain Manifesto* by Rick Levine, Christopher Locke, Doc Searls, and David Weinberger. (See Figure 4.2.)

expert in Nebraska he developed an interest in doing business with because of the way the man answered questions. "He was forthright, talked down-home common sense, always said his opinion was based on his experience of the last 40 years, and tried to steer people away from trying to make a quick buck every time."

Web sites convey personality, too. Linda Stone, director of Microsoft's Virtual Worlds Group, once asked a group of Internet-involved graduate students how many preferred to buy books at barnesandnoble.com rather than amazon.com. The answer: no one. They couldn't say why, but all preferred the experience of shopping at amazon. Stone then asked, if I offered you savings of $1 per book, would you switch from amazon.com to barnesandnoble.com? How about $2 less per book? She had to offer $3 less per book (representing hardly any profit left for the bookseller) before hands went up

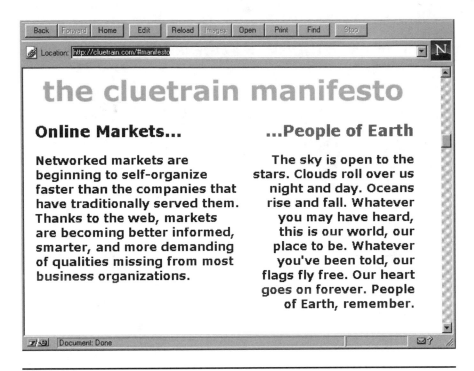

Figure 4.2.   The preamble of The Cluetrain Manifesto.

indicating that yes, they'd switch. According to Stone, through the way it was organized, its design choices, the kinds of information it conveyed and didn't in comparison to amazon, barnesandnoble.com projected a cold, get-your-business-done-and-leave impression, while amazon.com radiated a friendlier, stay-awhile spirit.

Since how you come across online will influence whether people will want to do business with you, think about the image you'd prefer prospects to have of you. I don't recommend that you choose a persona at odds with the way you normally are—you'd probably find such pretense difficult to keep up over time. Rather, you might resolve to be more patient or friendly than is your wont, or try harder than you would among chums to stay on your best behavior. "For me, being online is serious business," says magazine writer Jack Germain. "If I were to make an offhanded snotty remark it would reflect not only on me, but also on the magazines that run my columns."

According to Howard Rheingold, author of *The Virtual Community: Homesteading on the Electronic Frontier*, the intermingling of chitchat and commerce in electronic communication has precedents almost as old as civilization. "The agora—the ancient Athenian market where the citizens of the first democracy gathered to buy and sell—was more than the site of transactions; it was also a place where people met and sized up one another. It's where the word got around about those who transgress norms, break contracts. In a virtual community, idle talk—where people learn what kind of person you are, why you should be trusted or mistrusted, what interests you—is context-setting." In the online marketplace, *how* you are speaks just as loudly as what you say.

5

Making Connections

News Flash: SAVE YOUR TIME, SAVE YOUR MONEY

The forum is being flooded with messages from people TRYING to use the forum to sell something or develop business. If this is your primary purpose in using the forum, save your time. Nineteen sets of eyes of forum staff members see your ads and remove them from view. Repeat offenders are subject to losing forum privileges.

Paul and Sarah Edwards, Forum Administrators (SysOps)

If you had entered the Working from Home forum on CompuServe one day in the 1990s, this notice would have greeted you. (I condensed it slightly.) You'll find similar, though usually less strongly worded, mandates against sales pitches in contributors' guidelines for e-mail discussion lists. It reminds me of those signs, hand-lettered and askew, that a cartoon hero encounters at the foot of the long climb to the moated castle: TURN BACK NOW! Just as the intrepid hero gathers courage and proceeds, however, after reading this chapter you too will be equipped to safely forge on ahead. Armed with the knowledge of what will arouse the wrath of forum guardians, and what earns their blessing, you can blend right in with all the schmoozing *and* develop business.

Schmoozing Wins, Soliciting Loses

If the Yiddish word "schmooze" is foreign to you, don't worry. It denotes a cozy kind of conversation that people of any ethnic background or nationality can enter into and enjoy. Unlike some cold-blooded versions of networking that became popular in the late 1980s, its object is not collecting as many business cards or e-mail addresses as you can. Nor is electronic schmoozing aimed at making distant friends (though that often comes about as a by-product). Rather, it's an interactive tool for building remote—but otherwise real and beneficial—business relationships.

I doubt very much the Edwardses will mind my explaining to you the spirit and mechanics of schmoozing, because for this method to prove rewarding, you must in your heart and soul actually value person-to-person business relationships—which comes pretty close to the official purpose of a forum like theirs. Phoniness eventually rings as hollow on a computer screen as it does in a used-car showroom. And you'll quickly get bored if you cynically go through the motions of schmoozing with your arm ready to stretch out and grab the golden ring. So I'm assuming that you want to meet people who share your business interests and are prepared to spend time at your computer participating in discussion.

After pondering Chapter 4, you have an idea of where you wish to fish and how you'd like to come across. You still need to understand how to avoid committing the grand transgression of soliciting, because it's very easy to step over barely visible, rarely pointed out lines without realizing it. Let's begin by looking at two clearly acceptable examples of schmoozing and two examples of soliciting that would be decidedly unacceptable in most online discussion areas.

SCHMOOZE #1

To: all
From: Ron Tyler

Re: Etiquette?

Does anyone know the appropriate way to address a supreme court justice? Is it just "your honor" or something else? We got a reservation at my bed & breakfast inn from one, and I don't want to make a fool of myself! Thanks, Ron.

SCHMOOZE #2

To: Geri Burkhardt
From: Bruce Han
Re: ADA

I disagree with what you wrote about the disabilities act being a terrible burden on small businesses. In my seventeen-person accounting firm, we installed a ramp before we ran public seminars in our conference room and bought a TDD machine for an employee who lost his hearing suddenly. Total cost for both: $5500. The former gives us community good will (and one or two extra registrations) when we write on our brochures and ads "Wheelchair accessible." The latter saved us the cost of recruiting and training someone new.

Bruce Han

SOLICITATION #1

To: all
From: Ron Tyler
Re: Vacation ideas

With the incredibly frigid weather in many parts of the country these days, your thoughts may be turning south. If so, there's no friendlier, more interesting destination in Florida than Key West, and no friendlier, more interesting place to stay there than the Buccaneer Bed & Breakfast.

E-mail me for complete details on a special weekend package deal in Key West!

SOLICITATION #2

To: Geri Burkhardt
From: Bruce Han
Re: ADA

Geri: Did you know that the cost of compliance with the ADA is a legitimate business expense, and therefore fully deductible? Our full-service accounting firm specializes in helping small businesses like yours keep your hard-earned profits legally out of the hands of Uncle Sam. We're friendly, experienced, and affordable. Let me know if you'd like to set up a no-obligation appointment.

Did you notice significant differences? Schmoozing is purposeful business chitchat likely to be of interest to others, while solicitation involves a bald invitation to do business. Schmooze #1 consists of one of the most common forms of appropriate discussion, a business-related question. Note, though, that Ron's question sets his business in a highly favorable light likely to make others curious to know more. If a curious someone does ask, "Where are you located?" and then, "Geez, Key West—I was thinking of going there in April. Tell me about your B&B," he gets an opening to present the selling points of his business to his heart's content. Schmooze #2 consists of another common form of participation—contributing views on an issue. Here Bruce responded substantively to a comment by Geri and subtly injected the description, "my seventeen-person accounting firm." Over time if Bruce continues to post reasoned, socially enlightened arguments and experiences linked to his name and a phrase like "my seventeen-person accounting firm," regulars needing accounting services are going to turn to him.

Solicitation #1, addressed to "all," has no purpose or context other than conveying Ron's marketing information. It also has no discussion value or informative content—you wouldn't learn anything by reading it. Note too that it ends, like any good advertisement or direct-mail piece, with a call to action. Although schmoozy in tone, it comes across unmistakably as a sales pitch. It would therefore get attacked by the sentinels who guard their online arenas with a "No commercials" rule.

Solicitation #2 reminds me of classic ambulance chasing—as in lawyers going to the funerals of accident victims and tucking their business cards in the suit pockets of the family members. Here Bruce joins an ongoing discussion, but instead of furthering the interchange, he injects his selling agenda where it's beside the point. As in solicitation #1, Bruce recites his selling points and concludes with an invitation to call him. In addition, several phrases crop up in his note that one rarely encounters outside of marketing pieces, such as "small businesses like yours," "hard-earned profits," "the hands of Uncle Sam," "affordable," and "no-obligation appointment." Bruce does offer some helpful information about the deductibility of ADA compliance expenses, but he then switches unnecessarily to selling mode.

"People who haven't been working for themselves don't know that there's any other way to market besides advertising," says Alice Bredin, who writes a syndicated column on working at home. "To them, marketing means setting up a billboard somewhere by running big ads on radio, TV, or in a magazine, and if you can't afford that, well, online you can slap your message up in front of people's eyes and they are going to buy from you. Actually, the reverse is true. Being online is like being at a party, and the other people there aren't likely to buy from you if you just come up and tell them what you do. But after you talk a while about where you're from, ask them about their business, you exchange information, maybe then you've made a business connection." It's foolish to think that one note you wrote in half an hour is going to perform magic for you, says Bredin. "Instead, when someone posts a note, take off your salesperson's hat, or at least tilt it to the side, and give that person some help. Get a little relationship going, and they'll get a trial run with you that might get them wanting more."

If I've convinced you of the value of sticking to schmoozing and avoiding flagrant selling, here are some guidelines for promoting yourself indirectly and unobtrusively.

- *Do post questions that enable you to describe what you do.* It's fine not to know everything. Just make sure your questions aren't too elementary and don't cast doubt on your ethics. Investment banker Fred Richards says he sometimes sees questions "so basic that it's obvious the person asking has no experience whatsoever, like 'Is it cheaper to send things by mail or by UPS?' Just call and ask!" Another time, someone in mail order was asking about having to pay sales tax to other states, "Can I get around this?" Richards remembers giving this person a stern warning about the consequences of not going by the book.

- *Do answer questions from others you're qualified to address.* Even when the topic isn't smack on target with your service or product, your reputation with the group rises whenever you demonstrate that you know your stuff. Generosity makes a good impression too. Paradoxically, in this medium, selfless sharing of information sells.

- *Do contribute to discussions that put you or your business in a favorable light.* Taking a strong stand is fine so long as you can back up your position with facts or experiences and stay in control of your responses.

- *Do be constructive in tone.* Avoid sarcasm, put-downs, and personal attacks—even if someone throws verbal digs your way. See Chapter 17 on ways to avoid reputation-damaging conflagrations.

- *Do stay focused on the announced topic.* "Nothing is more irritating than to click on a thread marked 'FREELANCE WRITERS NEEDED' and find a discussion about restaurants in Omaha," says writer Kathy Seña, who adds that the problem has a name: "thread corruption."

- *Do offer valuable information.* Ron could have turned his "Vacation ideas" solicitation into a solid discussion starter by continuing after "there's no friendlier, more interesting destination in Florida than Key West" with a description of its attractions: the Hemingway connection, its typical February temperatures, the tolerant lifestyle, its accessibility by car and air, and so on. By setting himself up as someone knowledgeable about Key West, he's more likely to make a memorable impression in this medium than by pushing his B&B directly.

FAST FACTS

Schmoozing Success Story

Donna Cardillo of Wall, New Jersey, has attracted numerous valuable business opportunities by answering career-related questions on NurseNet, a discussion list for nurses around the world. After explaining to another subscriber how to construct a resumé, how to ace an interview or how to pursue nonmedical jobs, Cardillo signs off as an R.N. who does career development seminars. This has led to regional and national magazine publicity for her, speaking engagements, coaching clients, and sales of her audiotapes to nurses as far away as Japan. Total time expended for such results: about half an hour a day. Total cost: $0.

- *Do slip in off-hand curiosity provokers.* One of my first posts online succeeded in this category when I posted a message that mentioned the fact that my book *Smart Speaking* was going to be featured on the Oprah Winfrey show that Wednesday. Barb Tomlin, president of Westward Connections in Albuquerque, New Mexico, and at that time Board Leader of a Home Office Board, became curious enough to watch the show, ask me to tell her more about myself, and then invite me to become a featured expert on the topic of media and publishing.

- *Do balance getting with giving and showing off with humility.* Although author Charlotte Libov spends a good deal of energy online sniffing out publicity opportunities, she says she deliberately tries to give back as much help as she's received. "I share my contacts with people who have similar interests, and I take part in nonpromotional discussions," she says. "If I feel I've been promoting myself a lot lately, I'll hold back, or approach someone privately, by e-mail."

- *Do check messages frequently.* Glassblower Strat McCloskey of Newcastle, Delaware, got the opportunity to present a seminar when someone else couldn't make it at the last minute because he was the first out of 50 people to respond to the online appeal for a replacement.

- *Don't expect results from vague questions or answers.* "Nobody is going to respond helpfully to a question like, 'I need some help with taxes'. It looks lazy, as if you haven't put any energy into it yet at all," says Alice Bredin. "But if you make your question more specific—as specific as you can—people will respect that and put energy back toward you." Likewise, the more examples and details you can offer as advice, the more you showcase your expertise.

- *Don't use all capital letters, even in your headline.* Online, people consider that overexcited, the equivalent of shouting, and it makes them want to cover their ears—oops, their eyes. An extended patch of uppercase letters also slows down reading.

  ## FAST FACTS

  ### Schmoozing Success Story

  Linda Abraham of Santa Monica, California, has landed numerous clients who need her editorial services for college and graduate school admission essays by keeping her eyes open in forums where students hang out. "When I saw someone looking for help one day, I responded. This student became one of my best clients. A few weeks later, he referred someone else looking for help in the forum to me. Two others saw the exchange, and they too became clients," she says. "In addition, I received wonderful testimonials for my marketing literature."

- *Don't irritate discussion participants with advertising stunts.* Don't use gratuitous exclamation marks, empty superlatives, self-serving exaggerations, unsubstantiated boasts, and other symptoms of hype, such as words like "amazing," "revolutionary," "breakthrough," "unique," "fabulous," or "extraordinary." Avoid any sort of promise or offer, so that you keep a safe distance from the verboten territory of advertising.

- *Don't carry out "bombing runs."* Several online veterans used some variation on this term to denote the practice of scattering one message almost indiscriminately throughout various

Internet communities and then ending with, "If you want to know more, please e-mail me rather than reply here." Some go so far as to call this "spam"—a derisive term for completely untargeted mass electronic solicitations. The impersonality implied in your scatterfire is offensive enough. It's also insulting to the regulars to say you're too busy or not interested enough to hang around their neighborhood for responses.

- *Don't expect instant results.* "I've seen people come on a board, introduce themselves as a hot shot, and two weeks later they're gone. A week after that someone has a question for them, and they're not there," says Peggie Hall, owner of Peal Products in Atlanta, which sells marine sanitation products. "After I first went on a sailing forum, introduced myself, and started answering questions, it was three or four months before someone requested a catalog. In a year, though, we've done more than enough business to justify the expense of being online."

- *Don't mention fees or prices unless you are asked.* Even then, you might be better off providing them privately. A reasonable rule of thumb: If you don't normally include fees or prices in ads or a brochure, don't quote them publicly even when you're asked. One exception I can think of is a response to a discussion concerning prices. For example, no one will object if someone has asked, "Anyone know where I can get quality bulk 3½ inch disks for less than 50 cents each?" and you respond, "We sell name-brand disks, guaranteed, in lots of 100 for 32 cents each."

FAST FACTS

Schmoozing Success Story

Mike McBride of Smithfield, Rhode Island, joined forums, bulletin boards, and Usenet newsgroups, and began receiving public and private inquiries about his services. "This led to picking up several new clients," he says. "I also came in contact with someone who offered me a position as V.P. of Marketing along with an equity position in a new business, which is taking off because of the same dynamics."

- *Don't ask for the order.* Lawrence Seldin, author/publisher of *Power Tips for the Apple Newton*, got reprimanded several places online for using the words, "to order!" Complaints vanished when he said, "for more information, please contact me by e-mail." Instead of asking for the order, slip in some information that would catch the interest of someone in your target market, and let them approach you if they wish more information. If Ron Tyler added just a little to Schmooze #1, he'd probably inspire someone to respond, "You're in Key West? We were just talking the other day about going there. Can you send me a brochure?"

REVISED SCHMOOZE #1

Does anyone know the appropriate way to address a supreme court justice? Is it just "your honor" or something else? We got a reservation at my bed & breakfast inn from one, and I don't want to make a fool of myself out here on the sands of Key West! Thanks.

Ron Tyler, owner, Buccaneer Bed & Breakfast

Accept the fact that what gets perceived as a solicitation will vary from community to community. In borderline cases, the overall spirit of a note may determine whether it attracts criticism or not. For instance, in the following message Perry Smit let readers know that he's available to be hired, but he did it in such a charming way, tucked into an irresistibly friendly invitation, that none of the patrol officers where he posted it pulled him over for it.

I LOVE MY AMSTERDAM

Hello everybody,

I have seen a lot of cities: Sydney, Paris, Munchen, Brussels, Antwerpen, Frankfurt, etc. Beautiful cities but you never feel what you feel when you are in Amsterdam.

From the smell of the dogshit to the smell of the Heineken bier coming out of the cafes, it really got something. From busy businesspeople to the junks on the street. In one day you can see all kind of people from all over the world.

From the jingle bells of the trams to the chattering of people on the leidseplein. When you have never heard that noise, then you never been really in Amsterdam.

Amsterdam, you have to feel it.

When you have plans to come over, then let me know. If it is for business I can bring you in contact with the right prospect that you are looking for. When you want to come for a visit then let me know and I tell you more nice things that you have to see, hear, smell and to feel.

What are the nice things that I have to see, hear, smell and to feel when I come in your city?

Kind regards,
Perry Smit
International Business Services (Holland, Amsterdam)

Two hot prospects, planning a trip to Holland, responded, along with three people wishing to set up a similar service in their city and three people sending back humorous portraits of their beloved home town, Smit told me. I wasn't surprised.

Feeding a Fan Club

If you already have some standing as a Somebody, you can create a stir of interest in interacting with you merely by announcing your availability to answer questions. Washington, D.C., literary agent Bill Adler arranges what he calls an "online publicity tour" for his clients. After selecting appropriate electronic ponds, his firm posts a notice saying that so-and-so, the author of such-and-such, will be around from when to when to answer questions on the subject of X. During the appointed time frame, the author responds online to the posted questions. Because his firm keeps its own database of discussion groups, finding appropriate venues for the tour is a simple matter of searching the list by keyword. "There's been only minor back-lash," Adler says. "Everyone likes to have access to an expert."

You don't have to be an author to try this, of course, just have solid, authoritative experience ready to dispense through your finger-tips. If you offer to answer questions on an ongoing basis rather than for a limited time, you have the opportunity to watch an amazing dynamic take shape. Assuming you're at least moderately person-able, patient, and credible, other fish in the pond begin to refer ques-tions and point customers toward you along with priceless word-of-mouth praise. If you stick around and treat members of your "fan club" well, they will continue to do valuable marketing for you.

Tarry Shebesta, president of Automobile Consumer Services, Inc. in Cincinnati, Ohio, a nationwide new-vehicle buying service, joined CompuServe's Cars forum (see Figure 5.1) in 1992 and began an-swering questions from people looking for specific cars. He always

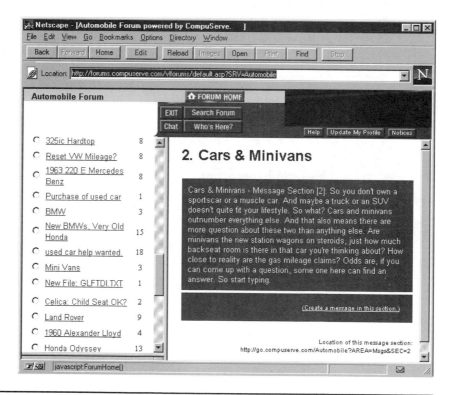

Figure 5.1. Down the left, some of the message topics in CompuServe's Cars forum.

made sure to offer facts about cars and car buying as well as, where appropriate, information about his company's quote sheets for bargaining and its full buying service. After six or seven months, he says, he no longer had to say anything about his company besides sign his posts, "Tarry Shebesta/ACS." "Someone would show up looking for a car, and a half dozen people would say, 'Call Tarry at ACS.' Just in the CompuServe Cars forum, there were soon 50 to 100 people who had directly done business with us. The rapport we built—you can't buy it," Shebesta says. "Besides, it feels good to be helping people."

To build and sustain a loyal following, advises Shebesta, consistency and dependability count, not only in the online information you give out but also in the way you treat customers when they contact you to do business. "Your customer service has to be top-notch. We're honest and we do what we say we do." Every morning and evening Shebesta would look through the messages on the Cars forum and answer those for him or those on automotive issues he knew a lot about, unless the tone of discussion seemed too argumentative. "When someone shows up and attacks buying services in general I don't get involved. Others do it."

Jan Melnik's online fan club took only one month to emerge. "I was the only highly experienced secretarial services business owner around who was also an author," she explains. Orders for her books on running a secretarial or resumé business, or for her newsletter arrived every day not only from forum members but from nonmembers who heard about her from her fans. "People are so hungry for information that this is less than soft-sell—it's no-sell," she says. "And I imagine it would happen for anyone who has professional advice to offer that's not readily available elsewhere." With a typing speed of 130 words a minute, Melnik finds it a cinch to blast off lengthy replies to public questions. The e-mail posed a bit of a burden, though, with people sending two- to three-page letters "pouring out their background. I answer every one and try to keep it personal, but I don't have time to write more than a paragraph or two back to them."

Like Melnik, Bob Coleman, who for a time wrote an official "Great American Ideas" column for Prodigy, tried to reply personally but briefly to the average of six e-mails a day he received from fans seeking advice. Although it might have saved him time with certain questions that he got again and again, he avoided prepackaged responses both privately and publicly because "when I first trolled around online, the canned responses really stuck out."

Coleman laughs that the two most common notes he got were variations on either "Dear Bob, No lawyer is going to sucker me into paying for him to draw up a contract" or "Dear Bob, I didn't use a contract and someone shafted me." He says it takes good interpersonal skills and flexibility to deal with questioners at all levels of sophistication, courtesy, self-discipline, and

> ## FAST FACTS
>
> ### Special Tip for Authors
>
> When you get fan e-mail, thank the writers for their comments and ask if they would take five minutes and post their comments at one of the online bookstores—amazon.com, bn.com, or borders.com. Almost everyone I made this request of did it, and I'm told that enthusiastic, substantive customer reviews make a difference to shoppers deciding which book to buy. They're far more credible than advertisements. Total cost: $0.

initiative. For him the payback included a unique kind of market research—"not structured or analytical, so that you get a good sense of what people really want to know." The second edition of Coleman's *The Great American Idea Book* included a new section on financing ideas because that proved one of the top three concerns of his online questioners.

Besides cultivating fans, who tend to be less experienced than you in your field, you can nourish relationships with peers online. Because I appreciate it so much when others do this for me, I make a point of putting in a good word where appropriate for other experts whom I feel I can vouch for. I can't prove this, but I'd guess that an aura of thoughtfulness associated with your name would help encourage valuable peer-to-peer referrals.

Schmooze-Compatible Announcements

I don't recommend trying to post a formal press release in an online area designed for discussion. Although less pushy than an ad, it's still "canned" and thus violates the flow and purpose of a forum, mailing list, or newsgroup. That doesn't mean you need to renounce notifying your market of relevant events, products, and opportunities. Just personalize your announcements, keep them short, and couch them in the buddy-buddy idiom of schmoozing. I've seen appropriately phrased contest announcements, seminar notices, requests for writers, new product introductions, and offers of survey results get by without complaints. Stress that you're letting people know something they've been trying to find out, not that you have something to sell.

Public relations pro Marty Winston used this approach in 1989 after convincing his client, Palindrome, to sell its superior tape backup software separately from the hardware with which it had initially been integrated. "I went into a Netwire forum and wrote, 'Hey, I just spoke with Palindrome (my client) about the Network Archivist, and they agreed to unbundle the software.' A couple of guys tried it and loved it and started talking it up as a solution. One of them was a reseller and put together a package of Palindrome together with someone else's hardware. I successfully launched the product without any advertisements."

Another way to tone down the "salesiness" of an announcement is to preface it with "People have been asking me…"—as in "People have been asking me when my PR seminar would be available on audiotape." Naturally this helps only if you've already been hanging around that area and you *have* been asked! If you're loath to appear even that self-promotional, you can ask one of your online pals to send you public congratulations. Self-deprecatory or tentative preambles like, "I hope I'm not out of line to…" and "Is this the proper place to…?" also take the edge off announcements.

Paradoxically, you come off as less offensively aggressive when you present something new of yours with an outright brag. In this quintessentially personal medium, it must be a distinctly human brag, though, not one that sounds pompous or bureaucratic. You want to come across as charming, disarming, or merely understandably excited about something wonderful that has happened. If many people know you, for example, you could post:

Guess what, friends, we're spreading! Accountability, Inc. just opened our third branch office, in Colorado Springs, in addition to our Denver and Santa Fe offices. As many of you know, our niche is small businesses needing tax return preparation, financial planning, and bookkeeping. We're thinking of starting to sell franchises next year. Watch out, H & R Block!

Or try a more modest brag:

> *A friend suggested the other day I tend to hide my light under a bushel. "When you achieve something wonderful you've got to tell people," he said. OK—gulp—I want to tell you guys that the 1.2 release of my human resources management software program, Workworks, is selling unbelievably. We've made sales to 240 of the Fortune 500 already, with more getting checked off our wall chart every day. We're having a one-year celebration tomorrow.*

Instead of waiting till you have an actual achievement to brag about, you can also attract customers by floating an idea. This worked for me unintentionally when I said I was thinking of putting together a flat-fee package of services and wondered how that approach had worked for others. Questions prompted me to explain what was different about my idea, and I picked up a customer for a $395 consulting package that was still in the testing phase. Don't forget, though, that if you reveal a hot idea publicly, you're revealing it to competitors who could snatch it right off their computer screens.

A variation of the float involves asking people for feedback, not on a business concept itself, but something related to it. For example, when you request constructive feedback on a draft of a press release, people get exposed to what's new and newsworthy about your business. Once a guy working on the final edit of a video asked publicly for advice on whether or not it should be indexed on screen and for help on whether he had left out anything crucial. "I'm not trying to sell you anything," he emphasized, and I agreed to offer my two cents on his outline. I was slightly annoyed to receive a gargantuan e-mail sales letter from him three months later, when the editing was finished and he was definitely looking for buyers. Be true to your word if you want to keep the good will of those you schmooze with.

Running a Column

When I was a philosophy graduate student at Cornell University in the 1970s, I had an idea I wanted to get across to the all-male faculty. Instead of making a speech to them—all champion debaters—or issuing a memo that they could glance at and crumple into the waste basket, I commandeered a section of the chalk board that took up one wall of the departmental lounge. In big letters I printed SEXIST QUOTE OF THE WEEK, and below that a quote from Aristotle. Every week for the rest of the year, I'd post a new quote from one of the greats, like Immanuel Kant, John Locke, or Jean-Paul Sartre. No one ever erased my messages or added graffiti. I didn't sign my name, but word got around that I was the one responsible, and once in a while in the lounge a professor would clear his throat and make a few nervous comments about the interpretation of a particular quote.

Cumulatively my efforts helped remind faculty of one of the more subtle ways in which women students were experiencing a hostile learning environment. My guerrilla communication tactic has an analogy for electronic bulletin boards and newsgroups where you're hoping to convert regular readers into customers. Issue periodic communiqués that challenge or inform group members, and you'll solidify a corresponding reputation.

I call this tactic running a column, because as with pieces appearing regularly under a byline in a newspaper, magazine, or news-style Web site, you build an audience by expressing a consistent point of view in a specific topic area. Columns should be short to very short, be spaced in predictable intervals, and include material you don't need to burden with a copyright notice. Compared with self-sufficient postings designed for permanent availability (see Chapter 11), columns are more ephemeral and provocative. You could also collect subscribers for your column, as discussed in Chapter 12. If they generate dialogue and mostly positive discussion, over time such columns will probably generate business for you too. Just make sure they're not blatantly self-serving or explicitly promotional.

A British consultant, who asked me not to use his name, called his series of online conversation starters the "International Business Quiz." Under the heading of "Int Biz Quiz ? #111," for example, was this:

111 In a program I saw, John Naisbitt (the Megatrend guy) lives up in some place in the mountains in a 1300-soul town. Nice, expensive houses. Everyone is on an InfoZone network. The British TV commentator seemed worried about this view of paradise. Seeing it as a form of escapism. In fact the whole program was expressing concern at the American approach to teleworking and the destruction of former societal structures. Naisbitt described himself as a "globalist"; some might see him as a little-towner. Your opinion please?

Elsewhere I saw a video producer launch a series with a note on how to produce low-budget infomercials—but then didn't keep it up. Perhaps he concluded that a lack of immediate response meant no one was reading and paying attention, which wasn't so.

Mike Holman of Queens, New York, saw his column, called "Info Highway Lessons" as more of an educational service than a provocation. A banker by day, Holman was working toward venturing out on his own by posting his weekly column in several African-American discussion forums, including the Usenet group soc.culture.african.american. "I'd had to learn on my own," he says, "with a high frustration level, and this is my way to give back to the online community. Some people feel that they can't obtain technological skills, and this helps make technology accessible to them. But I also believe it will benefit my business. Your business progresses when people know what you're contributing."

Whether you assume the role of educator or provocateur, an online column offers a continuing opportunity to win name recognition and respect among prospects. Suppose, for example, you're a commercial real estate broker. Once you find a group that contains a lot of prospects for your services, you could provide a paragraph or two or commentary on how the week's economic news might affect the buying, selling, and leasing of real estate. Or you could highlight a sale of the week (not necessarily yours) and what it shows about trends in the market. Or set up a series of myths about real estate to expose one by one.

FAST FACTS

Special Tip for Non-Authors

If passion about a topic gets you writing eloquently and at length to address a need or weigh in on a controversy, consider whether you can do a modest bit of revision and turn your online postings into articles. More on this in Chapter 11.

Let's say, on the other hand, that you're an editor who helps small business owners improve their sales letters, brochures, and ads. Once a week you could analyze (disguised, perhaps) a specimen that landed on your desk that badly needs your tinkering and polishing. You could reprint, as *The New Yorker* has for years, bloopers from newspapers or press releases. You could offer an educational series on punctuation—one week a light disquisition on the semicolon, another week do's and don'ts for hyphens. Short and informal notes win the day here.

Except in a moderated discussion list, you won't need anyone's permission to run the kind of column I'm talking about. Make it seem casual but consistent, and respond promptly to any objections, praise, and inquiries sparked by your messages. Like Miss Manners or Dear Abby, use the same header every time, and then below the heading, write, "Second (or twelfth) in a series." You'll know you've piqued the right kind of interest when people ask you how they can get a hold of previous installments, or the whole series. Compile them in a book for sale, or use them to lure people to your Web site, which of course would contain the series. If there's constant turnover in the group, you could even rerun the series after you run out of ideas, explaining in the first message of the reprise that you'd been asked to do so. For example, novelist Harry Arnston posted his 53-part "Novels 101" lessons all at once on Prodigy's Books & Writing Bulletin Board several times per year.

In most active groups, you'll get maximum effect if you space the installments at intervals of a week. Posted periodically at your Web site, a column offers a powerful answer to the question, "How do I get all those sightseers to come back?" If you resist the urge to make all of your past sallies accessible right there, those you hook won't have any other way to keep up besides adding you to their regular Net-surfing route.

6

Understanding the Medium

The medium is the message," wrote Marshall McLuhan in his 1964 book, *Understanding Media*, meaning that the material won't have the same impact on the cover of a magazine as on a flashing neon sign. Not only does every communication medium affect our sensibilities in subtle ways, it imposes an invisible grid of possibilities and pitfalls on participants and onlookers. McLuhan's perspective explains why people who listened to the 1959 U.S. presidential campaign debates on radio thought Nixon had won, while those who watched on TV hailed Kennedy as the winner—and why I got clobbered online by what I thought was an utterly safe, carefully reasoned, constructive message.

Puzzled by the way several people were using the word "scam," I looked it up in several dictionaries and presented a logical dissection of its meaning. To illustrate a point, I made the kind of argument I used to offer in college classrooms: "If you use the word 'scam' in this sense, then it would allow you to label a scam my course where I teach people how to get published, since in fact very few people do go on to get published, percentage-wise, after taking the course. Obviously, I don't believe my course is a scam and no one has ever made any such complaint." What happened next mortified me. Within a matter of hours, the thread evolved into a debate assuming that my course *was* a scam. Like the hapless Sorcerer's Apprentice who only made a disaster worse, the more I tried to mop up the damage, the more people spun off on their own, disconnected from my original post, discussing me in the same breath as bona fide scammers.

The lesson couldn't have been more dramatic: A discussion group is not a lecture hall. I had no power to set the ground rules or the context or to control what my audience did with the thoughts I shared. Their agenda could and did differ from mine, and while I could watch my comments being taken out of context and distorted, any protest I made about a misreading had no special claim to attention. As this example shows, the online discussion medium can trip you up if you don't appreciate its peculiarities. Here are the fruits of my observation and experts' analyses, along with ways to up the chances that you become the beneficiary and not the victim of your efforts to schmooze.

Joining the Stream of Pieces

To exploit the potential of the medium, you must understand the following characteristics:

- *Participants choose which discussion threads to read by their headings.* Unlike newspaper headlines, which appear immediately atop their articles, online headings almost always appear separately first, in a list detached from the content of messages. The more your heading points to the specific subject of your post and to your intention, the more likely you are to snag the audience you want. Consider, for example, these vague or lifeless headings and their improvements:

  Murky: Research question
  Clearer: Do you read fine print?

  Weak: Choosing a DTP program
  Stronger: Pagemaker vs. Ventura: help!

  Bland: Q about Who's Who
  Snazzier: What's what about Who's Who

What adman David Ogilvy wrote about ads in newspapers and magazines applies even more online, I believe: "On the average, five times as many people read the headlines as read the body copy." A length limit may force you either to use standard space-saving devices, such as "Q" for "question" and "DTP" for "desktop publishing," or to make some up. Whenever you respond publicly to someone else's message, of course, your reply bears their heading—unless you deliberately create an offshoot with a related heading.

- *In an environment of ever-looming information overload, brevity is at a premium.* You'll provoke irritation when readers wade through screen after screen of something that could have been stated in two sentences. State your piece simply and clearly and sign off, preferably within 20 lines or less. If you have much more than that to say, either apologize for running long at the beginning of your message or summarize what you meant to say and provide a link to the complete message at your Web site. Avoid the temptation, if your software makes this easy for you, to include the entire message you are replying to before you add your comment. Pare your quote of the previous note to the bone, so that it sets the context, then get to your point.

- *Newcomers to the medium and to your discussion can and will look in on an exchange at any moment.* This implies two imperatives if you're online to build your business. First, resist the temptation to become too clubby with others who post regularly. Avoid abbreviations and obscure in-group references such as "ROTFL—doesn't it remind you of Saratoga?—H.H." Indeed, I recommend that you never use special online slang like "ROTFL" for "rolling on the floor laughing" or "<BG>" for "big grin," no matter how prevalently you believe they are understood. Be inclusive rather than exclusionary, and you'll reap the rewards of a welcoming attitude.

Second, try to restate your business identity or business message in every followup post. You have tossed away a valuable opportunity when people come across a public message that reads in full, "Sure, I'll be glad to send you a copy. What's your address?" or "It costs only $20 a month for as much time as you want." Compare the effect of rewording those replies as "Sure, I'll be glad to send you a copy of our free report on keeping your tropical fish healthy. What's your address?" or "The Internet access provided by our company in 75 major metropolitan areas costs only $20 a month for as much time as you want." Unless your online area discourages the practice (see "Local Differences" later in this chapter), sign every post with at least your whole name and your business name, business slogan, or a revealing occupational title. For example,

Norris Kruntz, Financing for
"Unfinanceable" Upstart Businesses

Never assume the entire audience knows what you do just because the regulars do. Take a cue from skilled radio talk show guests who know that listeners are continually leaving and joining them and who therefore always toss in phrases like, "As I'm always careful to tell my therapy clients," or "As I explain in Chapter 2 of my book, *MegaBusiness Secrets.*" Sandwiched amid substantive information, this slides by as a clarification rather than as huckstering. Recognize too that even the regulars may have only a hazy understanding of your scope of business. For instance, over the space of a month or two, I interacted with a fellow who had created a product called Catalog-on-a-Disk. However, until we exchanged e-mail messages for some reason, I thought this was a singular disk-based catalog for specific products rather than a program for creating a catalog on disk, which would have interested me. Develop and test a brief spiel that truly communicates what your company does and then insert it as appropriate. For instance: "As you may know, we have created a program that anyone can use to place their catalog, complete with interactive order form, attractively on an IBM-compatible disk."

- *Anyone can comment or criticize.* Unlike online conferences (see Chapter 7), which may have a host, a guest, and ordinary participants, in a forum or newsgroup all contributions appear, at least initially, equal to each other. That means that

FAST FACTS

Schmoozing Success Story

When running a call center for Arizona Correctional Industries, Ron Bell tried schmoozing in forums where he could provide benchmarking metrics and information about effective techniques. By adding, "By the way, our call center specializes in these applications," he gained several new accounts. Bell also got useful inquiries when he added that the call center operated out of a prison, under the auspices of Episcopal Prison Outreach.

until people stop and ponder it, an uninformed or misinformed response carries the same weight as an informed response. Don't depend on any authority you may have outside of the group to add clout to your message. Instead, count on your online readers to be skeptical and irreverent. Only two factors make your contribution believed more than an opponent's: (1) how well your argument is reasoned or documented and (2) your reputation for reliability *within the group*. In the latter case, other members of the group may urge others to pay attention to you because you have previously demonstrated your trustworthiness. Still, credibility online is short-lived; you'll never be able to coast for a long while without pedaling in additional displays of know-how.

In some ways, cyberspace is a radically egalitarian environment. You have the right to mount a soapbox, but any brainless jerk also has the right to shout you down or ignore your brilliance. Other media upgrade you at least to a podium and a microphone. For example, if you share your information in a newspaper article, people can disagree in a letter to the editor, but not all of those get printed and you often get the privilege of the last word. Implicitly the article carries a greater claim to attention than the reply, unlike the free-for-all melee in an online discussion group. Similarly, most promotions you send out into the world lack any sort of talk-back feature. With online schmoozing you can't stop someone from tagging onto your message, "Hey, aren't you the one I sent $30 to last year and wouldn't refund my money?" All you can do is shout back "No!"

According to Bryan Pfaffenberger, author of *The Usenet Book,* Intel CEO Andy Grove stubbed his toes against the participatory nature of Usenet when he posted a message in newsgroups downplaying the flaw in Intel's Pentium microchips. That message got forwarded everywhere with comments attached like, "Can you believe this?" Grove's response might have had a different effect in another medium, Pfaffenberger says.

E-mail, more than snail mail, voice mail, or any other kind of communication, seems to place everyone at the same level. That's great when people respond with interest in how you can help them, not so great when people bombard you—or your suppliers and customers—with complaints for having somehow offended them. I believe this great leveling effect accounts for humorist Dave Barry's comment that he never receives letters through the mail that start off, "Are you the real Dave Barry?" as many e-mail messages that reach him do. (See Figure 6.1.) If you prefer the role of distant, lofty authority, disconnect your modem immediately.

- *Any message is fragmentable, and any discussion can get away from you.* The ability to take your words out of context is almost built into the technology, where someone can select any portion of a previous message to include in theirs. It's usually more difficult and sometimes impossible for a reader to go back and see those words in context. And since many people follow online discussions on an irregular basis, you can't assume that any rejoinder or correction will get seen by everyone who saw the unfair response. "Usenet in particular is like a yard full of snakes—at any time a snake can come up out of the grass and bite you," says Pfaffenberger.

John Glenn, publisher of a guide to translation agencies, heard those snakes hissing after he posted a very casual comment in a foreign language forum that was his prime pond for prospects. In a thread titled "pornography," someone asked a question about

Figure 6.1. Dave Barry on the Net

Japanese pornography that commonly appears in that country on CD-ROM. "I chimed in to say that they had them in the U.S. as well, I'd seen them in a CD store the other day. I'd joined the forum as 'John Glenn/Glenn's Guide', and that identity appeared automatically in the header of my reply." Of the droves of people reading that thread out of curiosity, one asked, "What is 'Glenn's Guide'?" and suddenly everyone drawn there was learning about his product in the puzzling context of pornography. "I got about 20 inquiries from that thread, but it was uncomfortable for me. Someone even suggested it was a good idea to get attention with the word, 'pornography', and I had to keep explaining that I hadn't done that."

- *You can't assume that only a certain audience group will see your message.* Although a certain online enclave may come to feel like a private group, don't behave as if it is. Another marketing consultant once made a nasty personal remark about me in a discussion list, probably knowing in the back of his mind that I had never appeared there. However, a client of mine forwarded the message to me. Flabbergasted by the consultant's poor judgment in saying something like that about anyone publicly, I retracted a recommendation I'd made to someone ready to hire him as someone savvy about online communication.

I saw this scenario play out once in a journalism forum, where writers griped on and on about editors, not understanding that some of the lurkers fell into the latter category. One writer who had just publicly bad-mouthed editors in general turned around and tried to sweet-talk an editor for a publication in his special area of interest. Privately this editor told me that she wouldn't give a writer with that kind of attitude an assignment in a million years.

Similarly, I once did a search on America Online using the word "consult" and turned up an extraordinary number of professionals who linked themselves with wisecracks designed more for other consultants than for potential clients. Try to imagine any of these impressing someone considering becoming a client:

FAST FACTS

Schmoozing Success Story

Mercia Tapping, president of *allergybuyersclub.com* found that schmoozing brought in customers even when conflict occurred. One day on allergy-related message boards she answered product questions by sharing her personal experiences, carefully avoiding blatant plugs for her own wares. "I incurred the vitriolic wrath of another vendor, who accused me of making up stories, which I found very offensive. Several other members of the board flew to my defense. Net result: My visitor count was up that week," she said.

— A consultant is someone who eats your lunch to tell you if you were hungry.

— Those of you who think that you know everything are annoying to those of us who do.

— Ask a consultant what time it is—he'll charge you a large fee, borrow your watch, and ask you what time you'd like it to be.

— The difference between consultants and prostitutes is there are some things a prostitute won't do for money.

Such confidence-killing slogans don't belong anywhere near your business identity. If you wouldn't include something in your professional Yellow Pages ad, don't put it online, even as a joke!

- *Contributions can and do show up 24 hours a day.* You're courting disaster if you expect the online world to have consideration for a 9-to-5, Monday-through-Friday, two-weeks-off-in-summer schedule. One of the most dramatic examples of this I've seen occurred when Sheridan, Indiana–based CBSI agreed to participate in a dialogue on a business board about its high-priced business start-up packages. The kick-off announcement went up on a Friday at noon, and it wasn't till almost 48 hours later that the CBSI representative showed up online. In the meantime, some extremely damaging claims about the company and numerous "Where are they?" notices remained visible to every visitor without any company response. I'm not saying not to sleep, just to be aware that rumors, inquiries, and complaints take no account of your convenience.

As a corollary to this, if you're soliciting business online, respondents will be getting in touch 24 hours a day, 365 days a year. Since telephone calls and faxes too—not only e-mails—will come in day and night, weekday and weekend, be prepared. Shutting down your company's fax reception when you go home for the night or the holiday is unacceptable, since people in Europe who don't know that it's Thanksgiving or in Nova Scotia who don't realize you're in Hawaii may simply conclude you've gone out of business. The same goes for companies that allow phones to ring forever outside of office hours. Yet if you're a home-based business and allow your business line to ring in your bedroom, the impression you give could be even worse. Before breakfast one morning I called an 800 number for a sample copy of a newsletter I'd seen discussed at a Web site. From the sleepiness of the "hello?" it was obvious I'd woken up the publisher. I wondered about the viability of a publication whose creator had either no money or no business sense.

- *A public question requires a public answer.* When CBSI finally did show up as promised on the business board, the owner of the company, George Douglass, responded again and again to specific, pointed questions with "Call our 800-number and get our tapes." Frustrated participants rejected that answer and repeated their questions, to more frustration. Whatever the rationale, such behavior appears evasive, shady, and manipulative to onlookers. Maintain your credibility by providing as much information as you can, along with appropriate qualifiers, such as: "Our literature contains full details, but basically with the XYZZ program a purchaser receives a Pentium computer, a modem, five proprietary software programs, a 453-page manual, and unlimited telephone support for $10,329." Or: "According to the ground rules of this forum I cannot give you specific legal advice. However, I can say that in several jurisdictions petitioners have gotten the courts to overturn prohibitions against giving Tarot and astrology readings for pay in one's home."

- *Where you can delete messages, be aware that they may never entirely vanish.* They may already have found their way into the archives of the system or of individuals, and system administrators may have easy ways of restoring deleted material, as we learned in the case of Lt. Colonel Oliver North in the Iran-Contra affair. Just how hard it can be to recall or correct misinformation online we know from the Federal Communications Commission, still dealing with protests stemming from an unfounded 1986 "modem tax" rumor. "Some days we get dozens of messages about the tax, sometimes just a few," sighs an FCC spokesperson. The best policy: Think before you press the Send button.

Local Differences

At a Chamber of Commerce luncheon people may be visibly impressed when you refer to your little law firm as a $4 million business, while at the Bar Association dinner, any mention of dollar figures may provoke raised eyebrows and significant glances. Similarly, the online medium is not monolithic, so figuring out one outpost's ground rules doesn't mean you've scoped out all of cyberspace. A method of schmoozing that works perfectly well in one locale may violate the norms in another province. The members of the group may be different, or distinctive traditions may be involved. You have to remain observant.

Online, Bryan Pfaffenberger illustrates this principle with the example of the newsgroup rec.backcountry, for avid mountain climbers. "If someone dies climbing, a friend is supposed to post an obituary of a certain type, because in this group death while climbing is noble, a kind of victory," he says. "If you didn't understand this and said how terrible the death was, you'd find yourself at the wrong end of flames."

Be especially sensitive to expectations about so-called signature files. Sometimes nicknamed ".sigs," on the Internet these function as the electronic equivalent of a business letterhead. Once set up by the user, they can get inserted automatically at the foot of all of his or her postings. For example:

****

Publicity/Marketing Consultant, Author, Seminar Leader
Marcia Yudkin, P.O. Box 1310, Boston, MA 02117, U.S.A.
1-617-266-1613; marcia@yudkin.com; http://yudkin.com
How badly do you need a Marketing Makeover?

****

FAST FACTS

"Spam" vs. Schmoozing

The epithet "spam" usually refers to unsolicited mass e-mail messages attempting to sell a product or service. However, in the context of newsgroups, forums, and discussion lists, it refers to the indiscriminate and perhaps inappropriate posting of the same canned message to a multitude of groups. If you have a message that's truly appropriate to a wide number of online locales, change the wording from posting to posting to avoid this charge. Better yet, monitor each group and introduce your message in relation to an ongoing discussion. This will almost certainly forestall complaints.

Since professors and researchers started this tradition, on the Internet, this format doesn't usually count as commercial promotion, unless you take it too far. How far is too far? Even the most staid discussion lists tolerate three-line signatures and regard eight lines as too much, and accept a simple description of your line of business but not necessarily a brazen sales pitch like "Call IDP for the best desktop publishing in Iowa!"

However, in some arenas you'll have to tone down a signature like the one here, or leave off everything but your name and a minimal identifier. "We had to make a rule against the Internet kind of signatures, because they were abused," says Janet Attard, who hosts a forum on America Online. "People were posting one-line messages and ten-line signatures." When in Rome, you might say, it's safest to observe what the Romans do and follow their example, being perhaps a teensy weensy bit more daring than the norm, if you like.

Another issue on which expectations differ is the extent to which people will put up with the same old questions. Participants in newsgroups and mailing lists are supposed to familiarize themselves with the FAQs—Frequently Asked Questions, available at the group's Web site or some other public location—and not to bother the regulars with questions answered there. Elsewhere, a question that has come up a thousand times before may receive an informative, courteous reply, although possibly a "canned" one.

Marshall McLuhan coined the phrase "the global village" to describe the effect of electronically linking people all over the world. Jay Linden, an Internet provider and consultant in Toronto, calls the Internet "the world's largest, most diverse small town." Perhaps we just need to change that to "villages" and "small towns" to remind us to check out the local customs before we hang out our shingle and walk up and down Main Street shaking hands.

7

Leading a Community

"When I went on Prodigy in 1992, I started a subject heading called 'Ask Lary Crews' and posted a variation on my resumé to explain why I had the audacity to offer my advice," mystery writer Crews of Sarasota, Florida, told me. "To my amazement, I got an average of 4000 questions over an 18-month period. After 18 months of paying an average of $25 a month to volunteer my help, I went through the roof when they announced a rate increase. So I tried America Online in June 1993 and instantly fell in love with the superior graphics, the lack of ads, the easy-to-navigate system. Again I opened my 'Ask Lary Crews' folder and started doing my volunteer work. Two months later, the leader of the Writer's Club asked if I'd be willing to be a writing consultant for the Writer's Club in exchange for some free hours. I said, 'You bet'."

Crews' official position on America Online has many counterparts throughout the Internet. If you have decent communication skills and expertise in a profession, hobby, or technical area, you might be able to wangle an exchange of your time and energy for a fiefdom, a title, and publicity for your other enterprises. Paid arrangements where you become a community leader for a Web site exist as well. Part III covers situations where you're king of your own online castle, but here you function more like a big shot or a chief within someone else's empire.

Recognition and Other Rewards

Except for the Prodigy detour, Lary Crews' story about how he got invited to become a community leader for the Writer's Club is typical. Different services have different names for their leading members, but just about everyone I spoke with who has held a position comparable to his had been invited. As with the Nobel Prize, it doesn't seem to help if you "apply" for the honor. Instead, you earn someone's attention, you get scrutinized, and you are chosen. That was certainly how I came to serve as a Special Contributor on the Business Board on Prodigy, where I was charged with stimulating discussion in my topic area, answering members' questions where I could, and helping to keep wayward members in line with the service's ground rules. Whether they're called hosts or "sysops" (system operators), community leaders need excellent communication skills, a cool head, and diplomacy, since they're counted on to help solve problems, not create them.

Trial lawyer Dan Kohane, who serves CompuServe's Lawsig forum as an assistant sysop, says that one of the rules he helps enforce is "You can provide legal information, but not legal advice." Information provides a legal context for a person's problem and points in several different directions, while advice zeroes in on the specifics of the situation. Sometimes those with the problem think that's a copout, and Kohane then explains the reason for the policy. Discussions on issues sometimes get quite heated, but only one message out of 600,000 was ever removed from the forum, he says—a direct racial or ethnic slur. "We don't mind controversy and disagreement. People think as a sysop I have an obligation to be neutral, and I do try to be a calming influence," notes Kohane. He also spends time explaining to people who wrongly believe their messages were removed where they actually went.

The grand host of CompuServe's PR and Marketing forum, Mike Bayer, credits PRSIG, as the forum is known by regulars, as having contributed more to his public relations career than any other one thing he's been involved with. Similarly, Merry Schiff, who sells a registered business opportunity for medical billing, says she gets "a big credibility boost from being a sysop on CompuServe's Working from Home forum. People have specifically told us that this impressed them."

On the other hand, the "don't call us, we'll select you" method of getting such a position may show recognition that the ideal forum helpers carry out their responsibilities as a mission or a semisacred trust. Gary Ellenbogen, for instance, told me that the spiritual guidebook *How Can I Help?* by Ram Dass has been a guiding force in the way he helps people stymied by their software in a technical support forum. "You need to recognize that when asking a technical support question, they make themselves vulnerable. They can be in a fragile or frustrated mood, or even angry, lashing out at the product. Instead of telling them what to do, you need to have the humble attitude, 'How can I help?' and give them what they need rather than what you happen to be good at. I also try to be a host rather than an authority figure, and to keep a sense of humor, especially when I don't know the answer. I get a big kick out of service, but you have to be able to do it selflessly."

On a smaller service, The Well, Boston-based freelance writer Fawn Fitter saw her online bill drop dramatically after she created and began cohosting a public conference, or message board, called Byline. "I had to persuade what's called the 'conference team' that there was a niche for it," Fitter says. "Although there was a writers' conference, it was more oriented toward fiction writers and the process of writing. Byline focuses on marketing your work. I spend even more time online than before, but they now waive my $15/month membership fee and I get 10 free hours a month." At Internet guide sites like about.com, which orient Web surfers to what's available on the Net in narrowly defined interest areas, topical hosts earn a cut of the advertising revenue attracted by their subsite.

Becoming a Big Cheese Contractor

What Fawn Fitter did on The Well represents a significant money-making opportunity. In 1992, for example, real estate journalist Peter Miller pointed out to the then-120,000-member America Online that they had nothing on the service covering real estate. Since virtually everyone lives in some sort of housing and since Miller had written numerous books on the topic, America Online readily agreed that this was an important topic to cover and that Miller was an appropriate person to set up and run a section of the service devoted to that topic. As host of the real estate area on America Online, Miller served, and got compensated, as an independent contractor. From scratch, he created the message boards, began stocking libraries, set policies, and recruited assistants to help run the area. As membership boomed, Miller added new features such as regular live conferences on different aspects of real estate. Although he told me it represents a "huge investment" of time and energy on his part, he explained, "It's another way to promote who I am and what I do, to make sure my books don't disappear from bookstore shelves after 60 days. When I started, fellow journalists asked me, 'Why are you bothering?' Now they ask, 'How can I get in on the action?'"

Most of the action now, of course, for those looking for such opportunities can be found at well-financed sites that hope a beehive of discussion will attract their best prospects to return again and again to the site. Community ring-leaders, says Greg Sherwin, co-author of *Connecting Online: Creating a Successful Image on the Internet*, "have an innate talent, not unlike TV talk show hosts, to break the ice, start a controversy, and moderate the exchange of opinion and ideas. These individuals are the scarcest resource, and as online communities proliferate, their talent pool continues to dilute." Jenna Woodul, cofounder and vice president of Talk City, Inc. (see Figure 7.1), which helps build communities for Web sites, agrees that community leaders are in greater demand than ever. "Hosts whose personalities reflect the brand's cultural attributes are usually found in the ranks of those who like the community and who return regularly. They show up and audition, if you will, by personifying the attitude and demeanor suggested by the brand or product. They become the role models for the community's behavior and tone, the talent scouts who encourage quality participation, and the recruiters of additional community leaders." The upshot: Demand appropriate compensation if you land such a position.

FAST FACTS

Do You Qualify?

These are the qualities most needed in a community leader:

- Diplomacy, tact, and a cool head
- Enthusiasm
- Dependability, general availability
- Wide knowledge of the field in question
- Ability to spark discussion
- Decent writing skill

Figure 7.1. Talk City Inc. helps build communities for Web sites.

According to Nigel Peacock of Tunbridge Wells in Kent, England, the greatest headache of community hosting is dealing with trouble-makers, such as what he calls a "confirmed con man," whom he locked out of his international trade forum. What constitutes disruptive or inappropriate behavior varies from site to site, with hosts having considerable latitude to define and handle violations.

Peter Miller calls his real estate area a "conservative" area in that "We don't accept everything that's uploaded to us. We only accept submissions that work, are relevant and valuable for our members, don't infringe any copyrights, and are up to date." When someone asks about or describes software, even if it's about real estate, "we send them elsewhere," he says. People do protest such decisions occasionally, and Miller explains that "no library or bookstore is required to put everything on its shelves, and we're not the place for something about, say, auto parts. On the other hand, we do allow messages saying that the area is lousy and the host is an awful person. Those we don't take down."

Janet Attard, who has hosted and managed online communities since 1988, likewise carries out policies to which some members object. "When someone uploads an ar-

FAST FACTS

Landing a Host Gig

Although most community leaders get hired after being observed in action, you could conceivably get such a position from a brand-new site by announcing your availability. Try a listing at one of these "talent markets" frequented by online adepts:

http://www.content-exchange.com

http://www.elance.com

http://www.freeagent.com

http://www.guru.com

http://www.workexchange.com

ticle, I look to see if it might have been written by someone else, and I might ask for proof of ownership or permission to upload it," she says. "I also look to see if it's an advertorial—one paragraph of text followed by a catalog of products and services. Several people who apparently bought 'reprint rights' to certain material have tried to upload the same article with different contact information at the end, and I don't allow that."

Besides dealing with conflicts, community hosts sometimes face the challenge of generating enough participation to inspire repeat patronage of the discussion area. Richard Hoy, who launched and built two successful discussion communities, the Online Advertising Discussion List and the ClickZ Forum, says he learned that to keep the exchange of ideas high in quality, a discussion moderator had to invite posts from "ringers" to inspire subscribers to jump in with their thoughts. In addition, he would sometimes take a more extreme position than he really held to get people worked up. "Clashing opinions often lead to knowledge about a subject being advanced. And that is what a discussion list should be all about—pushing the boundaries of knowledge about a specific topic," Hoy argues.

Making a Guest Appearance

Up to now we've been discussing asynchronous communication, where ideas go back and forth and around with breaks in time. Whereas electronic messaging resembles public letters, cybertalk, or "chat," is the closest equivalent to face-to-face or telephone conversation. Whether relatively formal and structured or so relaxed that you can endlessly interrupt each other, chat occurs in "real time." That is, the parties involved are all logged on and simultaneously present in some online location. Although your fingers do the talking and you can't see or hear the people involved in the session, online chatting has a cozy "getting-to-know-you" flavor. In the right setting, it can help you spread the word about what you do and help build business relationships. Many online communities offer organized chat sessions at which you can appear as a featured guest.

Very much like radio and television talk shows, Web sites and the online services offer guest appearances of celebrities, experts, and specialists. As with radio and TV, appearing as an online guest often puts your name in front of tens or hundreds of thousands of people who notice announcements of upcoming guest sessions but may not attend the actual chat session. For the event itself, you won't have to leave your office, worry about what to wear, or get concerned about controlling your nervous voice. Afterward, an edited transcript of the session may become available indefinitely to anyone who did not attend the session. "A lot of freelance writers see the transcripts," notes Lisa Kanarek, author of *Organizing Your Office For Success*, who has appeared in several online conferences. "It's a good resource for them." Don't take for granted the "before" and "after" segments of publicity, however; it never hurts to prompt your sponsor about pre-event promotion and whether or not a transcript will be generated for later public posting.

Although authors and luminaries of various sorts predominate among online guests, you don't have to be published or famous to make a guest appearance. A reputation helps, but all you really need is expertise or experience and willingness to share what you know with what may be a very specialized audience such as backpackers, Windows programmers, or people interested in Italy. For instance, if you're an intellectual property attorney, you might appear to answer questions about copyright for writers or software entrepreneurs. Don't be shy about volunteering to be a guest, because if you have something valuable to offer, your host benefits from the extra time people spend online to be with you.

Most venues call the event organized around your presence a "conference," but it resembles a radio or TV call-in show more than any other sort of guest–audience interaction. Basically, you answer questions during the conference from those assembled. Although you'll have a host or a moderator, you'll interact mostly with the participants. Unlike the radio or TV host, who lends his or her personality to the proceeding and shares the spotlight with the guest, online the host's role is mainly to keep the conference rolling along smoothly. Bestselling mystery writer Sue Grafton says she gets the same sorts of questions online as elsewhere—no better, no worse—"but it's an interesting way to reach people you might not reach otherwise. Lots of folks are plugged into the computer world, and they're a different breed of people." The major skill you need for appearing online that you don't need for radio or TV is fairly quick typing. The pace will be quick and relentless for the hour or two that you've agreed to be "on." For that reason Terri Lonier, author of *Working Solo*, calls an online appearance being a "guest typist."

Besides inquiring about pre-event publicity and a transcript being made of the event, here are some tips to ensure that your conference goes smoothly:

- *Get a telephone number or two to call in case something goes wrong.* You do not want people showing up only to find a discussion like, "Where's Rhonda? Gee, something must have happened to Rhonda. Well, folks, sorry, let's call it a night." If your modem happened to choose that evening to retire, at least you'd be able to call the moderator to pass your explanation on to the assembled multitude. Bob Coleman and Deborah Neville, authors of *The Great American Idea Book*, suffered an electrical blackout that made it impossible for them to turn up at an online guest appearance, but at least they knew someone to call who let the audience know the circumstances of the no-show.

- *Visit the conference space beforehand if possible, so you know how to get there and how to participate.* Graphic designer Heidi Waldman once agreed to moderate a desktop publishing conference on America Online and found herself wandering through rooms devoted to wifeswapping and worse trying to find the right place. "I had 'Aldus volunteer' on my I.D. It was embarrassing!" Following the precept that it's better to be safe than sorry, you might ask your host to meet you there at a certain time the week or day before to practice. Or attend someone else's conference, which would also provide a taste of the degree of interactivity you should expect at yours.

Lisa Kanarek told me that she received the questions for one conference ahead of time and got to choose the ones she wanted to answer. Indeed, one novelist confessed to me that he wasn't even anywhere near his computer the night he supposedly appeared for his chat session—he had received the questions from the coordinator and responded, whereupon the coordinator posted the Q&A session as if it were happening right then. If you want to let the audience know you're really there you might ask the questioner a question and maintain a dialogue—although "polylogue" might also be more accurate when five different conversations are zipping around, some completely independent of the honored guest.

- *Get directions and arrive early.* At sites with lots of chat rooms, if you don't know the name of your online destination, you'll never find it, and if you arrive after the room is already full, you may have trouble entering. Avoid putting your host in an awkward spot and making the audience restless by showing up prior to the announced starting time.

- *Make sure you double-check the time.* If someone tells you you go on stage at the Crystal Theater at 7 P.M. in Minneapolis, you know that means Minneapolis time. But if someone in Minneapolis tells you, who live in San Francisco, that the online conference starts at 7 P.M., is that 7 P.M. Minneapolis time, San Francisco time, or, according to a convention some businesses follow, Eastern Time? Find out.

- *Be prepared to give brief answers.* On the air, they call these short takes "sound bites." The online medium also prefers dialogue to monologue, and constant momentum. Limit your responses to three sentences at a time, tops.

- *Tell participants how to buy or get in touch.* A considerate host will every once in a while feed you lines like, "Marcia, please tell everyone how they can order your book, *Six Steps to Free Publicity*." If that doesn't happen, give out your ordering or contact information every twenty minutes or so, since your audience will be constantly changing as people enter and leave the conference. You can say, "By the way, if your local bookstore doesn't have *Six Steps to Free Publicity*, you can order it by calling 1-800-8YU-DKIN" or "Feel free to e-mail me at *marcia@yudkin.com*, or visit my Web site at *www.yudkin.com*."

Playing Host Online

The official conferences described in the previous section aren't the only "real-time" colloquies taking place online. Some individuals sponsor their own live schmoozing or professional exchange sessions. Wally Bock, publisher of the "Cyberpower Alert!" newsletter, hosted a get-together for professional speakers, trainers, and consultants for quite a time every Monday night on America Online. Most, although not all, of those who attended were fellow National Speakers Association members. "I wanted a place for people to go online regularly," he said. "It started off as a semi-NSA event, but then it became mainly my thing."

Bock e-mailed announcements of the weekly meetings to a list that grew from 12 to 140 people in less than a year. The sessions reminded me of the monthly networking meetings run for years by my chapter of the National Writers Union in a Cambridge, Massachusetts bar: People talked shop, greeted old friends, met new colleagues, and exchanged news about opportunities and problems in the profession. As host, Bock subtly but regularly reinforced his position in the vanguard of online developments.

Similarly, Nikki Sweet, a partner in the consulting firm Up Your Business! Inc. in Jupiter, Florida, took the initiative to organize networking meetings for other Toastmasters International members every Wednesday evening in a special chat room. Sweet got started by searching America Online's member directory for the word "Toastmaster" and sending e-mail invitations to each of the more than 200 members she found. From posting notes on the Internet in the newsgroup alt.org.toastmasters she received 30 inquiries a week, not counting the e-mail messages from people who had heard about the sessions from attendees.

"For me, business is all about creating relationships, and with live conferencing, it's as if you're really there and can express yourself to others spontaneously," Sweet told me. "One of my ground rules is that everyone must introduce themself, so that it's good visibility. Someone who finds out what I do might ask, 'Hey Nikki, I want to start a business but I don't know how to do a business plan,' and everyone in the room sees my answer."

A more structured model for online conferencing comes from Jeff Senné, a consultant in Fairfax, California, who specializes in sales leadership, team building, and strategic planning. Senné's vision involved an international community of consultants who use cyberspace to create strategic alliances so that teams of consultants can successfully compete against "the big guys." As part of that effort, Senné hosted two educational meetings a month online, one of them with a guest speaker who submitted a five-to-ten-page handout before the meeting to those on his list. Senné collected questions from those who showed up at the meeting and passed them along to the speaker, saved the proceedings, and e-mailed them afterward to everyone in the network. Senné's next step was developing a Consultants Online Directory on the Web as a sort of virtual mall of consultants. Asked how he expected this whole venture to benefit him, Senné replied, "Someone has to stand up and say, 'I know this and this and I'm willing to share it.' I'm an educator and want to educate people about what these new tools offer the business community. I'm doing all this as a volunteer, but it will give me personally an enormous resource pool to draw from."

Simply Chatting

A final variety of online talk that can benefit your business involves settings where you're neither host nor guest and there's no agenda, just a designated special-interest space. For instance, Dick Sine of Fort Mill, South Carolina, a stamps journalist and entrepreneur, logs on just about every night around 10:20 to attend a drop-in gathering in a conference room on CompuServe's Collectibles forum devoted to stamp collecting. Informally he fields questions about stamps from the 10 to 20 folks assembled—"dealers, collectors, journalists, some regulars, some newcomers, ranging in age from 12 to retirement, some from outside the United States. Conversation is wide-ranging, fellowship is excellent," he says.

Sine participates so religiously because he's found it useful in collecting information for his writing projects and developing new product ideas. "These kinds of chats offer contact with participants who don't necessarily know the stamp establishment," Sine explains. "If you want to have a market-driven approach, where else to get information than from the market? Also, I make friends this way. Later, when people want to buy, they prefer to buy from a friend."

Jan Melnick found it just as useful to attend chat sessions that were organized for people in the secretarial or desktop publishing business by colleague Deb Matthews every other Thursday evening. Between 15 and 20 people, mostly beginners and thus potential buyers of Melnick's book, *How to Open and Operate a Home-based Secretarial Services Business*, would show up.

Similarly, when writer Lary Crews has a few minutes to spare, he visits writers' chat rooms. "If I see an opportunity, I'll jump in and say, 'You know, I teach an online writing course', and then e-mail stuff about the course immediately to them. That's gotten lots of people to sign up," Crews says about his online course, "Writing the Novel." Also, more than 400 graduates, some of whom might be in that chat room, generate a lot of word of mouth."

If you enjoy talking, ask around online for live chat sessions in your subject area. Some are publicly announced; others, although open to visitors, require that you wangle a space on the invitation list. Behave as you would at any

FAST FACTS

Free Chat Services

If you want to run chat sessions for customers, clients, or colleagues, or add a chat room to your Web site, check out these free services:

- *http://www.beseen.com*
- *http://www.talkcity.com*
- *http://www.webmaster.com* (look for "Back Pack")

networking event—introduce yourself professionally and show as much interest in what others do and want to know as in any marketing message you weave into your conversation. Don't focus so much on business that you forget to relax and just enjoy being in the presence of others who are as fascinated by, say, Chinese cooking or furniture design as you are. Reach out person to person, come back, and people will remember you.

8

Answering Reporters' and Authors' Appeals

> *To: all*
> *From: Tracy Touchstone*
> *Re: article sources needed*
>
> *Hi everyone! I'm a freelance writer working on a story for a major business magazine on people who have been dragging their feet on going online but have finally made the leap to the Internet. If this applies to you, please e-mail me at the address above. Thanks!*

Don't pass over notes like this one. Feeding your story to a journalist may seem a farfetched, elusive way of wooing clients, but for many it proves more lucrative than, say, e-mailing one prospect who needs immediate help. In this chapter I'll describe the route between appeals like the one here and the warm, rewarding glow of media attention. I'll also describe more active tactics people have used to get their tale across to online members of the press. If you're thinking, "Not me! I'm not *People* magazine or *Wall Street Journal* material," hang on a minute. Even a humble Boonesville operation can deserve and reap the benefits of entering into the public eye.

Publicity 101

Most of all, media coverage bestows credibility. When you tout your own product or service, people discount your pitch—after all, that's you praising yourself. But when you're featured in a newspaper, magazine, radio show, or TV program, it implies objective worth, even when you initiated the contact. People presume experienced reporters know how to see through flimsy self-promoters. Kimberly Sheasby of Santa Fe, New Mexico, who bills herself as The Secretary Different, responded when a writer for the *Los Angeles Daily News* posted a note seeking people to interview who had made connections online that helped enhance their business. Not only did she appear in that newspaper, but also in the *Tampa Tribune* and other papers subscribing to the *New York Times* Syndication Service. "Without the online connection, my little one-person operation would have been hard put to get such national publicity. My local customers now look at me with awe," says Sheasby.

When media outlets feature you, your message reaches thousands, hundreds of thousands, or even millions of potential customers at no cost to you. Michael Burlingame, a history professor at Connecticut College, casually sent a copy of his biography of Abraham Lincoln to a reporter in Springfield, Illinois, who had helped him with his research. The reporter wrote a story about the book that went out on the Associated Press newswire and ended up in dozens of newspapers across the country, and even in David Letterman's nightly monologue. All those column inches and sound bites undoubtedly spurred the sales of his book.

Penfield, New York, consultant Marcia Layton also doesn't need to guess at the effect of national press coverage. When *USA Weekend*, a Sunday supplement with a circulation of 39 million, mentioned her as a specialist in writing business plans, her phone started ringing at 5:30 in the morning and didn't stop until she had received forty calls. "At least three clients came out of that," she recalls.

When you're trying to build a name for yourself, each time your public reads or hears about you, you come closer to—or cross—their threshold of recognition. Since more only brings more in this arena, I'm always delighted when someone posts a public message congratulating me for appearing in the pages of, say, *Entrepreneur* or *Home Office Computing*. Invisibly and inexorably the meter of reputation goes up.

These rewards aren't automatic upon any reply to an appeal like the one at the beginning of the chapter. You must be quick, informative, responsive, and confident to earn your turn in the media spotlight. Let's look at each of these guidelines in more detail.

- *Be quick.* "To take advantage of publicity opportunities, you have to check messages frequently and carefully," says Layton. "A notice may only be up for a short time." Cathryn Conroy, a senior writer for *CompuServe Magazine*, says that with a highly specialized request, such as in the RV forum for families who are living full-time in a recreational vehicle, she may receive only a few responses. "But for small business stories, I usually have to delete my message after 24 hours because I've gotten 50 responses. That's too much."

- *Be informative.* In your response, provide enough information for the reporter to determine whether or not your story is relevant for the article or chapter at hand. "Don't say, 'Hi, this is Bill from Montana,' urges medical writer Kathy Seña of Manhattan Beach, California, who really has received such responses from doctors. "Give your full name and affiliation and how I can reach you. Recognize that writers are confronting a deadline." Since some reporters will conduct their information gathering through e-mail and others by telephone, provide as many ways as possible for them to get through to you quickly, includ-

FAST FACTS

Schmoozing Success Story

One day when I couldn't find an article I'd read in *Business 2.0* at the magazine's Web site in order to include it with an article I was writing, I e-mailed a Letter to the Editor describing my frustration. Within two hours I received a reply from Jim Daly, the publication's Editor in Chief, explaining why the article wasn't yet at the site. Grabbing this opportunity to have the top dog's ear, I introduced myself more fully in a reply, offering to write for the magazine. Within a month I had a contract for my first article for *Business 2.0*. Your e-mail feedback may be read by important people!

ing after-hours phone numbers. When it comes to the substance of the requested information, "be quotable and not too dry," says Seña. "For instance, for a story on indoor pollution, the head of an emergency room referred to the image of the canary in the mine and said, 'It's the asthmatics who will let us know the planet's in trouble.' The artist used his quote as the basis for an illustration. I just keep coming back to this guy again and again as a source."

- *Be responsive.* Stay focused on the questions and needs of the reporter rather than your private publicity agenda. When I contacted the director of a media institute for this book, for instance, he seemed more interested in convincing me that the authority the institute was named after had been maligned in his lifetime than in finding out how he could be helpful to me. And the materials he offered to send me never arrived, not even after my second reminder. It's usually far better to offer too many facts, examples, explanations, and leads to other sources than to hold back. Indeed, the more information you provide that's relevant to the story, the more likely you'll be consulted at a later time on a related topic.

- *Be confident.* When reporters put out the word for examples, they aren't seeking businesses whose foibles and faults they plan to investigate and expose. Almost always, they'll cast you in a good light. Remember that sharing your successes with a journalist is just an extension of the kind of communication you're online for to begin with, says Jack Germain, a Barnegut, New Jersey, writer who does a lot of research online. "I'm never overwhelmed with responses when I ask for interviewees. The typical person online is leery of being quoted, just as someone who stands up at a public meeting to speak may get timid when a reporter comes over to them afterwards. People are unnecessarily intimidated by writers."

Cathryn Conroy says that many of those she interviews are reluctant to toot their own horn to her. "You have to brag to me, though, so I have something to write. And when I do write it, it goes in in third person, not as a brag. So don't worry, and don't hold back."

Publicity 707—Taking the Initiative

During my first year online, I probably saw at least a hundred direct appeals from writers and responded to perhaps fifteen. As you might guess, that response rate doesn't reflect shyness but the fact that I had little of relevance to contribute on many of the announced topics. At least seven of those fifteen times, my response led to a significant mention in a national magazine or another writer's book. Yet you don't have to merely keep your hunter's eye open and then pounce. As long as you're careful how you do it, you can also hunt for media personnel and contact them on their electronic turf.

Charlotte Libov of Bethlehem, Connecticut, for instance, is constantly thinking about opportunities to promote her book, *The Woman's Heart Book*. (See Figure 8.1.) On numerous forays into forums for journalists and broadcasters, she has sought and found people eager to interview her. "I've met about fifteen other health authors online, who will think of me when they're writing about heart disease, someone from the *Los Angeles Times* and a reporter from

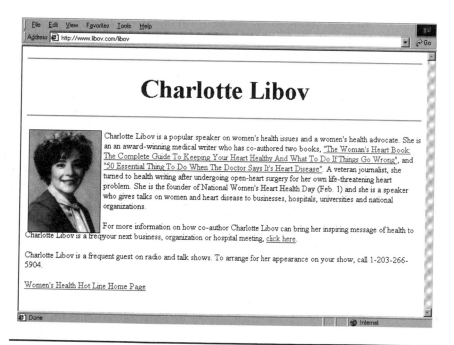

Figure 8.1. Charlotte Libov's online bio.

the *New Orleans Times-Picayune*, who wrote a piece about my book. I've gotten the most 'hits' among broadcasters, though, since they're so hungry for information—something like eight to ten radio interviews, including the 'Jim Bohannon Show,' which goes out to hundreds of stations and where I went on right after Dan Rather."

Libov emphasizes that when she finds someone who identifies himself as a talk-show host or a reporter, her approach is always low-key. "My e-mail messages are very self-effacing, something like, 'I don't want to disturb your privacy, I was just wondering if you would be interested…' Most people are receptive, and the broadcast people especially have steered me in the direction of appropriate health shows and said I could use their name."

Similarly, Marcia Layton ended up in *USA Weekend* through an enterprising electronic communication. She sent a note to the publicity director at CompuServe saying something like, "I just wanted to introduce myself and make you aware of the fact that I'm benefiting a lot from my membership in CompuServe, and if you ever have inquiries from journalists or writers, here's my story…." Not long afterward, the publicity director thought of Layton when a *USA Weekend* reporter asked for leads.

Jerry Harmon of South Lyon, Michigan, e-mailed the *Ann Arbor News*, 15 miles from South Lyon, a chatty pitch letter describing how and why his wife, who uses a cane due to multiple sclerosis, patented a line of colorful, fashion-accessory covers for canes. That letter produced a nice article, as did a similar letter mailed to his hometown paper, which ran an article in the section that goes to six different

FAST FACTS

Schmoozing Success Story

Editor Richard Lynch of Amherst, New York, landed a book contract when an acquisitions editor from Waite Group Press saw his replies to questions in a Photoshop newsgroup about the software program of that name. "I guess some of my answers struck a chord," Lynch says. "The editor asked if I thought I could write a book on Photoshop, and I said yes."

communities. "Some local people cut the article out and sent it to friends and relatives elsewhere who have M.S., and orders came in."

Kathy Seña, the medical writer, says she's seen doctors approach journalists along the lines of "Hi, I'm so and so, I do such and such, and if you ever need someone in my specialty...." Seña always files their information carefully. "They're a valuable resource, because these are people who want to talk to the media."

If you do decide to put your story forward to a reporter, contact him or her in the form of a brief, personable note—ten lines at most—rather than a formal press release. Beginning with an apologetic phrase like, "I know you must be busy, but!" or "I hope it's all right to use e-mail to let you know about..." starts you off on the right foot for this sort of intrusion. Someone who wants to know more will contact you for additional details. You want to avoid annoying those in a position to give your business publicity, and a simple informative note that can be scanned in 20 seconds will rarely impose a burden on the recipient.

Of more than 2000 journalists who write about the computer industry who were surveyed by publicist Marty Winston, all but 50 said they objected to receiving full-length press releases via e-mail. However, when press releases are distributed by special Internet services to reporters and producers who have asked to receive them, this prejudice apparently falls by the wayside.

Regular mail is still a viable medium for distributing news about your online activities to reporters, editors, and producers. My book *Six Steps to Free Publicity* (see Appendix B) contains samples and advice concerning traditional press releases. Don't overlook the trade press in your field—narrowly focused business magazines and tabloids such as *Coin-Op Industry News* or *The Gourmet Retailer*—when you've launched a specialized online community or created a new information resource for the Web. The media's hunger for information on trends and new developments in cyberspace has shown few signs of abating, so that almost anything new and different online can catch a reporter's fancy.

Laura Fillmore, president of Open Book Systems in Rockport, Massachusetts, showed me a full-page article about her company's Internet presence in *Forbes ASAP*, a high-tech offshoot of *Forbes* magazine. "Yes, they mention that we lost $100,000 last year, but if we were a shoe store losing $100,000 would that get us into *Forbes?*"

The Press Are Not Your Pals

An incident during my research for this book reminded me to end this chapter with a warning. Never let down your guard with a journalist and reveal information that would damage your company if it were broadcast to the world! Here's how the scenario goes: A writer calls to get your story and the two of you quickly build up some rapport. Twenty minutes later you're speaking as frankly as you would with a trusted colleague. But unless you're willing to see your dirty underwear hung out in public, watch your tongue. Many writers feel more loyalty to their readers than to you. I don't see my role as pulling off exposés, so when a source for this book confessed unethical behavior, I asked, "Are you sure you want that story connected to your company?" He said, "Yeah, that's OK." After thinking it over, though, I decided not to be the agent of his destruction and sent him back a note explaining why he shouldn't spill those kinds of beans with reporters, and why I personally disapproved of what he was doing.

Don't commit any of these potentially devastating mistakes:

- *Assuming that a "nice" reporter couldn't possibly do you wrong.* If Mike Wallace of "60 Minutes" fame showed up on your doorstep, you'd be on your guard. Yet a heart-to-heart confessional is never appropriate during an interview, no matter how well-intentioned and pleasant a representative of the press seems. Remember this basic rule: If you don't want your mother, clients, or competitors to know about it, don't mention it to the reporter.

- *Asking a journalist not to print something—in the same breath as saying it.* This still amazes me after two decades as a freelance writer. So many people say, "Don't put this in your article, but...." The reporter has no obligation to honor such a unilateral request. If you don't want it in the article, don't say it.

- *Trying to avoid trouble with a pompous "no comment."* This phrase became notorious during the Watergate years and will convey the impression that you're engaged in a coverup. Instead, explain why you can't answer the question, as in, "I'm sorry, that's proprietary information" or, "We don't release our sales figures."

- *Equating the end of note taking or tape recording with going "off the record."* Someone who has tucked away her notebook or turned off the tape recorder hasn't shucked her job. Remember: If you don't want it transmitted to millions, don't say it, even while you're walking her to the elevator!

Finally, prevent errors in media publicity by emphasizing details that matter to you. Writer Lary Crews told me, "Make sure you write a note to your copy editor that my first name really does have only one 'r'. Otherwise they'll 'correct' it for you." By taking this kind of responsibility, you up the chances that you'll be proud, not apologetic or angry, about your turn in the media spotlight.

PART III

Building Your Online Information Empire

9

Your Own Web Real Estate

When I talk about marketing electronically," wrote Studio City, California, consultant Bob Serling, "I mean actually placing an ad, getting a response, and attempting to close a sale. I don't mean customer support or long hours giving advice on [chat] forums." In 1995, this statement, in a column called "Marketing on the Information Superhighway: Truth vs. Hype," reflected prevalent skepticism that the Internet could ever mature into a selling medium. With more than $100 billion dollars a year now unquestionably changing hands through the Net, there remains widespread confusion about what kind of marketing and sales environment the Web represents. Is a Web site comparable to a print ad? Is it like television? Isn't it just a store or billboard in cyberspace? What's the best way to stake out territory on the Web and hawk your wares there?

In 2001, the World Wide Web continues to grow exponentially, with millions more sites already posted than any individual could ever visit in a lifetime. Big business has latched on to the Web, but it can serve your purposes if you're a smaller business or professional as long as you have reasonable expectations. A Web site won't magically triple your revenues once you slap it up in cyberspace and statically keep it there. Unlike a real-world billboard, no one drives by a Web site on the way to somewhere else. In the billboard metaphor, which ultimately fails to capture the marketing potential of the Web, you'd have to put up a billboard to tell people to go see your billboard, and a billboard for that, and so on—or build a highway connecting some already well-traveled road to yours.

Rather than trying to find a more appropriate metaphor, let's concentrate on three purposes a Web presence for your business can fulfill. Getting clear on your purpose or purposes provides a solid foundation for a Web site that works for you. First, you might expect your Web site to deliver leads, bringing you prospects who hadn't previously taken an interest in your products or services. Second, you might expect your Web site to supplement and support your other marketing vehicles by making it possible to view information about you or your firm instantly, 24 hours a day. Third, you might build a fully functioning online store in which people from all over the world can shop and place orders for merchandise by credit card. Although one site can fulfill two of these or all three purposes, you'll think most clearly about how to set up your site if you identify one of these three purposes as primary.

Lead Generation Through the Web

Joe Vitale, a copywriter based in Houston and the author of *Cyberwriting*, receives at least two very serious inquiries each week from his Web site (see Figure 9.1). Although he pays $98 a month for the site, he charges clients high enough fees that just one new account coming from the Web site would cover his Web costs for two years. "You can easily see that I don't even care if I sell many books from my site," he says. His results more than justify the cost of maintaining the site just for the purpose of funneling new prospective clients to him. Note that he follows up on Web leads the same way he would for a lead originating from someone who called after reading one of his books or hearing him speak—via phone, e-mail, and fax.

Lead generation through the Web can work well for consultants, agencies of various sorts, vacation spots, attorneys or accountants, art restorers—anyone who sells a complicated, expensive, high-contact product or service. From the lead's point of view, a successful match often begins with a need or problem and a Web search for the right individual, company, or establishment to solve it. In other cases the lead is merely searching for information and gets the idea of buy-

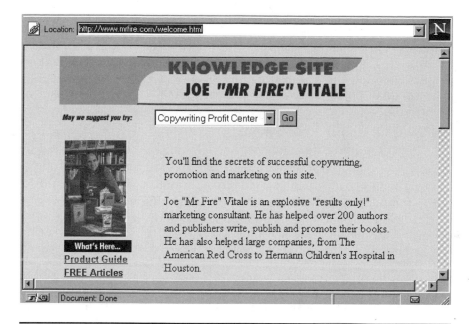

Figure 9.1. Joe Vitale's home page.

ing when something during the search hits a nerve. For instance, someone trying to decide whether to send mouse pads or cheese baskets as
corporate gifts might hunt for advice and end up hiring a corporate
gift consultant, not having known before the search that such folks
even existed.

Most companies aiming at leads from their Web sites create something disparagingly referred to as "brochureware": dull, company-
centered sales copy, often taken directly from paper-and-ink brochures,
explaining who they are and what they do. The headline presents the
name of the firm, and the rest of the page its capabilities, as if to a
hushed, darkened audience with their hands poised for applause. This
can indeed lure some shoppers who discover Web sites of companies
that fulfill their criteria for certain capabilities, location, price range,
and so on. If you were not already an active shopper, though, would
you spend the time to read a collective electronic resumé for Chefs,
Cooks, and Bottlewashers, Inc.? The more competitors the shopper
finds, the more something beyond brochureware has to reach out
and persuade the prospect to choose this possibility from many op-

tions. Moreover, brochureware doesn't attract the second kind of lead, those who can be nudged from vague curiosity to a resolution to buy.

For the most successful lead generation, I recommend a Web site that will attract information seekers as well as those consciously shopping. This means not only posting valuable educational content on your site but putting the educational, surfer-centered information up front and the promotional stuff behind. If you design restaurants, you would offer numerous articles and Frequently Asked Questions sections on restaurant design as your lead feature, and follow up with the ways in which you serve restaurateurs. From the visitor's point of view, this does a better job of establishing your uniqueness and credibility than the more common reverse option (company info first) or nothing but sales-oriented information.

To take an actual example, Dr. Jim Humphries, a veterinarian who answers callers' questions on syndicated radio and cable TV shows (see Figure 9.2), heads his home page "Welcome to Dr. Jim's Virtual Veterinary Clinic." The table of contents just below that has four headings: "It's our grand opening!—Who the heck is Dr. Jim?"; "Dr. Jim's Animal Clinic for Cats"—questions and answers; "Dr. Jim's Animal Clinic for Dogs"—questions and answers; and "Read My Disclaimer." Pet owners will spend more time there and return more often than if the site offered nothing beyond "Why you should hire Dr. Jim to treat your pet."

Similarly, Media Relations, a public relations firm, has created a subsite with articles of value for those hoping or planning to be featured in the media—i.e., its potential clients (see Figure 9.3).

FAST FACTS

Design Do's and Don'ts

- *Use* a color scheme that fits your business.

- *Use* high-contrast color combinations for text.

- *Use* navigation links that include what visitors want to find.

- *Use* proofreaders to catch spelling and formatting mistakes.

- *Avoid* having so many graphics that visitors wait forever to see what's what.

- *Avoid* complicated background patterns.

- *Avoid* requiring plug-ins, which visitors might not have.

- *Avoid* gratuitous animation.

Figure 9.2. Dr. Jim's Virtual Veterinary Clinic.

Visitors can read four feature stories on media relations, questions and answers under "Ask Dr. Publicity," and tips on publicizing a Web site. Only when readers explore further will they discover soft-sell material on the company.

Besides alluring content, the most indispensable other element your site must have to work well for lead generation is complete contact information—phone, fax, postal address, e-mail address, and the name of the contact person. This sounds too obvious to mention, but I can't count how many times I've searched a site in vain for the physical location of the company, a telephone number, or the name of the company owner or marketing manager. (See Figure 9.4.) Other times I finally found the postal address hidden away in some inconspicuous, obscure corner of the site.

With these essentials taken care of, you can enhance the pulling power and word-of-mouth potential of your lead-generation site by adding new content often and by adding interactive features such as quizzes, contests, or a forum. Up-to-date lists of resources in your topic area can attract traffic, as can book reviews, software reviews, and the like. Testimonial quotes and links to magazine or newspaper articles discussing you lend a tremendous boost of credibility.

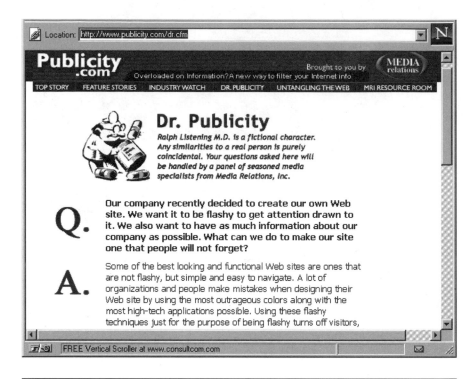

Figure 9.3. Media Relations' publicity information.

A Marketing Support Site

Let's say you own a coffee supply business on Cape Cod, keeping business customers stocked with the coffee blends they prefer, with coffee-making machines and thermoses, and with associated supplies such as cups, sugar packets, and napkins. Since you serve such a limited area, a Web site might not bring you a lot of new customers. Nevertheless, it might save you a lot of time and money. First, given a Web site you can run small ads in the Yellow Pages and local papers, providing your Web address as one way readers can immediately obtain prices and complete other details. Second, by providing forms allowing regular customers to reorder at their convenience, monthly delivery schedules, answers for frequently asked questions, and new products available, the site can cut costs and allow you to devote more time to locking up new customers and making sure old ones receive the level of service they expect.

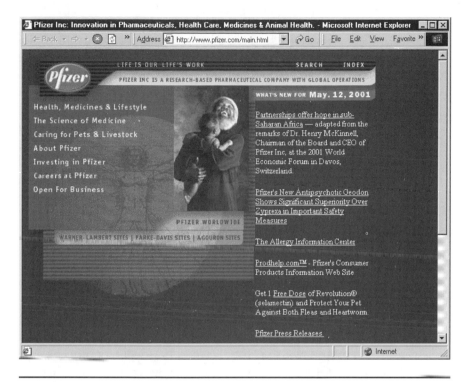

Figure 9.4. Pfizer's Web site includes no contact information at all.

Who else might benefit from a marketing support Web site? Let's say a standup comedian gets a call from the planner for a business conference who wants to know more before going ahead with the hire. While they're still on the phone, if the comedian can tell the planner the Web address, which has a photo, testimonial quotes, and a video clip of her in action, she's that much closer to the sale. A software firm can use the Web to make available more than would typically be included in printed manuals or sales literature: patches, macros, user tips, which program does what, projected updates, options and procedures for one-on-one technical help, training resources, and more. And any company with a walk-in location can save time and increase convenience for patrons by posting directions and hours of operation.

For a successful marketing support site, concentrate on making it useful to customers who have already heard of you, are on the verge of doing business with you, or already belong to your camp of customers or clients. Then make sure every communication vehicle about your company presents the Web site as a route for further, fuller details. Mention the Web address on the company voice mail and in the on-hold message. Put it on delivery trucks. Imprint it on pens and self-stick note pads that you give away. Solicit suggestions for making the site even more helpful. Can we check the status of our orders on the Web? You got it. How about a password-protected area where we can examine our usage patterns over the last year? Good idea! I know you don't have space in the catalog for each of the instructors' photos and class quotes, but how about at the Web site? Coming up!

E-commerce

If you sell products that can be selected, ordered, and shipped, you'll probably want to set up an online store. More and more, those who surf the Net feel comfortable plugging in their credit card numbers at a Web site and waiting for the merchandise to come by mail. How well your store succeeds depends on several factors: how shopper-friendly you make your catalog and the ordering process, how unusual or hard-to-find your offerings are, and the competitiveness of your prices.

A small business seems to do best selling online when serving a narrow niche with a cluster of products difficult to locate elsewhere. Atomic Books, an alternative bookstore in Baltimore, specializes in underground topics like UFOs, hacking, drug culture, comics, and so on. According to Bill Koch, who was involved in creating Atomic Books' Web site, even in 1995 it was bringing in "a couple of hundred dollars of sales a week. For a small business, that's like being open a few extra days a month, and it's extremely cost-effective," he said. Other narrow niches: equestrian supplies, recharged laser cartridges, custom-built hypoallergenic furniture.

The larger your inventory, the more mandatory it is for visitors to be able to search within the site for the precise item they're seeking, as well as to browse within meaningful categories. This may not come cheaply. The more complicated your offerings and the more integrated your online information with real-world situations, the more you'll need custom programming and database services to keep pace as prices change, product lines evolve, and shipping options or shipping prices change. Although "shopping cart" software is coming down in price, and some sites, provide electronic merchant services free, you'll still

FAST FACTS

Accepting Payment

I. *Credit cards.* If you sell right at your Web site, you should be equipped to accept credit cards. Your Web hosting company may have options for you, you might apply through your own bank, or you can deal with a credit card processing company. Some leads to investigate:

http://www.charge.com

http://www.acceptcreditcards.com

http://www.ibill.com

II. *Bank wires.* These are especially appropriate when you provide large-ticket services internationally. Just give your client your bank's name, its "routing number," and your account number to facilitate an electronic transfer of funds.

III. *Purchase orders.* Governmental organizations, not-for-profit groups, and corporations may issue a purchase order promising to pay after delivery of the products or services. I've found these extremely reliable.

IV. *Checks by phone (or fax).* The following services make this method of transfer of funds easier for merchants:

http://www.charge.com

http://www.phonechex.com

V. *Payment services.* These companies facilitate the exchange of money between online buyers and sellers outside of the Visa/MasterCard merchant system:

http://www.digicash.com

http://www.paypal.com

VI. *Old-fashioned checks and money orders.* Some individuals will prefer to print out an order form and send payment by postal mail. Why not accommodate them?

probably need professional help if you want to offer something more ambitious than a static Web catalog. Make sure your plans include keeping the site updated.

While online shoppers more readily type in their credit card numbers at Web sites now than a few years ago, you must still take the trouble to allay security concerns in the broadest sense at your Web site. Tell people they're placing their order through a secure server. Post your privacy policy, explaining that you never give e-mail addresses or other customer information to third parties. When they place an order, notify them that you received the order and inform them when it will be shipped.

If you don't already accept credit cards, you'll need what's called a merchant credit card account. Apply at your own bank first. You'll find approval easier if you have a decent track record with your regular bank and will perform some in-person transactions as well as some, you hope, online. No matter how much you reassure visitors of the safety of online ordering, however, some will prefer sending in a check or money order. So provide an order form that can be printed out and mailed with payment to your postal address.

Does Your Web Site...?

Compared to something you polish, complete, and send off to the printer, a Web site should always be a work in progress. You'll want to add content, refine rough edges, even rearrange the contents or redesign the look as you get feedback from visitors and colleagues. Whether you're just creating your site or re-evaluating one you've had up for a while, consider these criteria for quality and usability:

- *Do the pages load fast?* Web surfers are not settled into an armchair with a nice volume they've selected and previewed. With a slow-loading site, they're looking at a small blank screen not knowing how much longer it's going to take to see something, and they don't know whether or not it will be worth the wait. Most will click away elsewhere if your home page doesn't come up within the first half-minute. Dan Janal removed all the photos on the home page for his high-tech public relations firm in Danville, California, after he asked

FAST FACTS

E-Commerce Challenges

Before opening your online store, think through how you'll handle the following:

- *Taxes.* Check with your accountant about whom you should be collecting sales taxes from, on what, and for how much.

- *Shipping costs.* Will you estimate shipping charges by weight, by the number of items, by the amount spent, by how soon the buyer wants the stuff, or what?

- *Return policies and guarantees.* Under what circumstances will you accept returns? A generous policy encourages people to buy.

- *Contact information.* You should offer an e-mail address and phone number people can use to inquire about the status of their order.

himself, "Now would *I* stick around and wait a few minutes for these pictures to draw?"

- *Can visitors find what they're looking for?* A navigation scheme and categories that feel intuitive to you may not make sense to others. For instance, you might put your business hours and directions to your photographic studio under "Contact us," or "About us." (See Figure 9.5.) But if visitors call to say they couldn't find the information, you need to try a more explicit heading, such as "Our studio" or "How and when to find us." Since only about one in ten people will take the time to tell you their problem, even one complaint of not being able to find something at your site warrants investigation and tinkering.

- *Is there a way for visitors to phone, fax, or e-mail you with questions?* When I launched my Web site, I looked for everyone who had posted material by me, with the plan of asking them for a link. About one fifth of the time I couldn't find any clues to the identity or whereabouts of the site owner. These sites might as well have been the creations of hermits living in

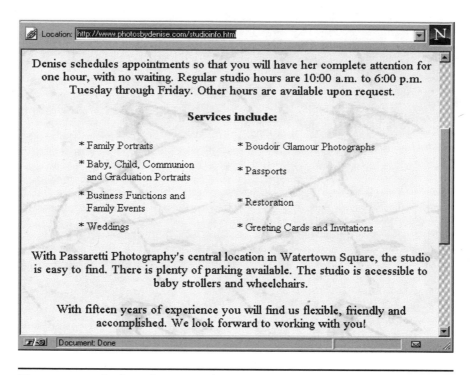

Figure 9.5.   Studio information for Passaretti Photography.

caves for all the good their efforts did them. Providing multiple opportunities and avenues for visitors to contact you makes sense whether you have a lead generation, marketing support, or e-commerce site.

- *Can anyone, using any old browser, access your basic features instead of encountering the equivalent of "Access Denied"?* Some people, with text-only or old browsers (see Figure 9.6), or special systems for the visually handicapped, won't see any pictures. If you provide what are called "alt-tags"—verbal labels for images and buttons—these people can still navigate and enjoy your content. Similarly, if you use cutting-edge multimedia features, don't stop those without the requisite software at the front door. Provide a link to someplace that enables them to download what they need to experience your cool stuff, and provide a substitute experience for those who won't or can't install plug-ins.

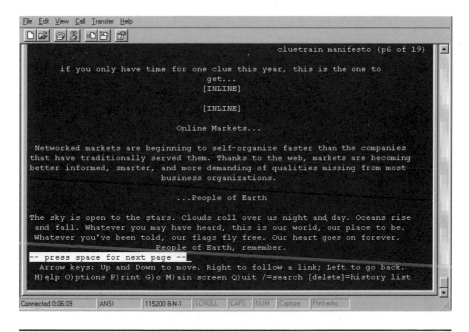

Figure 9.6. Figure 5.2 as seen in a text-only browser.

- *Does your site look at least moderately okay on other machines and with other browsers?* In a quirk of Web design that's shocking to novices, you can slave away at a harmonious design that appears hideous on other systems. Colors, fonts, and relative spacing may come up completely differently from your design. Originally at my site I chose sky blue as an accent color for text, which was perfectly readable with all the browsers I had easy access to. However, those using older versions of America Online and the latest Web TV told me they couldn't decipher words in this blue. This occurred, I later learned, because the default background, white to me, was gray for them, and eliminated a color contrast. I scuttled the sky blue accents.

A sign on your home page like "This site looks best when viewed with Browser XYZ.33" represents a poor solution to this problem. Similarly, ignoring someone who says your site looks awful doesn't make the problem go away. Once I mentioned to a colleague at a meeting that I found his site unreadable. He'd crowded it with four or five frames—devices that display multiple documents simultaneously, each with its own scroll bar. During a break in our meeting, I caught a glimpse of him at his computer, calling up his site. On his monitor, much larger than mine, everything that had seemed to me scrunched up, with portions of essential images and text half hidden from view, appeared nicely spaced out. He then clicked his computer off and never asked me to explain my comment. His site still has the problem.

- *Have you provided the content visitors need and want?* Make sure your Web designer doesn't view your site as an opportunity to show off. Design should support the promotional purposes of the site rather than call attention to itself. Similarly, the site should greet visitors in a "you" mode rather than relentless "me, me, me" or "we, we, we."

- *Finally, have you furnished enough information at the site to enable visitors to trust you?* As the famous cartoon puts it, "On the Internet, no one knows if you're a dog" (said by a dog). Chapter 15 goes into more detail about various ways to establish and maintain credibility online.

10

Power-packed Promotions for Your Web Site

Build a better mousetrap than your neighbor and though you build your house in the woods, the world will make a beaten path to your door." I don't believe this was true even when Ralph Waldo Emerson spoke this adage in the ninetenth century. It certainly does not apply to Web sites. In the twenty-first century, people are trying mightily to cope with information overload and the availability of more products and services than they could hope to enjoy in a lifetime. On the Web, surfers have millions of options, and it takes strategy, creativity, effort, and only sometimes money to lure them to your Internet location.

The three basic steps for drawing traffic are these, in the order in which you should perform them: First, create something worth visiting, revisiting, and recommending to others. Second, link with sites that already have the traffic you want. Third, promote your site like crazy off the Net, not only on it.

Become Web Worthy

Noticing what sites *you* visit and why can tell you a lot about features you can implement to make your site one that people visit, return to, and recommend to friends and colleagues. The more promotable your site, the bigger payoff you'll get from the promotional steps that directly invite traffic. Thinking about promotability prior to promotion will lead you to extra site elements that usually cost nothing but give you an angle to promote. No longer can you get attention for simply having a Web site. But if you're the first in your industry to offer a certain drawing card or you have the best directory of doodads, you've laid down the track for serious traffic. A site containing nothing more than "Here's who we are and how great our mousetraps are" can't compete with the appeal of these features:

- *Useful content.* The real estate agent who posts a "Guide to House Hunting for First-time Home Buyers" has an edge with that target market over someone who merely offers listings. The same goes for the educational software dealer who provides product ratings and reviews. Likewise the furniture restorer with the best set of links to Victorian design sites has the best shot at traffic from interior designers, architects, and people mad about Victorian furniture. Focus on the needs and interests of the visitors you're hoping to attract when you ponder the kind of content that will bring them in. Some options you should consider:

  - Articles, book excerpts, sets of tips, frequently asked questions

  - Reference information, such as Internet or real-world resources

  - Checklists for actions clients/customers take or should take in relation to your products/services

  - Case studies with educational value

  - Ratings, recommendations, reviews

  - Trivia, statistics, topical jokes, inspirational quotes

  - Sale item of the week

– Archives of your e-mail newsletter, if you have one

Thinking of content for your site as an ongoing endeavor makes you more promotable too, because the more you make changes and add new features, the more easily you persuade people to come back and to bookmark your site for return visits. Sometimes the very nature of your business suggests a schedule for updates, or the kind of changes that make sense. If you have a business sensitive to the seasons, content changes should relate to the current time of year. For instance, a personal shopper might post tips in July for dressing fashionably in hot weather, in September for a wardrobe built around the principle of layering, and in November for accessorizing last year's winter coat. If you sell software, you'd post the ever changing anticipated release dates for upgrades and new programs. Other obvious schedules for updates are daily, weekly, or monthly.

- *Interactive content.* Think fun, think participation, think involvement. Puzzles, quizzes, riddles, contests—all these encourage people to stick around for a while and to feel good about the company providing a good time. Even if you think "Fun doesn't fit our image," such gimmicks can work for you. A physical therapist specializing in services for the newly disabled, for example, could set up an educational "True or False?" quiz on disabilities that asks the viewer to guess the answer, then provides it through a pop-up screen. Surveys are another interactive feature suiting dignified businesses. (See Figure 10.1.) Ask people to register their views on some weighty topic and then provide, either instantly or after a certain date, the breakdown of how others voted.

You can increase traffic when you allow visitors to exchange messages with each other on a message board or forum. This might involve people describing problems and asking for solutions, people offering suggestions, recommendations, or the latest dope on phenomena of interest to your visitors—or even folks posting (with your encouragement) free classified ads pertaining to your topic area. For instance, an ice skating rink could invite skaters to swap stories about the Olympic greats

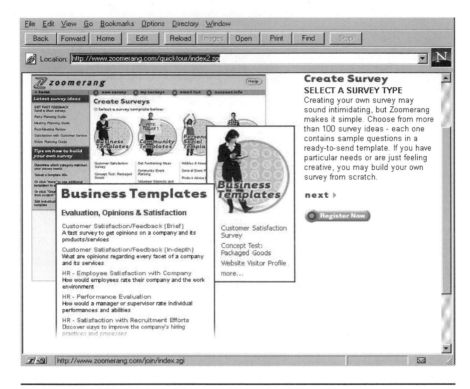

Figure 10.1. Zoomerang helps you create an online survey.

and to post notices about used skates and hockey equipment for sale or wanted. An online bookstore could simulate the kind of book club that meets in living rooms by choosing a book of the week and asking people to contribute their comments on the book.

Interaction might involve ways for visitors to hear from you again after leaving your site. You can boost return traffic by offering a signup to receive e-mail announcements of additions to the site—new articles, new specials, contest results, further installments of your case studies, and so on. Along similar lines, you could create a free reminder service specific to your industry, such as, if you sell to brides, checklists of things to take care of six months before the wedding, five months, four months, three, two, one month, two weeks, and the day before.

FAST FACTS

Free Puzzle-Making Resources

- Create a word-search puzzle from your words and clues: *http:// puzzlemaker.school.discovery.com/*

- Produce a topical crossword puzzle using your words and definitions: *http://www.connicomputers.com/crossword.html*

- Generate possible anagrams for any word or phrase you supply: *http://wordsmith.org/anagram/*

- *Real-time content.* Syndicators can provide licensed up-to-the-minute information such as localized weather reports, stock prices, currency exchange rates, sports scores, or lowest airfares that get installed automatically at your site. (See Figure 10.2.) This is such a powerful draw that it may warrant the expense. Suppose you're a lakeside restaurant where patrons arrive not only by car or walking but also by docking their boat there. A detailed local weather report including wind speed and the odds of a thunderstorm at your site along with your daily menu specials could persuade some boaters to cruise on over to your restaurant when they otherwise wouldn't.

Provide "In" Roads

Once you've created something people will want to visit and revisit, you're ready to cultivate traffic by linking your site with others in ways that invite visitors. Foremost among the possible routes to you from other sites are so-called "search engines" and Web directories. A search engine is a site like Alta Vista, Hotbot, Lycos, Excite, or WebCrawler (some of the most popular ones). They send out electronic robots to rove the Web and pick up information about Web sites for a master index available to searchers through its home page. Rather than waiting for such a robot to find you, you can also pur-

Figure 10.2. iSyndicate provides syndicated content for Web sites.

posefully register or submit your Web pages to these search engines. (See Figure 10.3.) A Web directory, such as Yahoo!, involves human beings who categorize pages much the way a professional librarian assigns books numbers in the Dewey Decimal or Library of Congress cataloging system. Most Web directories have acceptability criteria, so not everything submitted ends up being listed.

If your Web hosting service or Web designer doesn't include registration of your site in their bundle of services, then you should arrange it yourself for at least the top search engines (there are hundreds of smaller ones). For each page you wish to register, you'll need to

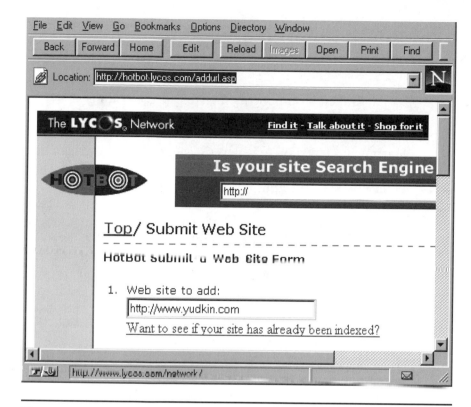

Figure 10.3. How I would submit my site to the search engine Hotbot.

assemble three ingredients before starting the process: the page's title, keywords for indexing, and a one-sentence description of the site. Then have whoever created your site insert these elements (technically called "meta-tags") into the site's code, where they get picked up by those roving robots but don't show up on the page to your visitors. Here's how these three components would appear when coded for the site of Nkomba Magola, a drummer:

> *<TITLE>From Ghana to Delaware: Nkomba Magola, Drummer </TITLE>*

> *<META name="keywords" content="drum, djembe, Nkomba Magola, Delaware, percussion, African, Ghana, music, drummer, drumming, performers">*

*<META name="description" content="Nkomba Magola,
African artist on the drum, now based in Delaware; CDs,
performance schedule and audio clips.">*

With these components inserted in the coding at the top of the
site, Magola would go to the search engines, look for a button that
says "Add URL," and type in his Web address. He's then registered.
Starting in a few days, whenever someone typed "African drumming"
or "Delaware music performers" in the search engine, the title and
description would appear among the listings. Clearly, success with
the search engines derives partly from anticipating what people seeking sites like yours search for. Beyond that, search engines keep the
specific formulas they use to rank sites top secret. Even firms that
promise top ranking in search engines have only moderate success.
While gaining a number one position when someone typed in "African drumming" would benefit Nkomba Magola, gaining the forty-
third position is not the end of the world. Don't get obsessed with
your placement in search engines.

To get listed in Yahoo! and other Web directories, go to the
directory's search page and look for a button that leads to the instructions. Specialized directories for niches such as foreign trade,
sports, hotels, and geographical regions exist and deserve your entry.
To find those appropriate for your site, type *directory* then your topic
area into Yahoo! or one of the search engines.

Unlike the process of getting your site listed in search engines, which
with its black-box calculations can feel beyond your control, soliciting
links is a human-to-human process. You simply find sites that have a
section for recommended resources and send an e-mail requesting a
link. When your site includes useful resources for your target market,
emphasize those in your link request. Someone who clicks to your article or tip sheet would then have the opportunity to look around the
rest of your site and become a customer. For instance,

Dear Webmaster [or the site owner's name, if you can find it],

*I discovered your site today and was interested to see that
you offer a page of links to financial information for
women. My site includes an article called "How Working
Women Can Calculate Their Retirement Needs." I hope
you will add it to your list of recommended financial*

resources. The URL is http://www.womensmoney.org/ calc.html.

I'm a financial planner with 18 years of experience, and my company specializes in helping women plan for retirement. Please let me know if you need additional information, and thank you for your consideration.

Sincerely,
Meredith Jackson
mjackson@womenscash.com

How do you identify promising candidates for links into your site? The best starting point is a list of resources for your industry or niche that someone else has already compiled, which should turn up relatively quickly through a search engine. Less obviously, find a couple of sites that contain useful resources on your topic and appear to be popular. Then go to a search engine and find the instructions for determining who has linked to that popular site. (See Figure 10.4.) Chances are that if you have comparable offerings, anyone who has linked to the popular site would also be willing to link to you. Remain on the lookout for new link possibilities during your regular Web surfing and reading of trade or specialty magazines.

Two types of sites call for divergent strategies in soliciting links. The first type of site, sometimes produced by a hobbyist or not-for-profit group rather than someone running a business, functions almost completely as an information hub rather than a commercial site. Such sites tend to agree liberally to links, since they aim simply at comprehensively serving their sector. Sites run by businesses tend to

FAST FACTS

Web Awards

Being named "Best of..." can give you a big publicity boost. These awards are some of the most prestigious, but there are hundreds more:

- *http://www.webbyawards.com*
- *http://www.gii.com*
- *http://www.cool.infi.net*

Cost to apply for and receive an award: $0.

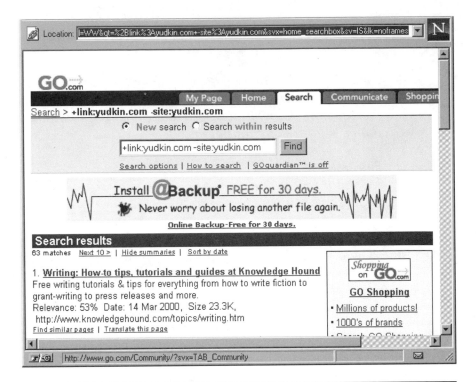

Figure 10.4. At go.com, how I would search for sites linking to mine.

view links more strategically and may agree to a link only on condition that you link back to them. They may decline altogether if they perceive you as competition. You may have better luck getting links from commercial sites by linking to them first, informing them, and then requesting a return link. Even with commercial sites, however, if you've produced a "must-have" resource and describe it persuasively in your e-mail, you'll succeed in obtaining links.

Also investigate whether appropriate Web rings exist that you can join (see Figure 10.5). These structures pass traffic along in a circle from one member site to another, and they cost nothing to join. Upon becoming a member, you place a graphic link at your site that allows your visitor to hop along to the next site or to a random spot on the circle. Most Web rings focus on a special interest, such as waterskiing, witches, or watch collecting, but others facilitate more random site jumping, such as Web rings for University of Wyoming

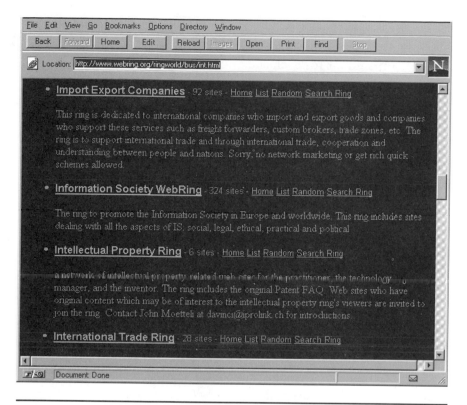

Figure 10.5. A few Web rings.

alumni or for men named Wyatt. Normally each ring provides one-click access to the ring founder, whom you can ask to join.

Don't overlook the opportunity to get links from the sites of organizations you belong to. Some charge for the privilege, but others include it as a perk of membership.

When you've pursued as many link opportunities as you can, consider paid advertising as a method of directing more of the traffic you want to your site. Currently the supply of advertising space exceeds demand from advertisers willing to buy them, with even the most popular sites not selling all of their ad slots. That means, never automatically pay the asking price for Web advertising. Always try to negotiate your way to a better deal. Usually Web ads take the form of banners—graphic boxes that contain a few words and urge surfers to click over to the advertiser's site. You pay either a set fee for the banner to remain for a certain length of time or a certain amount for each click through to your site. When considering advertising, you'd be wise to think through carefully which sites might deliver the kind of traffic you want and to try to contact some current advertisers to see how happy they are with what they've gotten for their money.

Spread the Word off the Net

The final way to make sure your Web investment offers adequate return is strangely underutilized. Simply, apart from the Internet make sure everyone who hears about your

company also learns about your Web site and gets a good reason to go take a look. You undoubtedly use stationery and business cards—do they list your Web site? Does your company's printed newsletter include features about what you've posted on the Web? How about your Yellow Pages ads? Your newspaper or magazine ads? Your on-hold and voice-mail messages? ("To read how we've helped other clients in your industry, you can visit our Web site at *www.us.com*.")

Some companies have gotten traffic rolling and spurred word of mouth by sending out postcards about their new Web site and giving reasons to visit. Incentives like the chance to win a trip or a computer by visiting a certain page have worked well for some businesses. You can send Web page postcards (see Figure 10.6) not only to your own

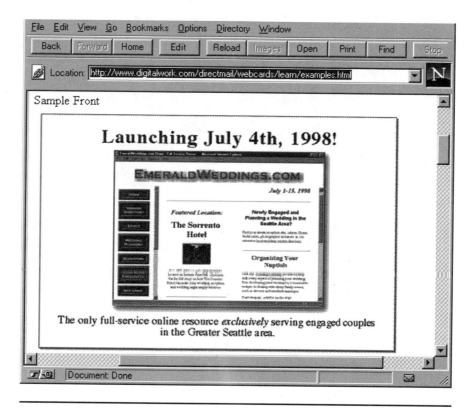

Figure 10.6. You can order Web site postcards at digitalwork.com.

customers and clients but also to carefully selected prospects you've hand-collected or to those on lists rented from mailing list brokers. *Dynamic Graphics* magazine published a postcard that cleverly started off, "25 Ways to…" and presented tips 1–4. To read the other 21 tips, you had to visit the site. Postcards make sense because they cost so little to send, but you can also refer to what's on your Web site in sales letters, ads, product inserts, and so on. You get in the habit of using your Web site to best advantage when you consider it one more marketing tool in your arsenal to integrate with all the other marketing you already do.

If you've followed my advice earlier in the chapter and created unique, useful features for your site, you should also pursue media coverage. I got my e-mail newsletter written up in the Sunday *Boston Globe* just by sending an e-mail to the columnist who wrote about local doings on the Net. A formal news release mailed or faxed to appropriate newspapers, magazines, and authors of annual reference books can produce results too. Remember that the mere existence of your Web site isn't news, so you want instead to highlight its distinctive features and how they benefit your target market. Here are some sample news release headlines to put you on the right track:

FAST FACTS

Places to Promote Your Site Offline

- Voice mail, on-hold message
- T-shirts, hats
- Paper pads, mouse pads, pens
- Bookmarks
- Stationery, business cards
- Panel trucks, license plate holders
- Ads, direct mail, Yellow Pages
- Billboards
- Fortune cookies

- The Extra Store Now Offers Sports Regalia in Tall and Large Sizes for Sports Fans

- Alabama Gardeners Now Have 24-hour Advice Available at *www.alabamagardens.com*

- Furntours Makes Furniture Shopping Easier with Free Online Directory of Factory Outlet Stores Nationwide

- Child Custody Strategies for Men Detailed at *www. keepchild.com*

Sample Successful Press Release

For: eBoard, 20 Rowes Wharf, Suite 409, Boston, MA 02110. Contact: Gordon Brott or Brad Peterson (617) 739-7378.

FOR IMMEDIATE RELEASE

The Simplicity of E-mail, the Accessibility of the Web: eBoard, New Hybrid Internet Tool, Enables Groups to Coordinate Better—for Free

Boston, MA, June 15, 1999 – A family planning a reunion, a soccer team scheduling games and practice sessions, a teacher making class assignments—until now they've had several unsatisfactory choices for coordinating times, places, who'll drive who and where, what's due when, and so on. Old-fashioned postal mail or take-home flyers easily get lost and take time to duplicate and distribute. A Web site requires more effort and skill than most ordinary folks have and than these tasks require. E-mail to multiple addresses is easy to use, but also can get lost, especially when someone has one e-mail account at work and another at home.

eBoard, a new hybrid of e-mail and the Web available at *www.eBoard.com,* solves the problem. At no cost and in less than five minutes, anyone can create a private Internet bulletin board that members of a group can access when ever they need to, independent of whatever e-mail account they are on. "The eBoard interface is as intuitive to use as tacking up a notice on a physical bulletin board," says Gordon Brott, cocreator of the site. "Our testing shows that anyone who knows how to use e-mail and get to a Web site can create, modify, or simply read an eBoard."

Photos or graphics in JPEG or GIF format can be posted as quickly and easily as a text message, making eBoard useful for families or friends sharing snapshots, maps, diagrams, and so on. eBoards require a password to view, and can either be modifiable by any group member or only by the person who created the eBoard.

Applications are endless, adds Brott. "Friends coordinating a camping trip, a community organization planning activities, a support group scheduling meetings—even restaurants notifying staff of who's working when each week and letting patrons know daily specials.... Every day we hear about users creating new uses for eBoard. It's the fastest, easiest way to post material for a group online."

Anyone can establish an eBoard or view samples by visiting *www.eBoard.com* on the Web.

11

No-cost Online Postings

I wrote a piece of Windows code that solves a common problem and posted it in a forum library," says Terry Richards, a computer consultant in New Brunswick, New Jersey. "From there it spread all over the Internet. The code is free for private use, but I charge for inclusion in a commercial product. The real benefit, though, comes from people who have seen my work and want to hire me to have other things done. After I posted the code, customers from all over the world got in touch. I was able to quit my regular job, and now I work from home and travel at their expense. The really great thing is that they call me—I never have to make a cold call! It has completely automated my marketing."

If you have a friend or relative who ties up their phone line for hours downloading software, you may have thought that the obsessive pursuit of files was limited to the computer field. Not so. Twenty-four hours a day, people hunt online for free tips on everything from recovery after bankruptcy to vegetarian nourishment for kids. In addition to or instead of a Web site, almost any business can benefit from making reports and articles available for free to hungry information seekers.

In 1995 direct-mail specialist Susanna Hutcheson of Wichita, Kansas (see Figure 11.1), told me that she posted one article a month

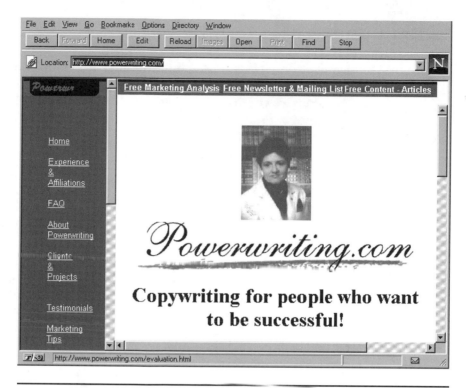

Figure 11.1. Susanna Hutcheson's home page.

in more than a dozen appropriate places all over the Internet. In an average week, these brought her 3 to 5 faxes, 5 phone calls, and up to 20 e-mail inquiries. "These are *very* serious prospects," she said, "especially those who pick up the phone. Some of them have read all of my articles and not only know I'm competent, but feel they know me." Around 5 percent signed on as clients, willing to pay her fairly high writing fees.

Unlike the intensive ongoing time commitment necessary for effective schmoozing, seeding your material around the Net involves doing something once and then passively reaping the benefits. If you've already written various things for different purposes, it's a cinch to adapt them for posting. Here's how to take full advantage of the power of the online environment to put evidence of your talents in front of those who need you precisely when they are searching for help.

Pulling Treasures from Your Drawers

In hooking electronic treasure hunters, the first step is to dredge up or create something they'll be overjoyed to find. Include an invitation to readers to contact you to buy something, hire you, or at least talk business. Finally, post the file and describe it so that serious prospects for your business will want to peruse it. Just remember that your information will be posted outside of a sales environment, so people will be expecting your material to have a ratio of at least 95 percent valuable information to 5 percent marketing or sales information.

You may have something you've already done that can serve as a lure for customers or clients online. Think about these categories of temptation:

- *Samples or excerpts.* With software the sample might be a demo version that motivates users to buy the full-featured edition or a clever solution that inspires those needing programming to call, as with Terry Richards. If you publish any sort of newsletter, have authored a book, or have created a company "white paper," make tantalizing free extracts available.

- *Adaptations.* If you've ever presented a seminar, your handouts may serve as a perfect skeleton for a piece worth posting. Perhaps you wrote a client proposal that you can turn into a problem/solution piece on your industry. Maybe you already have a fact sheet such as "Myths and Realities about Pawnshops" or a customer briefing like "How to Choose a Printer"— just transform it into the format recommended here. Even a list you've compiled, such as bookstores that welcome self-publishers or famous quotes on procrastination, can qualify if the list relates to your area of specialization. I converted four press releases from my files into an article format, posted them, and in the first three months received seven or eight requests to print them in business magazines.

- *Original articles.* If you can't find hidden wealth in your file cabinet, write something. Six hundred to one thousand words— the length of a magazine column—is ideal. "Short enough to prevent boredom, long enough to be substantive," suggests

Susanna Hutcheson. For best results, keep the focus practical and reader-oriented, as in

- Twelve Ways To Keep Your Aquarium Fish Happy

- How To Be Your Own Private Investigator

- What You Should Know about Home Inspections and Why

- Eight Investment Mistakes You May Be Making

- Backcountry Camping Without Deprivation

- Do's and Don'ts When Upgrading to Windows 2000

In-depth reviews of books or other resources may also give you a chance to show off what you know.

Become a Content Provider or Consolidator

This no-cost strategy often meets with incredulity when I begin to explain it at seminars, but I assure you that it works. Remember how Tom Sawyer turned work into an adventure and got his friends to paint the fence he was supposed to do as a chore? Similarly, although the norm is that everyone pays for Web space, you can turn that expectation upside down by changing the perception of who's doing a favor to whom. You can arrange for your postings to appear many places on the Web if you figure out which noncompeting companies or organizations need your content and present yourself as the solution to their problem.

More and more, Web creators realize that valuable information often does a better job of attracting traffic than does the mere opportunity to shop and buy. As some put it, "Content is king." But many companies and organizations have no deep file cabinet from which to pull already created content and little time to write or compile new material. Along you come, offering free ready-to-post content of interest to the visitors they want to attract. For a brand-new site, a package of content—related articles, lists of Internet resources, etc.—is irresistible. For established sites, just one alluring information piece might do the trick. Offer to provide a new information piece every month and you help solve the problem of how they can encourage Web visitors to keep coming back. In return for your content, all you require is a paragraph at the end about what you do and your contact information along with a live link that takes the visitor to your own Web site, if you have one.

For best results, think strategically: What kind of outfit would benefit from the information you can provide? Suppose you're a veterinarian: Pet shops, breeders, kennels, and pet food companies have Web sites that need traffic builders that you can furnish. Indeed, any one of those players in the pet industry could benefit by supplying content to the others. Or let's say you own a bed & breakfast in Key West. Other tourism-related sites for your area that have straight promotional content might jump at your offer of a "This month in Key West" feature or articles like "Offbeat Key West" in exchange for a link to your site and/or a final paragraph touting your B&B. If you sell a bonsai growing kit, garden supply or interior decorating sites might appreciate articles like "How to Care for Bonsai" or "Why Bonsai?"

I get approached at least every other month by a company that has seen my material online and wants to know if they can use it at their site to help attract traffic. The variety of kinds of businesses inquiring shows that Web owners do think strategically along the lines I'm suggesting. Companies approaching me about marketing articles included a stock photo agency, a mortgage consortium, a high-end color printing firm, a Spanish-language business portal (which will be translating my stuff), and a promotional products supersite.

Sometimes you'll be in a position to create a larger win-win deal. For almost two years, I had a free Web site from a television program, "The Job Show," for which I did a weekly call-in spot. Our arrangement was that I collected resources and articles for job seekers, by others as well as by me, and in exchange I could have a portion of the site with which to promote myself in any way I liked. I later created my own site only when the show went off the air and it became impossible to post updates and new information. In addition, I had a free mini–Web site through Salesdoctors with my photo, articles, and promotional information in exchange for my articles (see Figure 11.2).

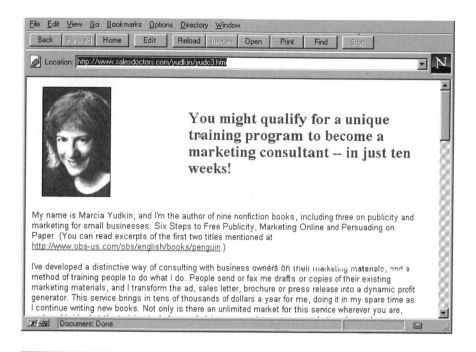

My name is Marcia Yudkin, and I'm the author of nine nonfiction books, including three on publicity and marketing for small businesses: Six Steps to Free Publicity, Marketing Online and Persuading on Paper. (You can read excerpts of the first two titles mentioned at http://www.obs-us.com/obs/english/books/penguin.)

I've developed a distinctive way of consulting with business owners on their marketing materials, and a method of training people to do what I do. People send or fax me drafts or copies of their existing marketing materials, and I transform the ad, sales letter, brochure or press release into a dynamic profit generator. This service brings in tens of thousands of dollars a year for me, doing it in my spare time as I continue writing new books. Not only is there an unlimited market for this service wherever you are,

Figure 11.2. Salesdoctors.com let me promote myself where it posted my articles.

Barbara Brabec, author of *Homemade Money* and other books for crafters, whom I mentioned in Chapter 3, struck a similar bargain. "Of course I was wrong about 'too old to go online'," she wrote me when we got back in touch after several years. "I was just too old to want to have to figure out how to do this myself, when all I really wanted to do was write. So the good Lord solved my problem by putting someone in my path who was delighted to do all this stuff for me in return for my presence on her Web site. It has been a

FAST FACTS

Some Business Sites That Accept Articles from Outsiders

- *http://www.expertarticles.com*
- *http://www.ideasiteforbusiness.com*
- *http://www.marcommwise.com*
- *http://www.4freecontent.com*

win-win situation from the get-go, as she has the technological expertise and I have the ability to attract visitors."

So unclear is it who benefits most from this kind of deal that you can even label yourself a "content provider" and license your content to Web sites for a fee like a syndicator. Although you might assume that if you're offering, say, information on makeup and dress to photographers, only one photographer would want the info at their site, that's not true. No one travels far for a business portrait, so photographers in dispersed geographic areas do not compete with each other. Thus a photographer in Bangor, Maine, wouldn't care if colleagues in Portland, Oregon, Billings, Montana, Phoenix, Arizona, and Columbus, Ohio, post the very same information at their sites, since most visitors to any one of these sites would never see any of the others. Charging for content may or may not supplant your original promotional purpose.

Fear of Freeness

A popular saying on the Internet proclaims, "Information wants to be free." Deciphered, this means, "Many people believe all information should be free because so much of it already is." If you sell information in some form—software or books, say—this aphorism may give you the willies. Relax. Yes, cyberspace has more than its share of bootleggers, cheapskates, and pirates, but with intelligent marketing you can get back a hundredfold what you give out for free. What will motivate people to pull out their credit card or sign a contract with you when they received something gratis?

1. *They liked what they saw and want more, which they can't get without paying.* Compare a test drive at a car dealer or coming attractions at a movie theater. Or you can provide information free for a while before you announce a membership, sales, or subscription fee. PR pro Dan Janal calls this the "heroin marketing strategy"—give it away until they're hooked.

2. *They want convenient packaging or delivery.* Although we can read the newspaper for free at the library, we'd rather pick it

up from our doorstep and read it at breakfast. Similarly, we may prefer to have each issue of a magazine arrive in the mail without our having to go navigating around cyberspace to download it. Laura Fillmore, president of Open Book Systems, points to what happened when her company posted the complete text of Tracy LaQuey's *The Internet Companion* on the Internet in 1992. "Counterintuitive as it may seem, giving the ASCII files away spurred the print sales of the book. Who wants to read hundreds of pages in ASCII?"

3. *They want customization of the information.* No matter how detailed your advice, it can't cover every nook and cranny of someone's individual situation. With almost any subject, if you know enough and can communicate and apply your expertise, people will pay high fees to have you help them understand and put into practice what you know. Your consulting business will boom as you disseminate free information. I was happy to learn that a large number of public libraries in the Boston area carry my books, even though for each person who checks one out, I receive no money. Nevertheless, those readers can and do sign up for my seminars, recommend my books to others, and call me to arrange to pay for guidance on their unique project. The same thing occurs with files I've made public in cyberspace. John Perry Barlow, former lyricist for the rock band The Grateful Dead and a theorist on intellectual property, alludes to the potential free products have to attract paid clients for services when he asks, "Who needs copyright when you're on retainer?"

4. *They want it before it's released to the masses.* Some magazines that post the complete contents of each issue online appear to keep a one-issue lag so that just about the only way to read the current issue is to buy it. Quoting Barlow again, "Most information is like farm produce. Its quality degrades rapidly both over time and in distance from the source of production." Many who truly value the information don't want to wait, just as some folks will pay to call a 900 number to find out if they won the day's lottery rather than suffer the suspense until the winning number appears in the next morning's newspaper or on the wall board of the convenience store.

Preparing Your Material for Posting

Except for software programs, prepare all the following components to each article or set of tips:

- *Title.* A confusing or vague title decimates your chances for getting read. Compare, for example, "How Does Your Client Want to…" with "Sales Letters Without Fear!!!" The latter, posted in America Online's Small Business Center, was downloaded 1525 times in three months, compared to the former's 601 downloads in an entire year. Remember that your article title competes in a list of other titles for readers' attention.

- *Byline.* Under the title, the words "by Yvonne You" (your name goes there) visually emphasize your role in creating and offering the information. For best response, don't omit the byline.

- *Copyright and distribution terms* (optional). To prevent your piece from being misappropriated, it's wise to insert a copyright notice and a statement of the extent to which you wish to encourage, control, or forbid reprinting and distribution. For example,

  Copyright 2001 Jim Author. Not to be reprinted, resold, or redistributed for profit, except with written permission, but may be freely distributed electronically provided that the entire file, including this notice, remains intact.

- *Your text.* Follow the instructions in Chapter 14 for greatest readability. Use short paragraphs, subheads, an extra return between paragraphs, and a line length of 60 characters or less. Make sure it's straight text (so-called ASCII) without any formatting codes.

- *Tactful marketing pitch.* Here's your chance to motivate people to call or write you. If you provide a service, describe what you do, specifically and interestingly. Don't include prices, but do include contact information, and keep this section to seven lines or less.

You may be asked to provide a description of the file and keywords by which the file will be indexed. I always include "yudkin" along with the topics as keywords so that someone who finds my work and likes it can easily retrieve it all. For instance, here are the title, keywords, and description for one of my uploads:

Get Your Press Release Read and Used

[Keywords] press release publicity marketing news media yudkin

Get your media message out of the trash can and onto the front page or the evening news by avoiding the four most common mistakes in press releases.

Tips from Marcia Yudkin, author of *Six Steps to Free Publicity* (Plume Books).

A related strategy involves creating a free printed booklet and announcing its availability via "snail mail" during schmoozing in forums or newsgroups. Whenever she spots relevant questions in a sailing forum, for instance, Peggie Hall of Peal Products in Atlanta responds, "We've written a piece that's not sales literature called 'Marine Sanitation: Fact vs. Fiction.' We'd be happy to send it to you if you e-mail us your address." During winter, the off-season, Hall says she receives about 20 requests a week for it, "and it's led to more than enough sales to make it worthwhile." Though many have asked her to upload the entire piece for immediate general access, she doesn't think that would work as well for her. "I want people's addresses and the opportunity to send my sales literature along with the 'Fact vs. Fiction' piece. I want people to discuss it with me, and that wouldn't happen as much if they just downloaded it."

In some cases you can post informational pieces or offers to send them to newsgroups and mailing lists. Since these groups are not designed as permanent repositories of information, they offer distribution more comparable to publishing in one issue of a newsletter than placing it in an electronic library. Tread very carefully here, since you could quickly get overwhelmed with complaints if the regulars perceive your offering as inappropriate, irrelevant, or overly commercial.

Make sure your file is very short—750 words or less, is very high in hard-to-find information pertinent to that specific group, and includes a signature file or a no-sell signoff with how to get in touch. See the section on columns in Chapter 5 for more suggestions. If it's longer than 750 words, you should instead post the piece on your Web site and offer just a note in the newsgroup or mailing list inviting people to read it.

A much longer file earns a welcome in newsgroups when you call it a "FAQ"—Frequently Asked Question— and design it in that spirit and format. FAQs are highly appreciated throughout the Internet, often archived, and widely read, spread, and recommended. They lend their creators worldwide visibility and name recognition among Internet aficionados. Terry Carroll, a law student when he created his FAQ on copyright law, mentioned in the FAQ that he was looking for a job and listed the FAQ as a credit on the resumé that landed him a position. "Its big value," Carroll says, "was that on the CNI-Copyright mailing list, where I'm well known in part because of the FAQ, when I announced I was looking for a job, I got a number of recommendations of firms that were looking. A partner in an Oregon firm who read the FAQ invited me to send a resumé. Later, someone from a major legal publisher wrote, inviting me to send a resumé, but by then I already had a job."

Influenced by Carroll and another FAQ author I interviewed in the first edition of this book, in late 1995 I composed a set of 24 questions and answers called The Freelance Writing FAQ and organized it in the format prevalent throughout the Internet. Only question #24, "And who are you, anyway?" said anything about me

---

FAST FACTS

Just the FAQs

A few of the topics on which FAQs exist:

- Beer
- Calendars
- Diabetes
- Fuzzy Logic
- Investments
- Martial Arts
- Nonlinear Programming
- Privacy
- Shamanism
- Woodworking

personally or my publications, although my ulterior motive was to keep my 1988 book, *Freelance Writing for Magazines & Newspapers*, in print. I can't prove that the FAQ accomplished that feat alone, but in 1996 my royalties from the book reversed their decline. In 2001 the book tied to my FAQ was still selling steadily, even though the book itself had not been updated since 1988.

After completing the FAQ, I posted it to several writing-related newsgroups. Within two weeks, one complete stranger volunteered to automate its posting to that group every three weeks and another asked my permission to post it at her Web site. Five years later, the updated or original FAQ appears on well over a dozen writing-related Web sites (including, finally, of course, my own—see Figure 11.3) and is recommended with links at several dozen more. I believe

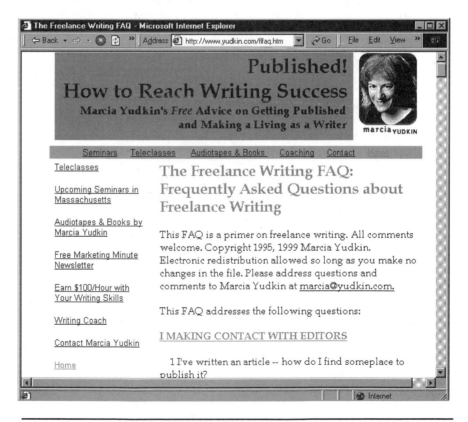

Figure 11.3. Just one location of my Freelance Writing FAQ.

that anyone who provides useful question-and-answer information on a topic of vital importance to some audience would have a similar experience when creating a FAQ.

Another option uses low-tech e-mail by offering a free document to anyone who sends a message to a certain e-mail address. A program called a "mailbot" or an "autoresponder," set up by your Internet provider or by a Web-based service, robotically shoots back your information to any and all who write there. The Internet equivalent to a fax-on-demand system, this saves you the trouble of dealing with every inquiry individually. While most people use this technique for straight marketing pieces or sales letters, there's no reason you can't set up a mailbot to offer a bait piece that inspires prospects to hire you.

Seth Godin created a system like this to promote his book, *Permission Marketing*. Ads in business magazines included an e-mail address to write to that would send off several sample chapters of the book. Once you set up the mailbots, you can promote the availability of your bait piece via your signature file, discussion list postings, media publicity, or offline direct mail. For many people, e-mail gets read in a more leisurely mindset than do Web pages, and e-mail is more easily saved, stored, and responded to than material at a Web site.

12

Attracting Business Through E-mail Lists

Control. Exposure. Responsibility.

These represent the rewards and costs of creating your own e-mail publication, where you are completely in charge. You set the policies, determine the focus, choose the frequency, assemble or invite the content. If you want to flat-out sell, you can. If you want to outlaw mention of a competitor's name, that's up to you. Just don't believe that if you build it, visitors will automatically come. You'll need to promote it and solve technical and customer-related problems to keep callers coming back. Here are three e-mail delivered options to think about, along with the unique benefits and pitfalls of each.

Emperor of a Mailing List

The accepted terminology for starting and managing an Internet e-mail discussion list is "owning" the list, but I like the imperial metaphor because by creating an online environment, you get the right to say, "Here's what this is and isn't, and if you don't like it, join another list or start your own." Quilting artist Melissa Bishop of Coram, New York, had exactly that motive in mind when she launched Interquilt, one of three mailing lists she has started.

"Quiltnet, a very large list, goes through periodic upheavals with people getting very intolerant of off-topic discussions or beginners making posting mistakes. I didn't like its unfriendliness," Bishop says. "Quilting is a very social activity, and I saw the need for a list that welcomed newcomers and allowed the warm chatty talk that goes along with quilting." Making clear that she wasn't intending to replace the established list, she posted an announcement of her new group to relevant newsgroups and sent it to members of Quiltnet. Within three days she had 250 members. Her other lists are the Pfaff Sewing Club and Ragdolls, a cloth dolls club.

Most lists are programmed to run automatically on large computer systems using either Listserv or Majordomo software, both available free on the Internet, so that subscriptions get processed and messages sent to the list address go out to all list members without any human intervention. There are also Web-based e-mail list management services, for free and for fee. Bishop, by contrast, keeps her lists only partially automated—to give her more control, she says.

People who write to Bishop asking to be put on the list have to read a statement about the purpose and ground rules of the list and send back an application acknowledging that they understand its spirit and expectations. Once she has placed an applicant on the member list, her software automatically sends any properly addressed message from a member out to the entire list. A message from a non-member goes just to Bishop, however. She fine-tuned the programming by using friends for guinea pigs. "I drove them crazy for a couple of weeks until I got all the bugs out," she says.

Because her lists run from a server at the university where her domestic partner works, Bishop cannot allow any commercial messages. Nevertheless, she considers the lists a business venture—without profit. Probably the closest nonelectronic equivalents are organizing a business or professional organization and publishing a participatory newsletter, both of which likewise bestow credibility and visibility among members of a target group.

For Glenn Fleishman, then president of an Internet services company called Point of Presence, the opportunity to stand out among peers and spread one's point of view were clear benefits of the work he invested in the Internet Marketing discussion list, with thousands of subscribers. His work on the list attracted interviews from *Forbes*, the *New York Times*, the *Wall Street Journal*, and *Internet World*, which marked him as a leader in the industry and gave him another chance to evangelize for his cause, the soft sell. "The list gives me an opportunity to sell my company, but also to sell my world view," Fleishman said.

Instead of distributing all submitted messages automatically to members of the list, Fleishman moderated the discussion, rejecting about half of the 50 to 60 daily posts that came in every day, many of them for being repetitive, some for being inappropriate sales pitches. For better or worse, his filtering made him more of a personage than the owner of an unmoderated list. In 1995 Fleishman said he spent about 10 hours a week on the list, down from 20 to 25 when he first started.

Bishop calls her lists moderated to a slight extent in that she will explain after the fact to someone who had sent in an inappropriate posting what she was doing wrong—although the person who sent a chain letter to one of the lists got summarily kicked off. "Chain letters are illegal and drag down computer resources across the globe," Bishop says. "There were thousands of headers at the foot of the message from everywhere it had been, and it clogged the mail queue of the whole university system, designed to serve more than 20,000 students, staff, and faculty."

Serious technical glitches bedeviled the launch of Stefan Gruenwald's bio-tech mailing list in February 1995. Four hundred subscription orders arrived the very first day, causing the system to crash three times. "I had to keep doing backups, and even so some subscriptions got lost. For the first two weeks, it was a mess," Gruenwald recalls. During the launch, his job as director of molecular biology for a San Diego biotechnology firm took him out of town, and he had to try to straighten things out on his portable computer in his hotel room every night.

Although work on the list continued to take him about two hours a day, Gruenwald felt good about his effort, having signed up 1500 or so subscribers in the first year and having received more than 200 thank-you notes from people grateful for the existence of the list. "I thought we needed a way for academics to tell biotechnology professionals about their discoveries and things they want to license. Otherwise we wouldn't know what they have in the academic pipeline." Gruenwald adds that heading the list gives him a powerful vantage point on what's happening in his field and has made him much better known in the bio-tech community.

Similarly, John Audette, whose I-Sales list (see Figure 12.1) filled the gap when Glenn Fleishman closed down the Internet Marketing list, found that his list, launched in November 1995, helped him build a reputation online. "I didn't really have a company at that time and thus I-Sales was not really begun as a marketing tool. Since then the serendipity has been fantastic: I-Sales has become a great forum as intended, and it helped to establish Multimedia Marketing Group as a credible interactive agency. Was this my master plan for I-Sales? No way (I wish I was that smart). I just followed the 'give, then take' model. Find a way to make a contribution—it will yield great dividends later." Audette notes that running a list "puts you under an international microscope," so integrity is a must.

Another list owner, Terry Oakes, says that he just manages to eke out the necessary list-maintenance time for his six lists, given his full-

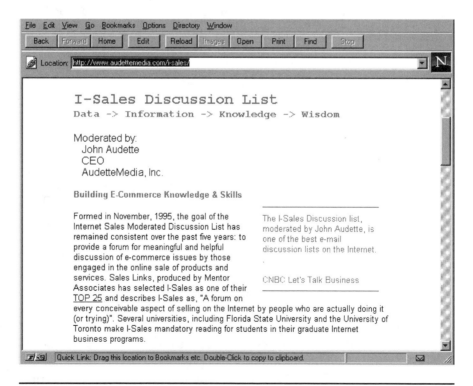

Figure 12.1. The I-Sales sign-up page.

time job as production coordinator of the printing shop at the University of New Brunswick in Canada. Daily maintenance includes dealing with messages that bounce back to him when the recipient's mailbox is full, forcing him to guess whether the recipient has left school for the summer, has allowed messages to pile up temporarily for some reason, or is the victim of a systemwide computer breakdown.

But Oakes has been giving short shrift to another pressing need—trying to keep flaming (verbal personal attacks) to a minimum. "Since I'm very busy at work, it's hard to find the time to write properly diplomatic and constructive letters to intervene and give direction to Litho-L, the most active list, on desktop publishing and printing," he says. One of the other lists, on letterpress printing for people who own vintage printing presses, has more than 200 members worldwide, all so gentlemanly, he says, that that list pretty much runs itself. "I'm an Internet fanatic," he explained when I asked why he started so many lists. "When I get involved in a hobby I tend to dive headlong into it."

Like Fleishman, Gruenwald, and Audette, Oakes says that his lists give him high visibility in his field of expertise, printing and publishing. "People write to me with questions, saying they see my name everywhere," he says. Although he acknowledges that for-pay lists aren't common, Oakes is mulling over the possibility of charging a subscription fee for a list that involves bids and tenders for printing.

One bit of advice emerging from these stories for those aspiring to become emperor of a list is to be sure you're ready technically and equipped to handle anything that might go wrong with the software or system you're using. Oakes suggests enlisting the help of a co-owner or two to make the work manageable. Gruenwald says it's hard to find a helpful service provider because a commercial provider company doesn't make much money from housing a list

FAST FACTS

Finding Topical Discussion Lists

Mailing lists aren't as well indexed as some other features on the Internet, but these directories can get you started hunting for the lists that might prove profitable for you to join:

http://paml.alastra.com

http://tile.net/lists

http://www.topica.com

and a university system won't allow commercial postings. Like Melissa Bishop, you should carefully think through your list guidelines before getting started. It helps too to know your audience. For instance, would they tend to view commercial messages as a service or a plague?

Bishop caters to an expectation specific to the quilting world by providing subscribers to her list who send in an unusual fabric swatch with a membership card that earns them discounts at quilting shops. If you've targeted a niche that perceives a need for your list, you'll get subscribers at once by notifying the grand old list of lists and posting schmooze-compatible announcements (see Chapter 5) in appropriate newsgroups and related mailing lists. Everyone I spoke with said that after the initial surge of subscribers, word of mouth made it unnecessary to keep publicizing the existence of the group.

Publishing an E-zine

In contrast to the traffic-cop duties of running a mailing list, the e-zine option turns you into more of an electronic publisher. Modeled on a magazine but delivered by e-mail without photos and illustrations, an e-zine contains several articles by various authors and goes out on a regular schedule to a set of subscribers. Generally e-zines are free, supported by topical advertising, and have a Web site where people can subscribe and unsubscribe, read back issues, and find related resources and products. Few e-zines publish any more often than weekly, because they involve a lot of work.

Like John Audette of I-Sales, Florida sales consultant Art Siegel had no grand plan when he launched an e-zine called Salesdoctors as a vehicle for learning about the Internet. Published every Monday, Salesdoctors contained several articles in each issue, donated by recognized sales and marketing experts in exchange for publicity at the associated Web site. All articles published since the 1995 launch, totaling more than 6000 pages, were archived at the Salesdoctors Web site. No wonder it received more than 60,000 visits per month. Organizing contributions for the e-zine and keeping the site updated took Siegel and three others about 70 hours a week. Unfortunately, shortly after Siegel sold all the holdings of Salesdoctors to another company, the new owner decided to dismantle the site.

Toronto writer Debbie Ridpath Ohi published the e-zine Inklings every other week for about 45,000 subscribers (see Figure 12.2). Like a magazine, each issue contained a letter from the editor, new Web sites of interest, markets that needed writers, subscriber questions answered by one of the e-zine's nine experts, an article, and ads. As with Salesdoctors, the content was original to and exclusive to Inklings. Ohi paid her contributors a small honorarium, and subscrib-

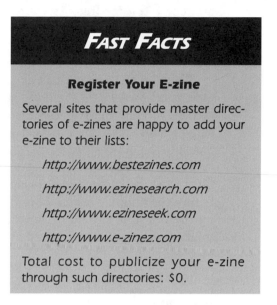

FAST FACTS

Register Your E-zine

Several sites that provide master directories of e-zines are happy to add your e-zine to their lists:

http://www.bestezines.com

http://www.ezinesearch.com

http://www.ezineseek.com

http://www.e-zinez.com

Total cost to publicize your e-zine through such directories: $0.

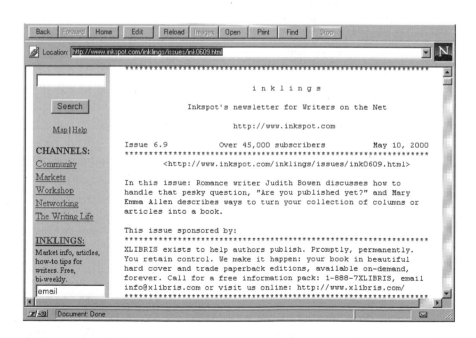

Figure 12.2. Inklings, an e-zine.

ers received it for free. As with Salesdoctors, not long after Ohi sold her company to Xlibris, the new owner froze the site and stopped publication of the e-zine that had performed such a great public service for writers.

What's the business benefit of all the work involved in publishing an e-zine? Siegel said he could trace at least $250,000 in consulting income directly to his publishing of Salesdoctors. "But I get the most satisfaction from the e-mail I get from readers saying how much Salesdoctors has helped them," he said. Don't embark on such a venture unless you have good editorial skills, can meet deadlines issue after issue, and are willing to keep the venture going for a year or more before the tangible benefits begin trickling in. And if you're motivated by the desire to provide a service as well as to build a business, you might think twice before selling your baby off to the big guys!

An E-mail Newsletter

Your third option, an e-mail newsletter, differs from the first two in that all the content comes from you. For attorneys, consultants, social workers, decorators, and other professionals, this is a perfect way to cultivate loyal fans of your expertise. It works equally well for mail-order businesses, software manufacturers, retail stores, and rock groups. When you write it in a personal voice and fill it with customer-centered content, you maintain top-of-mind awareness among subscribers and win new recruits for your fan club through the pass-along factor.

Mitchell Levy, president of ECnow.com, created a weekly newsletter that accomplished this purpose for the Passport Wine Club. Each week, 5,000 subscribers received a personal message in the form of a travel journal from the club owner. Not only would he describe why he liked the wine from the vineyard he'd visited that week, he'd also include an anecdote on how he found his way (or didn't) to the vineyard and would discuss which foods went best with the wine. By including a link to the online store where the wine could be purchased, the newsletter sold wine. More important, "Over time the newsletter built credibility and trust," Levy says. "After receiving the newsletter for a couple of weeks, the subscriber felt comfortable signing up for membership in the wine club or buying a membership as a gift for another."

I launched my e-mail newsletter, "The Marketing Minute," when I was doing a minute-long weekly call-in spot for "The Job Show," a television program seen throughout New England. Since I was writing a weekly script anyway, I wanted to get more mileage out of it. After I set up the e-mail list, people could subscribe from the show's Web site, but I believe most of my initial subscriptions came from a postcard mailing I did to people who had been in my seminars or whom I'd met networking. When "The Job Show" went into a hiatus after a few seasons, I continued weekly publication and focused more attention on making my efforts pay off. By adding a special offer every week, usually tied in thematically with that week's tip, I turned "The Marketing Minute" into a profit center with no evidence of any discomfort on the part of subscribers. (See Figure 12.3.) Three years after launch I had more than 3,000 subscribers.

One iron-clad rule I follow is never adding people to the list unless they explicitly request a subscription or they sign up directly themselves. Otherwise one runs a serious risk of alienating the people one is trying to attract. A colleague confessed to me the disaster that occurred when he ignored this guideline. He compiled a list of companies and individuals whom he wanted to receive his message of the week, then sent out his first issue. Within hours, people began replying to the newsletter in the vein of "What IS this?" or "I didn't ask to get this—take me off the list!"

Unfortunately, the mailing list had been misconfigured technically, so each of these annoyed missives not only went to the list keeper, but also to everyone else who'd been put on the list. Thus, as the day went along, many recipients who didn't get put off originally did get irked as annoyed messages multiplied and became increasingly shrill. "It was a nightmare," the colleague told me. "People even telephoned and yelled at me." Compounding the calamity was that my colleague's message contained numerous typos and spelling errors—all in all creating an unfavorable impression among the very people he'd hoped to influence positively.

Another egregious mistake with an e-mail newsletter came to my attention when a friend mentioned she'd joined the list of a well-known marketer and was being overwhelmed with interminable screaming "Buy this! Buy this!" messages from him every day. The

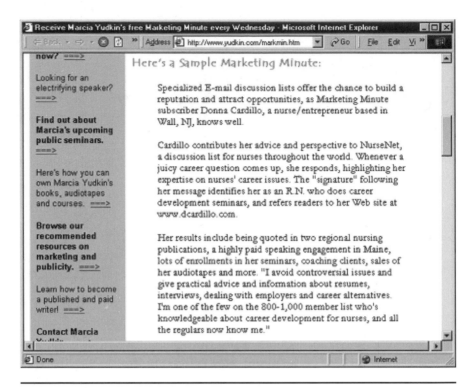

Figure 12.3. My Marketing Minute sign-up page includes a sample issue.

card deck from which she'd signed up promised "Free Marketing Tips by E-mail"—"but I can't find a single marketing tip in there," my friend said. "Can you?" She forwarded two issues to me, and I found it as unreadable as she had, screen after numbing screen of loudmouthed offers—4,000 words' worth, or eight single-spaced pages thick with capital letters when printed out. And no, it didn't contain any marketing advice. Nor did it predispose my friend to consider seriously any of the offers.

Where that marketer lost credibility by delivering something contrary to what he'd promised, I've seen others sabotage their e-mail newsletters by failing to keep to the announced schedule. When the newsletter says that it's published monthly and then you let several months go by without sending an issue, you inspire doubt that you would fulfill a paying contract on time. Another newsletter baffled

---

FAST FACTS

The Opt-in, Opt-out Controversy

Some Internet marketers believe it's acceptable to send mailings to anyone and expect them to unsubscribe if they object (the "opt-out" position). Others hold that getting prior permission for e-mailing is required ("opt-in"). I side with the opt-iners. Read more about the underlying reasoning in these articles:

- Mailing by the Rules, by Emily Avila and Greg Sherwin, in the archives at *http://www.clickz.com*

- Speaking The Opt-In Language, by Kim MacPherson, in the archives at *http://www.clickz.com*

- Ten Rules for Permission-based E-mail Marketing, by MessageMedia, at *http://www.messagemedia.com/rc/ten_guides.shtml*

---

me for a while because the sender signed it with only her first name. Did she think most people had only one "Ruth" in their lives? Several others send multipart missives several times too long for the e-mail medium. You'll get the maximum payoff from subscribers if you keep each message short (less than 500 words in all) and increase the frequency to weekly or biweekly rather than monthly, as long as you can keep to that schedule consistently.

Since I believe that an e-mail newsletter can have a bigger impact on your business over time than a Web site, here are a few ideas for content:

- Beauty spa: New products, new treatments, skin-care advice

- Bookstore: Monthly, an author Q&A and upcoming in-store appearances

- Church: Thought of the day or the week

- Custom tailor: Each season, tips on new designs, updating outdated clothes

- Landscaper: Amusing story of client problem solved

- Music teacher: For parents, kid-friendly concerts coming up

- Nutritionist: Low-salt, low-fat recipes

- Restaurant: Every Monday, daily specials for the coming week

- Software manufacturer: Updates now available, user tips

- Web designer: Three useful new sites and a tip of the week

Making Your E-mail List a Profit Center

Often getting a payback from your discussion list, e-zine, or e-mail newsletter is as simple as providing valuable content on a regular basis. This reminds clients as well as those on the list who haven't bought from you yet that you exist and have the ability to solve problems for them. As with a paper-and-postage newsletter, you should find over time that it boosts your repeat-business quotient and people calling to ask, "Do you do XYZ?" Provide valuable content and you'll also find subscribers forwarding your material to others who have an interest in your area of expertise.

In many cases you can cash in on your electronic list by combining useful advice with a special offer, either a limited-time discount on regular items or services, or a specially priced package put together specifically for your list. With my "Marketing Minute," I found that crafting a different special offer every week brought subscribers into action mode when a particular invitation and price got them thinking about the marketing help they needed. Offers tied to the week's marketing tip, such as a new business bio for $150 when I'd described imaginative ways of highlighting business credentials, did especially well. When I saw a slowdown in my work schedule coming up, I would announce a deeper discount than otherwise, and when I couldn't see space in my schedule for weeks I'd run a product offer that wouldn't require time on my part.

Once you attract more than a thousand subscribers, you may be able to make money by charging for ad space on your list. For instance, if you're a music teacher sending periodic messages to parents of your students, an ad from a local music store or instrument repair shop makes perfect sense. A sponsor or advertiser would normally expect a paragraph or so within or at the end of your message, including complete contact information and Web links, as well as the same copy and links at your Web site, where applicable. Don't inflate subscription numbers in your eagerness to find advertisers. Word gets around quickly online when people feel burnt.

Ad rates on e-mail lists vary widely. When Randy Cassingham had more than 150,000 subscribers to "This is True," a weekly compilation of nutcake news stories, he charged advertisers $500 a week for a spot on his list, while the I-Advertising list charged $850 a week to reach about 8,000 subscribers. Since standard rates don't exist, it will be up to you to make the case for the value advertisers will receive from exposure to the specific population you've gathered. The more elite or otherwise hard-to-reach your crowd is, the more you should be able to charge.

Note that when you rent out space in your list, e-zine, or newsletter, no one else actually gets their hands on the e-mail addresses of your subscribers. This is vital! I don't recommend that you follow what may appear to be almost the equivalent strategy, of renting out your subscriber list, the way print magazines do through mailing-list brokers. On the contrary, you should assure subscribers periodically that you never under any circumstances provide subscriber e-mail addresses to anyone else.

Finally, you may be tempted to capitalize on the loyal list members you've attracted by charging for subscriptions. Sometimes this does indeed work, if you can offer timely, must-have information available nowhere else. Ralph Wilson's free "Web Marketing Today," with 60,000 subscribers (see Figure 12.4), allowed him to spin off a for-fee "Web Commerce Today," with 35,000 subscribers paying $49.95 per year. But the Internet is littered with the remains of entrepreneurs both large and small who overestimated the public's willingness to pay for words in an intangible medium. You may be better off concentrating on building an audience for a free, advertising-supported electronic periodical.

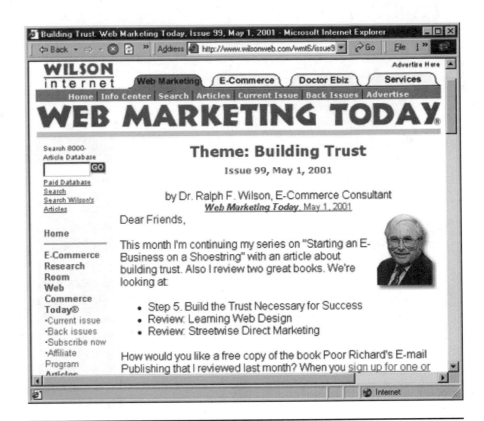

Figure 12.4. Web Marketing Today, another e-mail newsletter.

13

Harnessing Pass-along Power

Walk into any fast-food establishment, order a hamburger, and I'll bet that the next words out of the mouth of the person working the counter will be some variant of "Would you like fries with that?" Just as that question augments the restaurant's profits from someone already clinched as a customer, certain techniques parlay the winning over of one customer into the recruitment of several others. In the Internet marketing world, such techniques go by the name of "viral marketing." Not only does that term carry nasty connotations, however, it exaggerates the extent to which cute or useful online innovations spread automatically, like influenza. Nevertheless, many equivalents to "Would you like...?" multiply your marketing reach with minimal effort on your part. Here's how to encourage people who come within your sphere of influence to widen the circle for you.

A Send-it Mechanism Spurs Referrals

Just as people who order a burger may remember on their own to request French fries, people who visit your site may take the initiative to tell others about the site, send them specific pages and print pages out to send around the office. But unquestionably, suggesting that they do so, and making it easy for them to do it with just a click or two magnify the odds that they'll recommend and pass along your stuff.

For instance, MarketingtoWebMarketers.com, a portion of the larger site MarketingSherpa.com, invites visitors contemplating its current table of contents to tell a friend about the site (see Figure 13.1). The person who becomes enthusiastic about the site and wants to notify someone else about it just fills in her name, adds the friend's e-mail address, and presses "Go!" Note the reassurance below this feature explaining that recommending the site in this way will not expose the friend to spam. As shown in Figure 13.2, on top of each article, MarketingtoWebMarketers.com also includes an equally easy-to-use option to send that single article to a friend.

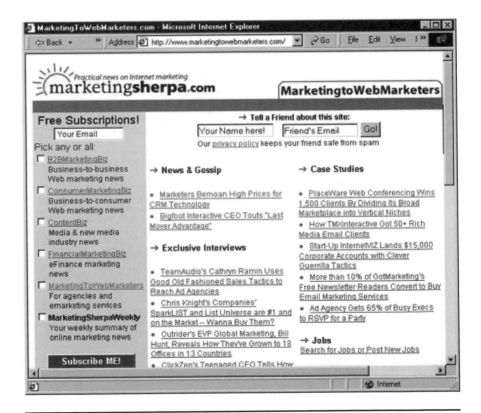

Figure 13.1. MarketingtoWebMarketers.com invites readers to tell a friend about the site.

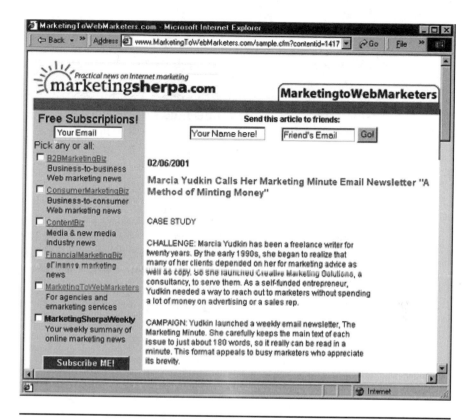

Figure 13.2. Above each of its articles, MarketingtoWebMarketers.com invites readers to send the article to a friend.

Here are some variations on this theme that you'll want to consider:

- Tell a friend about the site

- Tell a friend about a particular product or special offer

- Send this article to a friend

- Send this page (not an article) to a friend

- Send a friend a link to this article or page (not the whole article or page)

- Send a friend a link to this article or page with comments

- View a printer-friendly version of this article or page

The last option reformats the page without ads running down both sides of the piece and minus much of the clutter at the top and bottom of the site's pages as viewed online. The theory is that a cleaner-looking, more compact version will more often get printed out and saved or routed to a co-worker.

Fortunately, a good number of free scripts and services make it easy to add such recommendation capabilities to your site. In choosing which ones to implement, favor those that enable you to customize the wording of the e-mail message that goes out to the friend. For example, putting yourself in the position of a friend who's interested in Civil War history, the second recommendation here—customized for your site and with the e-mail subject line "A message from Marilyn Mensch"—would make a much better impression than the first one, which is generic and stiff.

> *PASSABLE: Your friend Marilyn Mensch suggests that you visit the following site: Civil War What-ifs at http://www. civilwarwhatifs.com.*

> *BETTER: So you're a Civil War buff! Your friend Marilyn Mensch has asked us to let you know that our site, Civil War What-ifs at http://www.civilwarwhatifs.com, offers mind-twisting speculative history, games and commentary, along with calendars, tips and bulletin boards for the re-enactment community. Please visit us at your convenience by clicking http://www.civilwarwhatifs.com. We respect your privacy and have not retained your e-mail address for further contacts.*

The exact placement of the sending apparatus on your page may make an enormous difference in how often visitors use it. When the recommendation mechanism is at the top of the page, it attracts notice when someone has just arrived and not necessarily begun exploring or reading. At the bottom of the article or page, however, the recommendation opportunity comes to the visitor's attention when he or she is emerging from a glow of absorption in your content.

Thus, when you think someone will survey the offerings at your home page and feel immediately excited about letting someone know what you're up to, put the link near the top of the page. When the recommendation urge will probably surface after reading, put the send-it-on option just below the spot where they probably will finish reading.

I learned this lesson about placement when a reader of my "Marketing Minute" e-mail newsletter suggested that my invitation to forward the newsletter to friends and colleagues probably wasn't having much effect in the e-mail subject line, where I placed it every week. After all, he pointed out, when people are reading the subject line of an e-mail they haven't read the contents yet. And after they have read the contents, the subject line may be out of sight, out of mind. Why not put that invitation inside the newsletter, just after the week's featured content? I did exactly that, since it made so much more sense. Placing the invitation to forward in the subject line resembled asking "Would you like fries with that?" when someone walked into the restaurant, not after he'd ordered a burger.

FAST FACTS

Send-it-on Scripts and Services

The following sites provide some sort of apparatus to send a recommendation for your site, or the contents of a page, to a friend for free. Some require you to display their logo, some not.

- Birdcast

    http://bignosebird.com/carchive/ birdcast.shtml

- Bravenet Announcers

    http://www.bravenet.com/samples/ announcer.php

- Let 'Em Know Automated Traffic Generator

    http://www.letemknow.com

- Mail2Friend

    http://www.jokhoo.com/mail2friend/

- Recommend-It

    http://www.recommend-it.com

- Tell a Friend

    http://www.cgi.net/

- TenZero Instant Invite

    http://www.tenzero.com/invites.htm

Should You Offer Incentives and Gimmicks?

Many Internet commentators take it as a given that you can't get results from word-of-mouth marketing without offering rewards for recommendations to friends, such as a free download or the opportunity to win a prize. They also reckon that if people are in the mood to pass the word to one friend, you might as well encourage them to do so to five or ten friends. In my view, however, these two assumptions put together open you up to the possibility of disaster.

If you're marketing for long-term results, rather than hit-and-run traffic, rewarding people for recommending your site to as many people as possible lowers the likelihood that the e-mail addresses they enter belong to people who genuinely would be interested in your site's offerings and indeed that the e-mail addresses truly represent the recommender's friends. How would it benefit you if someone wanting more chances to win a Las Vegas vacation recommends your how-to-beat-the-odds-at-blackjack site to someone who doesn't even gamble? On the contrary, inappropriate or bogus recommendations can backfire on your site in the form of complaints you must deal with directly, spam complaints to your Web host, negative word of mouth, and sabotage. In addition, offering rewards for multiple recommendations may reduce your credibility to those who see that offer but don't get involved. They may wonder why you need to pile on incentives for recommendations—the content isn't appealing enough in itself?

I even see a possible backlash from giving away a cool gimmick that you invite people to send along to their friends as something entertaining in itself and designed to serve as publicity for your product or service. These are usually set up to be sent by e-mail either as links to the cool content on a Web site, or as the cool content bursting with animated color right in the e-mail. When I've received something of the first type, requiring me to click to a Web site to see that it's a thank-you greeting card, I wished the person just said "Thank you" without wasting my time on the gimmick. And when I've received an e-mail of the second type while out of town at a hotel, I've become incensed that someone's idea of a nifty greeting took fifteen minutes to download and cost me more than $10.00 in long-distance charges.

Offering rewards for recommendations and encouraging multiple recommendees may work fine for you. Scope mouthwash, for instance, created online ads that allowed consumers to send an animated e-mail "kiss" to friends. The embedded premise: Scope mouthwash brings people "kissably close." According to Jeffrey Graham of Dynamic Logic, people were soon sending Scope kisses all over the world, resulting in a measurable increase in awareness of and intent to purchase Scope. I'm warning only that you need to know your target audience and consider possible negative repercussions.

Whether or not you use incentives and gimmicks, make sure you follow the lead of MarketingtoWebMarketers.com and reassure users of your recommendation system that you don't make any other use of the friends' e-mail addresses.

Some lucky companies have a "spread-the-word" effect built into the very structure or purpose of their product or service. This makes for exponential growth in patronage of the site or service without having to explicitly ask users to recommend it. For instance, sites that offer on-site sharing of photos from weddings or reunions will inevitably have users e-mailing the URL for their photos to friends and relatives, thus exposing them to the service. The same goes for sites enabling easy construction of family trees, free e-mail services (Hotmail is the classic example, with every Hotmail e-mail including a line promoting it), free message boards, etc. If this approach fits what you do, make the most of those built-in recommendation opportunities. But if not, don't strain to draw the analogy. Highly paid professionals find this sort of coup difficult to pull off.

Self-Syndication Spreads Your Influence

If you have ever read the "Dear Abby" advice column or the "Doonesbury" cartoon strip, you've encountered the phenomenon of syndication. With syndication, a content creator hands over distribution of content to a third party, who signs up clients and negotiates and collects fees, passing along 50 percent or so of monies collected. Then the content creator can concentrate on writing or drawing, receiving income that rises with the number of outlets running the column or cartoon strip. On the Web, companies like iSyndicate.com and Screaming Media distribute everything from weather reports and sports scores to parenting columns and political analysis to Web sites

FAST FACTS

Start Your Own Affiliate Program

If you have a product that you're already profitably selling online, you can multiply your sales by creating an affiliate program through which others sell or recommend your product for you and receive commissions for doing so. Amazon.com started this years ago, calling it an Associate Program. It sounds wonderful—enlisting an army of sales representatives whose sites also promote your products 24 hours a day, 365 days a year.

However, administering such a program reliably requires either a lot of labor and know-how or specialized software, which does not come cheap. The cheapest service or software I found for setting up your own affiliate program costs $500. So, save this option for when you have considerable earnings from product sales to reinvest. And make sure you have set up an escape clause in advance in case some neo-Nazi site wants to be your affiliate and you find that horrifying.

Here are three affiliate set-up programs to look at:

- AssocTrac

    http://www.marketingtips.com/assoctrac

- ClickTrade

    http://www.clicktrade.com

- Commission Junction

    http://www.cj.com

in a similar fashion. Some of their offerings are free to recipient sites, while others are billed on a quarterly basis.

New self-syndication tools allow anyone to distribute their own content efficiently and widely on the Web if they can cultivate the demand for it. Although they can certainly charge syndicatees, I believe that in the current economic climate syndication works best as a publicity strategy. I learned about this strategy from Ralph Wilson, who has hundreds of sites running his free Doctor Ebiz question-and-answer column (see Figure 13.3). Anyone who wants that content for

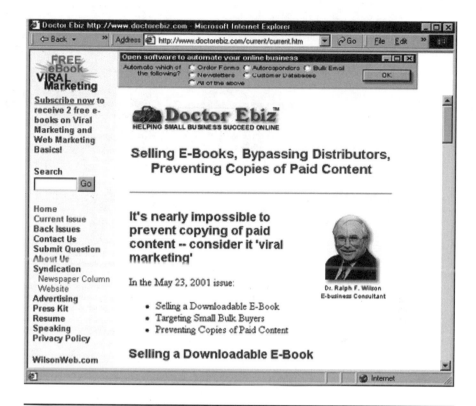

Figure 13.3.   Dr. Ralph Wilson syndicates his Doctor Ebiz column to scores of other Web sites.

their site gets one line of javascript code to place on one of their Web pages, which automatically causes Wilson's current Doctor Ebiz page to appear there almost instantly, at the syndicatee's site. Wilson created an attractive template for his column, containing low-key links to his other offerings, and when he updates the content once a week, all of his syndicatees automatically have the fresh column as well.

Any kind of content that you can create on a regular basis can be syndicated in this fashion, from pet horoscopes to sports commentary, and it's a stupendous way to enlist other sites to help spread your influence. Inspired by Wilson, I created a similar syndication setup for my "Marketing Minute" e-mail newsletter, and within a month I had both long-time and new fans running my content exactly as I had formatted it (see Figure 13.4) at their sites.

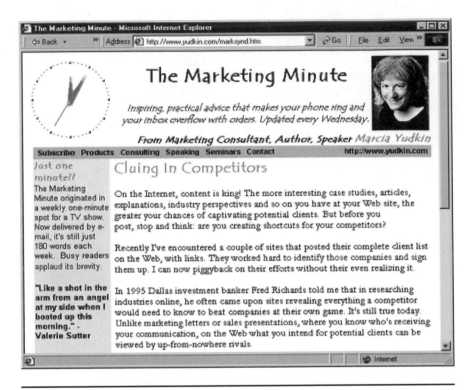

Figure 13.4.   I syndicate my Marketing Minute newsletter to other Web sites in this format.

Technically you accomplish the syndication delivery through a special program or script that generates the code that you give out to syndicatees, which pulls up your current content at their remote sites. Wilson uses a program called MasterSyndicator. Others use free scripts that require technical prowess beyond the average Web user's knowledge. I use a self-syndication program my husband created for me, and that we are releasing commercially because it's easier to use than both MasterSyndicator and the free scripts.

If you don't mind trusting syndicatees to format your content properly, you can also distribute your content through regular old e-mail. Note too that this way it's hard to enforce guidelines on how long they can post your material. I had an experience with a site doing unbelievable things to my content that made me shy away from this distribution method. I'd given the site permission to post one article of mine

---

FAST FACTS

Self-Syndication Solutions

- MasterSyndicator software

  With self-installation, $99; with installation, $159

  http://www.mastersyndicator.com
- Self-syndication javascript tutorial

  Free, requires familiarity with HTML and javascript

  http://www.purplepages.ie/site/articles/article.asp?faq=6&fldAuto=67&page=1
- Self-Syndicator software

  About $129, no installation or special knowledge required

  http://www.yudkin.com/marketing.htm

---

for free, and when I saw what they'd done, I had to vehemently retract my permission. They posted it without any capital letters, all in lower case, beginning like this:

> *not long ago i read about an internet company that had handed out yo-yo's bearing its brand to well-heeled diners hanging around outdoors waiting to get into a chic restaurant. the yo-yo's didn't work properly, however, so that a playful gesture created a ridiculous scene of frustrated yo-yo'ers.*

To my eyes, this made me look like an idiot. To them, this was the outcome of making my work consistent with their brand identity. Sorry, this was not consistent with my branding, I retorted, and fortunately they complied with my removal request.

Offers With Pass-Along Power

I'd like to wrap up this chapter with a brief catalog of other methods of using customers to bring in others like them that aren't specific to the Internet but could just as well be used at your Web site or in your e-mail newsletter as in traditional media. My favorite of these is offering a major discount if someone brings along a friend. Restaurants encourage newcomers by distributing coupons for the second dinner free in a party of two, knowing that the second person might never have stepped foot in the establishment otherwise. Seminars do the same by giving 25 percent off when two people sign up together. At your Web site, you might implement this strategy by making gift purchases half off when also buying something for oneself. Or you could provide free gift certificates with purchases over a certain amount.

Mail-order companies have long been in the habit of asking on each order form, "Do you know anyone else who would like a catalog?" If people are ordering physical goods online, you could include in their delivery a mail-back postcard with that question. When they call to place an order, you can ask that at the end of the information-gathering process.

Another common promotional technique off the Net is distributing doodads (pens, T-shirts, mugs) bearing the company's name and message. You can use your Web site and e-mail newsletter to distribute these to those who become your customers. However, in line with the theme of this chapter, consider promotional items that are more likely than others not only to serve as reminders to those you give them to, but also to come to the attention of others. For instance, self-stick notes branded with your logo, tag line, and contact information would often find their way onto documents circulated around an office or to others. Amazon.com once slipped a couple of pads of these in with an order, and I happily used every last one. Another giveaway with pass-along power is postcards with some low-key promotional message on one side, such as a picture of your Web site, or of your products, and enough space on the other side for your customer to use it the way they would a postcard of the Champs Elysées.

PART IV

Problems and Solutions

14

Online Style Tips

When desktop publishing boomed in popularity, people who had never taken the slightest interest in fonts, leading, or point sizes developed new habits. They learned how to select an effective typeface; emphasize points with boldface, italics, or spacing; and create a formal, "official" look by justifying the right-hand margins. People are again getting excited about the ability to send formatted files containing sound, pictures, and animation by e-mail. Progress doesn't always march forward in a straight line, however. If you have become skilled at producing a sophisticated layout or multimedia communications, you also need to know how to abandon all your new tools and generate readable electronic text with nothing more than the features available on an old-fashioned manual typewriter.

ASCII—The Digital Lowest Common Denominator

When you're e-mailing an unknown party or placing messages on electronic bulletin boards, you have no idea what kind of computer or software people will be using to retrieve and read your contribution. Your brilliant ideas become accessible to all when you incorporate them in a standard, limited set of characters and symbols called

ASCII, pronounced "Askee" and short for American Standard Code for Information Interchange.

So-called "pure ASCII" or "straight text" includes all the everyday letters and numbers on a computer keyboard, plus a few extra symbols that you probably have no reason to bother with. It lacks any formatting codes for particular word processing programs or other software applications, and it lacks any font choices or any layout or placement tools besides the return key and the space bar. In Microsoft Word, it's the kind of file you get when you choose the option "MS-DOS text." "Boring, boring," you say? I admit it's a limited palette, but just as a skilled designer can create an elegant impact in black and white, you can learn to keep people reading and help them absorb your message using these universal, low-tech tools.

If you insist on sending something that looks nicer to you, your recipient can get puzzling garbage. For example, here's what your message could look like if you don't strip the extra codes inserted by certain word processing programs to denote curled apostrophes, quotation marks, long dashes, italics, and nontypewriter symbols:

> *Don^A't be disappointedúÇ'there are only seventeen widgets left. They^A're only Æ250 each!*

Even worse, here's what your respondent might see if you send your message in HTML, the coding system for Web pages:

```
<HTML>
<HEAD>
<META HTTP-EQUIV="Content-Type"
CONTENT="text/html; charset=windows-1252">
<META NAME="Generator" CONTENT="Microsoft
Word 97">
<TITLE>Don't be disappointed – there are only seventeen
widgets left</TITLE>
</HEAD>
<BODY>
<FONT FACE="Arial Black" SIZE=4><P>Don't be disap-
pointed – there are only seventeen widgets left. They're only
£250 each!</P></FONT></BODY>
</HTML>
```

Jeanine Graf, host of "The Job Show," the first integrated online, TV, and radio job fair, invited viewers, listeners and Web surfers to e-mail their resumés for forwarding to appropriate employers, but all too many proved unreadable, because they were sent either as unopenable attachments in a format that turned into pure gibberish in e-mail or with spacing that became unreadable. Now that several widely publicized virus attacks have spread through e-mail attachments, which preserve all formatting in the original program, many people will not open up an e-mail attachment from someone they do not know.

Keep in mind too that if the recipient doesn't use the program and program version you use—or uses a Mac where you use a PC or vice versa—the attachment might as well have a "Ha-ha, Just Try and Open Me!" sign on it. Forcing the recipient to read an attached file is equivalent to saying, "Here's my information, in invisible ink. To read it all you have to do is soak it in a pan of lemon juice and then blow air on it with a hair dryer for two minutes."

One of the biggest frustrations for some people online is that although you can send a message from Seattle to St. Petersburg in a flash, in e-mail or online postings you can't emphasize important points *with italics*, with **boldface**, or even <u>with underlining</u>. That last makes ASCII even more primitive than a typewriter. Here are three alternative means of emphasis, demonstrated with a signature line I used when I first went online:

- Marcia Yudkin, Author, *Six Steps to Free Publicity* and six other books

- Marcia Yudkin, Author, _Six Steps to Free Publicity_ and six other books

- Marcia Yudkin, Author, SIX STEPS TO FREE PUBLICITY and six other books

The first, my favorite method, consists of surrounding the text you wish to stress with asterisks. In the second, you surround it with single underlining signs, and in the third, you type it in all capitals. Caution: DON'T EVER USE LONG STRETCHES OF CAPITAL LETTERS. NOT ONLY ARE THEY VERY HARD TO READ,

PEOPLE EXPERIENCE IT AS THE EQUIVALENT OF SHOUT-
ING—WHICH IS AS ILL-MANNERED ONLINE AS IT IS OFF. (Isn't
it a relief now to be looking at normal type again?) It's almost as bad
to use all lowercase, as i am doing now—for different reasons. "One
guy who types all in small letters, I wonder if he is drunk," says Paula
Berinstein, an independent researcher in Los Angeles, California.
"Another person I can tell is trying to type fast and spend as little
time online as possible to save money." Using standard capitalization
conventions with an occasional very short stretch of all-capitals helps
to keep the reader's attention on the message rather than on the so-
briety, frugality, or manners of the messenger.

Although you can't include a graphic logo in text messaging, I
have seen a text version that fulfills a similar function—letting the
reader know in a split second who the message is from. Author Bob
Coleman is the only person I know who opened every message with
"Howdy!" In the same way, certain people who always indent their
name and other identifying information distinctively create a subtly
recognizable all-text look. Can you come up with your own text-
based trademark, the equivalent of always showing up in a certain
color or having an inimitable voice?

Formatting for Readability

When it comes to setting up a file or e-mail message to be universally
readable, you have a number of tools available that can help, including the space bar and the return key, which can make an enormous
difference if you use them appropriately.

Use the space bar instead of the tab key. Avoid creating indentations
with the tab key. If you want to arrange text on the screen or the
page, use the space bar instead. Tabs can cause visual mayhem because they are interpreted differently on different computer systems.
If you have your tabs set to every three spaces and I have mine set
every eight spaces, a file segment that looks like this to you:

Here are the three biggest fears of those shopping for a used car,
along with some remedies:

1. being cheated on price   statewide price charts
2. being saddled with a "lemon"   30-day guarantee
3. being deceived about car's problems   independent evaluation

may look like this to me:

Here are the three biggest fears of those shopping for a used car, along with some remedies:
1. being cheated on price
statewide price charts
2. being saddled with a "lemon"   30-
day guarantee
3. being deceived about car's problems   independent
evaluation

The damage is equally serious with an Internet signature, which might look like this when you create it:

```
* * * * * * * * * * * * * * * * * * * * * * * * * * * * * * * * * * * * * * * * * * * * * * * * * *
*   Marcia Yudkin          Publicity Coach          Writer   *
*   P.O. Box 1310          Boston, MA 02117          U.S.A.   *
*   marcia@yudkin.com                         (617)266-1613   *
*        Helping professionals & entrepreneurs since 1988     *
* * * * * * * * * * * * * * * * * * * * * * * * * * * * * * * * * * * * * * * * * * * * * * * * * *
```

But if those spaces were marked by tabs, that might come up on someone else's screen like this:

```
* * * * * * * * * * * * * * * * * * * * * * * * * * * * * * * * * * * * * * * * * * * * * * * * * *
*   Marcia Yudkin          PublicityCoach
Writer     *
*   P.O. Box 1310          Boston, MA 02117
U.S.A.      *
*   marcia@yudkin.com              (617)266-1613                    *
*        Helping professionals & entrepreneurs since 1988
*

* * * * * * * * * * * * * * * * * * * * * * * * * * * * * * * * * * * * * * * * * * * * * * * * * *
```

Not anywhere near as neat, don't you agree?

Keep your line lengths at a maximum of 60 characters per line by using the return key. Different systems for writing and reading messages handle word-wrapping (the system for arranging text line by line) differently. Some interface programs for online services and the Internet automatically wordwrap anything you write within that interface, while others don't. Problems occur when a paragraph that looked perfect on your screen before you sent or uploaded it gets crammed into a text reader with a shorter line length. Instead of this:

> The key to success in used-car sales is understanding the considerable fears prospects bring to the lot, including most of all getting cheated, stuck, or lied to.

your recipient might see this:

> The key to success in used-car sales is
> understanding the
> considerable fears prospects bring to the lot,
> including
> most of all getting cheated, stuck, or lied to.

The shorter line length and the next tip also help with reader-friendliness.

Use shorter paragraphs than you ordinarily do, with an extra space between them. Almost always, online text gets read on screen single-spaced, which feels crowded and tiring unless you provide visual relief. Compare this, from an electronic sales letter of mine:

> Right now I'm eager to pass along what I've learned about how to get priceless media coverage dirt-cheap. Whatever product or service you are offering for sale, you undoubtedly face the challenge of finding customers or clients. Sure, advertising is an option, but it usually costs a fortune even to test the waters. And buyers these days remain justifiably skeptical of the content of your ads—after all, it's what you yourself are saying about your own company!

With this:

Right now I'm eager to pass along what I've learned about how to get priceless media coverage dirt-cheap. Whatever product or service you are offering for sale, you undoubtedly face the challenge of finding customers or clients.

Sure, advertising is an option, but it usually costs a fortune even to test the waters. And buyers these days remain justifiably skeptical of the content of your ads—after all, it's what you yourself are saying about your own company!

Doesn't the second version seem more inviting? Shorter, well-spaced paragraphs keep the reader going at a decent clip.

Use headings, particularly in sales letters and files to be posted at Web sites. Any electronic text that goes on longer than a page becomes easier to scan, both on screen and when printed out, when it contains subheads. As long as the subheads are just two to five words, they stand out well all in capitals. You also help the reader keep on going when you organize information into bulleted or numbered lists. Here, as throughout this chapter, your goal becomes easing the effort of reading long stretches of text for someone whom you hope to gather into your sphere of customers or clients.

Addressing for Memorability and Legibility

I'd like to add some suggestions for naming e-mail and World Wide Web addresses, where you have a choice. Unlike the postal service, which delivers mail that's misspelled or illegible to the average person, computers can't guess that a comma really should be a period or that "Msra" should really be "MrsA." If you've ever tried to read an e-mail address off a handwritten fax or to get certain Web addresses over the radio or the phone, you know that some addresses are darned hard to communicate accurately. Avoid these elements in addresses if you can, which exacerbate problems for some users:

• *Unusual ASCII characters, such as "~," "^," and "_."*

Do you have any idea what to call these characters in words? From my long-ago study of Spanish, I know that the first of these is called a "tilde." But the first time I saw it in a printed address I mistook it first for a hyphen and then for a printing blotch. As I originally typed this chapter, I discovered that I couldn't type a tilde by itself because my usual word-processing program reserved it for a special function involving hyphenation. It also took me quite a while to locate that symbol on my keyboard. Imagine the trouble a tilde would cause me, then, if I had one in my World Wide Web address and tried to type it into a letter! Indeed, one of the testimonials printed in the front of the first edition of this book had the "~" left out of its address when the typesetter, who'd probably never encountered its use, ignored it.

The second of these obscure characters might be called a "caret," but that word denotes a proofreading symbol placed under, not above, a line of type. Or maybe it's called a "circumflex," after the accent mark used in French? It was once described to me over the phone as "the wedge that's above the '6' on the keyboard." The third sign I have no idea what to call—"two vertical dashes stacked on one another"? And although that's what it looks like on my keyboard, on paper it comes out from my computer as an unbroken vertical line.

- *Underline marks and extra dots.* Worse, in some e-mail systems and on a Web page, anything typed in the format of an e-mail address appears on screen with the whole unit underlined. If there is an underline sign in the e-mail address it will mistakenly look like a space. The underlining sign is sometimes hard to distinguish from an errant splotch or a hyphen. The same distortion may occur if you include extra dots within the left half of an e-mail address, such as in firstname.lastname@domain.com.

- *Eccentrically mixed upper- and lowercase characters.* These help a password remain obscure, but in addresses may keep people from connecting electronically with you. They're also very tedious to explain verbally. The safest policy is to stick to lowercase, since that's the general custom on Unix systems. When I hear Tom Brokaw say I can send him an e-mail at "nightly at nbc-dot-com," I don't need to look at the TV screen to know that he means "nightly@nbc.com."

- *Hard-to-spell words.* My photographer, Denise Passaretti, wisely decided not to choose "passaretti.com" as her domain, even though the address was available. Having been in business since 1989, she knew how often people got stuck over whether "Passaretti" had one or two s's, r's and t's. Instead she selected "photosbydenise.com," to which she only needs to add "all one word" for people to find her on the Web from a conversation on the phone or during networking.

  Compare Passaretti's decision to the hundreds of times I heard the name of a particular sponsor on public radio along with the Web address (pronounced, never spelled): I assumed it was the "Pugh" Charitable Trust at "pugh.com" or "pughtrust.com." Only when I happened to see a reference in print to the "Pew" Charitable Trust did I realize that that alternate spelling even existed as a possibility. Even then I got the URL wrong, as it's actually www.pewtrusts.com, since the official name of the organization ends with "Trusts" rather than "Trust." I have a good ear, but never in those hundreds of listenings did I hear the final "s" on the name of the organization.

  Before committing yourself to an electronic address, make sure it's something you can easily pronounce and convey to someone over the telephone or on the radio, and that it will be easy to pick out and use when someone sees it in print. A good test for the latter is type it out and handwrite it, then copy the page on your fax machine and see if you can still read it accurately at a glance. If you do get stuck with an address that is easy to get wrong, alert others explicitly to its quirks.

Writing for the World Wide Web

Whatever you write for the Web will usually get marked up and converted into copy with a colored title in a nice font and text that includes boldface and italics where appropriate. It would be easy to assume that you can therefore take texts originally written for print, hand them over to your Webmaster, and go on your merry way, enjoying the results of them being posted online. Sorry. Reading text on the screen is uncomfortable for many people. And in the Web environment, impatience is a constant undercurrent and distraction is always one click away. Given these two factors, you should scrutinize and edit or rewrite everything originally written for paper before putting it up on the Web.

Dense text that went over fine in an academic journal won't get read by many on the Web. It takes too much effort, and people are not surfing with the patient attention they have when curled up in an armchair or propped up on pillows in bed. They can send the file to themselves to print out and read on paper wherever and whenever they like, but even then it won't be as readable as when professionally typeset in book form. Bottom line: For the Web, shorten your sentences, shorten your paragraphs, and make the style more informal. And add subheads. (See Figure 14.1.)

Traditionally, every paragraph focuses on one central idea, so that you develop that idea fully before starting the next paragraph with a new central idea. To make your paragraphs short enough for readability on the Web, free yourself from that rule of paragraphing. Instead, divide that cohesive, nicely organized paragraph into two when it contains more than five sentences, or when it goes on for more than ten lines. Even better, adhere to a seven-line limit for optimal readability of paragraphs. Deliberately creating shorter paragraphs for the Web has influenced my writing for paper as well. I used to write much longer paragraphs than you'll find here.

Finally, where you have control over Web page design, don't run your columns the whole width of the screen. Five or six inches—sixty characters or spaces—is the widest text people can read comfortably on computer. Once you become an experienced surfer, you'll see that the best sites almost universally follow this guideline.

Online Sales Copy Tips

When you're trying to sell outright online—as opposed to "schmoozing"—you want to use most of the techniques that have been proven to work in direct mail writing. In just a few pages I can't turn you into a copywriter par excellence, but I can highlight the most important principles that bring you paid orders.

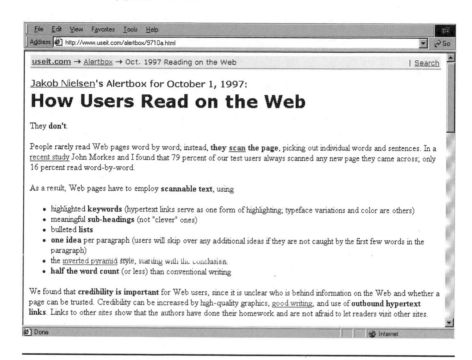

Figure 14.1. Jakob Nielsen offers valuable tips on writing for the Web.

- *The clout of headlines.* On the Web, the functional equivalent of headlines appear not only at the spatial top of distinct pages, but also in the verbal links and in the titles that appear in someone's browser when they access your page. Compare the lure of "Full-Strength Quality at Half Price" with "Our Products and Services" and you'll understand how much more power a distinctive headline can pack. Make sure that the headline tone is compatible with your professional image. Direct-mail pro Sheila Danzig can scream out with "I made $16 million!!" but Marcia Layton's much pricier, professional service fits well with the low-key, straightforward "Need a Business Plan?"

- *The old two-step.* Instead of trying to get orders directly from a Web catalog, invite people to inquire for more information so that you can convert these leads to sales with a multipage, in-depth sales letter. That is, keep the description of your product to four lines or so, ask people to "Click here" for more information, and then get them a detailed sales pitch that they

---

FAST FACTS

Invest Time in Proofreading

Web usability expert Jakob Nielsen has estimated that for a 10,000-employee company, the cost of one poorly or incorrectly written headline for an internally oriented Web page amounts to almost $5,000. Your cost for poorly written copy or mistakes in marketing copy is lost customers. Vigilance matters!

---

can read when they are mentally out of browsing mode. Pack the letter full of substance as well as sales talk. As marketer Chris Brandlon puts it, "When people ask for more information, give them an education, not just a sales letter." Mere "Buy now! Hurry! Offer expires in 48 hours!" does not work in the information-rich online environment.

- *Test, test, test*. Intuition, experience, and study do not give anyone the ability to forecast what words, what punctuation, what offer will get the greatest response. Would you have guessed, for instance, that the headline, "Here's a Strange Way To Learn Music" outpulled "A Few Months Ago I Couldn't Play a Note" by a wide margin? John Caples (see Appendix A) provides scores of illuminating examples, highlighting the monumental sensitivity of readers to minuscule differences. My favorite is the headline "How to Repair Cars—Quickly, Easily, Right," which did all right, but changing the single word "Repair" to "Fix" while keeping everything else the same increased orders 18 percent.

- *The personal touch*. When writing text for an autoresponder file or follow-up e-mail that will land in people's electronic mailbox, use the time-tested format of a letter. That means including a date, salutation, dynamic opening paragraph, closing, signature line, and a P.S. The one extra ingredient you should add is a selling headline, perhaps the very one used in your ad, at the beginning. When you can, customize your standard reply letter for each recipient with his or her name in the salutation. Lawrence Seldin, author of *Power Tips for the Apple Newton*, did this until he got tired of customizing each reply. Within a week he received his first negative feedback ever, and promptly returned to adding "Dear ...." Some autoresponder utilities can now insert the addressee's name automatically.

- *Conversational tone.* Rather than a formal, off-putting brief or a simple but distant list of prices, establish a connection with your respondent by explaining your offerings as if you were telling a friend about them. Alfred and Emily Glossbrenner's mailbot sales piece, for instance, starts off with a spread-out W E L C O M E! and then says, "This file is being brought to you by an autoresponder that lives at books@infomat.com. It will tell you how to get your hands on some truly wonderful computer books, if we do say so ourselves." The letter continues with the same casual voice, distinctive with personality.

- *Many contact points, many payment mechanisms.* In your note, make it possible for people to order by phone, by fax, by e-mail, by mail, by returning to the Web site, and in any other way you can imagine. Insert all your contact information obviously and more than once. An order form that people can print out and fax or send helps, as does your announcement that you accept major credit cards, checks, money orders, and cash. As explained in Chapter 16, wherever you advertise online, you may attract international attention, so be prepared with overseas shipping prices and a foreign payment acceptance policy.

- *Guarantees.* As Chapter 15 demonstrates, online prospects have plenty of reason to be more suspicious than elsewhere. Reassure them with a way they can find satisfaction if you let them down. Counterintuitive as it may seem, the stronger and longer your guarantee, the less likely you are to have to deliver on it. "When I first started out in mail order, I offered a three-day guarantee," remembers Sheila Danzig. "This didn't instill confidence in the buyer, and pressured those who did buy it to return it right away, before the deadline passed. With a thirty-day or one-year guarantee, people take their time, and then forget—although if you sell a bad product, you'll get returns even if you don't mention any guarantee."

- *Provide an incentive for people to act now.* Regardless of how much they need your help, human beings procrastinate and then fail to act. Special prices if they order in the next ten days, strict expiration dates for offers, and so on help them break through their inertia. Rob Cosgrove, of Precision Data Corporation in Memphis, Tennessee, has found that nonelectronic response methods, such as fax on demand or an 800 number, move people more effectively toward a buying decision than a mere mouse click. "When we can get them to stop typing at us, we can sell," says Cosgrove.

- *Take care with layout, spelling, and descriptions.* All people have to go on is the text in front of them, and if it's verbally, aesthetically, or logically a mess, some will not respond. See the suggestions earlier in this chapter for making plain text as easy as possible to read and absorb.

15

Inspiring Trust

Imagine coming home from work one day and finding a simple copied flyer tucked in your porch door. Larry's Lawn Service: Completely Taken Care of While You're at Work. Since your grass is long and you're out of gas for the lawn mower, you read on. "Larry" (no last name) is offering to mow your lawn whenever it needs it and you're too busy. All you have to do is leave a message on his voice mail any weekday morning and leave an envelope containing $15 in cash under your front mat. When you come home from work, the lawn will be immaculate.

Hmm, you think. Fifteen dollars is very reasonable. There's a chance he'd pick up the envelope and abscond, of course, but you'd be just $15 out. Unless... "While You're at Work": Could it be a scheme to find out when you won't be home, and then rob the house?

In a nutshell, that's the kind of dilemma into which you put potential customers and clients who encounter you online. They encounter only the messages you've set out for them, which could be mere words and empty promises. From those bits and bytes, they have precious little evidence to judge, first, are you for real? That is, are you a genuine business person capable of delivering goods or services? Second, will you do what you say without ripping folks off? Your challenge becomes reducing their leap of faith in you from a bound across a chasm to a safe baby step forward.

Are You For Real?

Let's think about what Larry could have done to reassure you that he really had a lawn-mowing business.

1. *Provided a full name.* This should go without saying, but Larry violated this axiom. With his full name, you could have looked him up in the telephone book, learned his street address, and driven by to see whether his was a neatly clipped lot or a weedy yard strewn with rusty mufflers. Listing his address along with his name would have saved you a step and implied he had nothing to hide.

2. *Made himself available by voice.* An answering machine isn't anywhere as reassuring as a person who picks up the telephone or returns your call. Larry has several options for making himself more trustable here: mentioning on his taped message that he'll return calls during his lunch break or in the evening; mentioning hours on his flyer that he's more likely to pick up the phone; or best of all, providing on both his flyer and his answering machine a cell-phone number where he can be reached at any time. A telephone number doesn't help credibility much when it functions as a dead end, but when it's a route to a live voice you can interact with, it's the next best thing to meeting face to face.

3. *Met you in person.* Come to think of it, why couldn't Larry have gone through the neighborhoods on a weekend, rung doorbells, and explained his service face to face? "When we meet someone and shake their hand, look them in the eye and talk to them for a while, we tend to feel a higher level of comfort about doing business with them," says Ivan Misner, author of *The World's Best Known Marketing Secret: Building Your Business with Word of Mouth Marketing.*

4. *Given evidence of stability.* If Larry could draw your attention to a truck with Larry's Lawn Service painted permanently on the side, that would help. During his doorstep visit, it would have loomed behind him. A photo of the truck on the flyer

would imply stability. A slogan like "Serving Huntington Beach Lawn Owners Since 1990" might have helped as well.

5. *Reduced your risk*. Larry could have offered to mow the lawn during the day and come back in the evening to make sure you were satisfied and *then* collected payment. Or, taking a lot more risk onto himself, he could offer monthly billing by mail. If Larry mentioned that he was bonded, you probably wouldn't worry as much about him breaking into your house.

6. *Offered checkable credentials.* Truly suspicious potential customers wouldn't be satisfied with anything less than the names of people they know or know of who can vouch for Larry. Almost as effective would be stating that he belonged to the Better Business Bureau, or that he was a certified lawn technician, second grade, and a member of the National Lawn Care Guild.

I've gone on at length with a hypothetical example because I believe that Larry's case reveals both the challenge of establishing trust in cyberspace and many of the remedies. "We have to work much harder at presenting an image of stability, normality, and integrity than we would if we were, say, an ice cream parlor," says Rob Cosgrove, owner of Precision Data Corporation in Memphis, Tennessee, which markets aggressively its software and business manual for starting a remote computer backup service business (see Figure 15.1). Cosgrove or his staff check their e-mail many times a day and respond immediately with personalized responses, not sheer boilerplate.

"Quick response means an awful lot to people," he says. In addition, Cosgrove offers as much information about himself and his company as possible—"phone numbers, URLs, physical address, e-mail addresses, my life story, the works. I'll even talk with people who call if I'm available. Many people tell me that honesty and availability were a deciding factor in their purchase. Some people say, 'Thanks for being a real person for a change,' which makes me wonder what other companies are doing." Besides responses to his own online ads, Cosgrove receives about five e-mails a day asking if another aggressive marketer, Sheila Danzig, who lists him as a satisfied customer, is "for real."

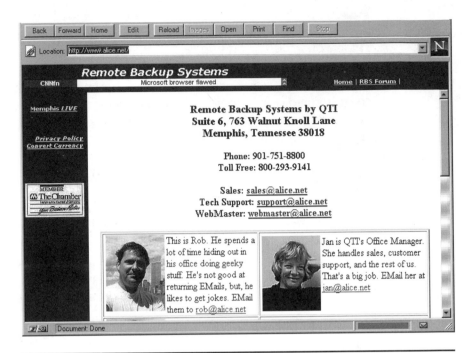

Figure 15.1. Home page for one of Rob Cosgrove's businesses.

Because of its impersonality as a communication vehicle, online advertisers have a hard time engendering trust. World Wide Web sites in particular have less interaction and more "face," says Kansas State University professor of management John Bunch. "Lots of people have created home pages where it's difficult to find out where the business is located and who the principals are. That sets up legal hurdles for cautious customers, since whenever a business relationship falls apart you can't sue unless you know where the other party is located physically." Schmoozers don't face as great a challenge because the more you respond to textual messages as yourself, the more you gather reality as a distinct individual. Since expertise is awfully hard to fake, whenever you exhibit your knowledge, wisdom, and perceptiveness during an exchange of ideas, you also add to your aura of solidity. Whether you're advertising or schmoozing, however, remember that before people send you any money, they must feel confident that you have an established existence apart from cyberspace.

Don't make Larry's mistake. Exhibit as many of these signs of solidity as you can, and you'll be on your way to credibility.

- *Physical address.* To many, a street address feels more reassuring than a post office box.

- *Personal names.* Cybernauts prefer doing business with "Rob Cosgrove of PDC" than with "PDC." Similarly, "Ostrichman" might be a great chat handle, but "Smythe Davies/Ostriches to Go/Houston" works better if you want people to send away for an ostrich-farming manual.

- *Reachability.* Provide as many routes to the real you as you can—phone, fax, e-mail, beeper, and so on. Make sure these routes work as they would with highly capitalized businesses—that your five-year-old daughter isn't the deliverer of your answering machine message and that a fax sent to you in the middle of the night doesn't encounter a sleepy "hello?"

- *Responsiveness.* Reply as quickly as you can to inquiries—within 24 hours whenever possible. Don't slouch around for the FTC-mandated allowance of 30 days before filling mail and telephone orders.

FAST FACTS

Post a Privacy Policy for Greater Trust

A 1997 study by TRUSTe found that any posted privacy policy increases visitors' willingness to share personal information by 50 percent. If the policy states their personal information will not be shared, it doubles or triples visitors' willingness to buy from the site.

In your privacy statement, explain what personal information your site collects and who if anyone you share that data with.

Be honest, since the Federal Trade Commission has begun investigating and penalizing sites that violate their own posted guidelines.

- *Indicators of stability*. Online these include credit card processing capability, recital of your number of years in business, membership in professional and civic organizations, media mentions, willingness to provide a client list or references, and so on. Before the existence of amazon.com, I invited people to check me out in their public library, where at least one of my books was likely to be available.

- *Tangibility*. Offer to send additional information by mail or fax. To the extent that these materials appear to have been prepared with care—professionally printed rather than a copy of a copy of a copy, or verbally and graphically exact rather than slipshod in spelling and design—you reassure prospects that you're not a 12-year-old running a computer prank.

Will You Deliver?

Let's not forget that you could exhibit all the trappings of a thriving business and still be unable or unwilling to fulfill your claims. So besides the evidence that you exist, you must substantiate your competence and reliability. Although this requirement applies to almost every method of marketing, certain online vehicles enable you to satisfy it almost automatically. That is, people learn of your existence in a way that also demonstrates your professionalism. Regular substantive and constructive participation in a forum, mailing list, or newsgroup can prove that you know how to solve problems, that you have a depth of knowledge and experience, and that you have integrity.

Many online communities ruthlessly expose fakers, who offer misinformation, endorse shady business tactics, or lack follow-through. So mere longevity and consistency in an online pond implies you can be counted on. If thoughtful onlookers observe respectful rapport between you and other professionals, they'll conclude you're probably not incompetent or a huckster.

Similarly, informational postings that contain creative ideas or descriptions of previous solutions can show beyond doubt that you're not any old consultant. In effect, such postings get samples of your work onto the computer screens of prospects. Skepticism fades when someone downloads a software patch of yours that works or a dramatic before-and-after editing lesson. A consortium of strategy professors and consultants called Strategyweb makes available at their Web site an old transcript of a client session as a credibility-boosting sample of their mentoring.

Beyond opportunities to show off what you've done, be ready to use the trust-building techniques that always work in traditional marketing: fully attributed testimonials, credentials, client lists, press clips, and, if appropriate, money-back guarantees.

On Virtual Business

Since 1981, when I sold my first freelance article, I've been doing business through the mail and by phone, often never meeting in person someone promising to pay me for performing such-and-such a piece of work. Thus I'm used to the idea of making long-distance deals, sealed by signatures exchanged by mail or by fax. But I know from talking about this at how-to-get-published seminars that the suggestion of doing business without face-to-face contact strikes many people as a baffling surprise. A consultant who gets high fees from Fortune 100 corporations didn't believe me when I said I'd interviewed consultants and lawyers who had found work online. Successful virtual business builds upon both sides' comfort with technology and the intensity of their electronic contacts.

Debbie Dewey, a special projects manager and private investigator in Fairport, New York, who had been online for about nine years, told me she had an excellent business relationship with someone in Switzerland with whom she'd done nothing other than exchange e-mail. "I would go into a joint venture with this person, although we've never even spoken on the phone," she said. "I go with my gut instinct, and because of my investigative experience, I'm good at seeing through people." Similarly, in 1995 Pat Pisarski, whose company ExpresSearch, Inc. set up bulletin board systems for other businesses, did almost all of her work long-distance. She said then, "We've never encountered a prospect who expressed concern about not having met us in person. This is the wave of the future."

There appears to be a natural progression from electronic communication to telephone or fax and then to in-person meetings, but in some business realms the prehiring sniffing out does not need to reach the third or even the second stage, while in some other business arenas it does. Years before eBay made online auctions commonplace, Bob Schmidt, a freelance copywriter in Orlando, Florida, bought and sold limited-edition ceramic figurines through "collectibles" bulletin boards. "You describe what you have and either post a price or hold an auction, asking people to submit bids," he explained. When the deal concluded, the buyer would send a cashier's check through the mail that might be as large as $1,000.

"Most buyers don't even get on the phone," Schmidt noted. "They have a precedent of answering classified ads. Once about twenty people were taken in by a guy who collected their money and never delivered the goods, but generally, people online are trustworthy." On the other hand, Stefan Kolle, an Amsterdam-based finance consultant for the entertainment industry, points out that while he has lined up sources of financing for feature film projects online, the finalization has to occur face to face. "No investor will give money to someone he hasn't met," he says.

FAST FACTS

Four Ways to Obtain Testimonials

1. Pay attention to your e-mail. If you have decent online offerings, sooner or later you'll receive unsolicited praise. Simply ask the person sending the praise if you can use his or her comments publicly.

2. Survey your clients or customers, and ask permission to use the positive remarks as blurbs.

3. Pay attention to thanks during phone calls with clients or customers. If you hear praise, ask your caller to repeat what he or she said, write it down, and use it after asking permission.

4. Call repeat buyers and ask them what they like about doing business with you. Again, obtain permission to use what they tell you.

Cost of credibility-boosting testimonials: $0.

16

International Considerations

Around the time I first went online, a friend approached me with a proposition: He wanted to help businesses get publicity on the Internet, and he needed a guinea pig. Was I game? Of course. Our experiment would involve announcing the availability of a free sample issue of a creativity newsletter I was then publishing. A librarian working for him drew up a list of about 20 mailing lists and newsgroups that seemed appropriate, and we crafted a note that he would post with his Internet I.D.: "Would this be the right place to mention a new newsletter called The Creative Glow: How to Be More Original, Inspired & Productive in Your Work? You can get a free sample issue by e-mailing your address to Marcia Yudkin at...."

E-mail responses began showing up the very day of his posting—from the United States, Canada, South Africa, Taiwan, Hong Kong, New Zealand.... I gritted my teeth. At around $1.40 each for postage rather than $.29, the foreign requests held the potential of being budget-breakers. Very dumb of me, I thought, not to realize that free exposure on the Internet meant costlier marketing than the print media coverage I was used to getting in the States.

If your business has been confined within your national borders, you probably won't instinctively foresee the adjustments in strategy, approach, and arrangements that are necessary in dealing with customers globally. With the greater use of the Web, we rarely have to mail any sort of samples or brochures internationally. Nevertheless, careful planning is still necessary whenever you put out the word electronically. So many people are linked up with each other that if you put out something valuable, you can't expect your news or your offer to stay confined within your locality or your country. Don't skip this chapter! Keep reading, first for the hard-and-fast challenges you need to think about, then for the more subtle ones.

Open Up to the World

In some cases doing business across national borders isn't much more complicated than dealing with someone far away within your own country. Business plan writer Marcia Layton picked up a client in Saudi Arabia online and says there weren't any problems in the relationship. "We worked with a contract, with one third of the fee due at the beginning, and he paid in U.S. dollars from a U.S. bank. Faxes were more expensive, but e-mail kept the cost down. And conversing by e-mail was easier than it might have been by phone, since on the computer there wasn't any accent."

In an international medium, you don't want to alienate or exclude clients solely because of geography. If you put up signs that amount to "No foreigners," you could come across as an ill-mannered hick. But you want to be careful because problems with international communication and payment can rear their blazing heads. By learning about pitfalls others have fallen into, you can avoid putting up unnecessary barriers while appropriately protecting yourself. Here's a checklist to get you started.

- *Have you enabled distant prospects to get in touch with you?* In the last two decades, most Americans have gotten into the habit of always including their telephone area code in business communications, but as Oakland, California, translator Ines Swaney discovered during a European trip, other blunders are possible. "I was particularly proud of my fax number because I'd discovered that the numbers spelled a certain word, so that's how I listed it on my business card: Fax ###-cutewrd—### being the area code and the other seven characters being the word I had discovered. The whole thing fell apart when I handed my card to someone in Hungary who I hoped to do business with in the future. I had assumed that our equivalency between numbers and letters on the telephone keys was universal—and it's not."

For Europeans and Asians, you must not only avoid things like "508-CALL-N-US," but 800 numbers without a regular area-code number too, because 800 numbers generally don't work overseas. So that folks can figure out when to call your office, it's helpful too to always include your geographical location along with a telephone number. Within the United States, people can look up your area code to learn your time zone, but overseas that may be cumbersome.

- *Have you adapted your product and your Web ordering procedures to foreign needs?* Tim Bourne, president of Structured Information Analysis Methods Limited in Hemel Hempstead, England, complains that American software manufacturers often neglect to make their parameters customizable for international paper sizes, telephone number formats, postal codes, and date formats (e.g., 31.3.99 instead of 3/31/99). "Products that include spelling checkers without a choice of dictionary are worse than useless here," Bourne adds, "and often you don't find out such things until after you buy."

Likewise, New Zealander Simon Young hit a dead end when he tried to order what was billed as a free copy of a book but couldn't input his address. "I filled out the fields okay until I got to 'state'. I looked for the 'none' option. Not there. I scanned the page again to see if this offer was only for U.S. subscribers. Nope, didn't say that anywhere. So I tried to leave the field blank. Error. Drat. Well, I guessed the closest U.S. state to New Zealand is Hawaii, so I tried that." Of course Young never received the book. Make sure you enable buyers or registrants to have a four-digit postal code rather than a five-digit zip code—or no postal code at all. The same goes for states and provinces, which some countries, such as Denmark, do not have.

- *Have you investigated and posted appropriate foreign shipping charges?* Tim Bourne cites a magazine subscription offered at $20 in the United States and $80 in Europe, which seems to be way out of line with additional mailing costs. Don't just pluck a foreign shipping charge out of your uninformed head. It's pretty simple, once you think of it, to call United Parcel Service, DHL (a big international air freight company), or the post office to find out how much a parcel of a certain size and weight would cost to send to a sample destination overseas. Shipping across an ocean may not cost as much as you would guess. I was surprised to learn that mailing two of my books "airmail printed matter" to a purchaser in Germany cost less than $6.00.

- *Have you described acceptable payment methods?* For products, the easiest way to pay across borders is via credit card, which eliminates worries on both ends about currency exchange. "The transaction is charged in the currency of the supplier,"

FAST FACTS

Make Your Site Internationally Friendly

- After your address, list your country instead of presuming everyone knows it.

- During registration or ordering procedures, provide enough options and space for people with extra-long foreign addresses that don't follow your standard pattern.

- Use more generic labels like "Zip/postal code" and "State/province."

- If you normally use toll-free numbers, provide regular phone and fax numbers too.

- Include the country code before your telephone number (for the U.S., that's "+1").

- Indicate which currency prices are stated in.

- Describe shipping options and prices for overseas buyers.

- Where appropriate, state measurements in both metric and English systems.

says Bourne, "and the customer is billed in his own currency. The currency conversion occurs at close to the current commercial rate—in my experience it's a better rate than changing money at a bank. I have credit card customers in Australia, New Zealand, the United States, Canada, Japan, Saudi Arabia, and most countries in Europe."

If you can't accept credit cards, or you want to put out the welcome mat for foreigners who might not have Visa or MasterCard, you must be very clear and specific about payment methods. Before setting a policy, you might be wise to speak with your bank about its fees for options like checks in foreign currencies from foreign banks, in your own currency but drawn on a foreign bank, and in your own currency drawn on a foreign branch of a bank based in your country.

Bob Schenot, who self-published *The Shareware Book*, thought this through thoroughly before releasing the electronic text of his book on how to market software through the try-before-you-buy method in 1992. Knowing that the electronic text would find its way to many obscure locales, the New Hampshirite quoted prices for the book in French francs, Canadian dollars, English pounds, German marks, and Japanese yen as well as American dollars. "My terms are cash or international postal money orders in those currencies but *not* checks. One third of international orders arrive in cash," he says, "so round numbers make things easier." Although Schenot's foreign prices used 1992 exchange rates, his profit margin was high enough to cushion any disadvantageous effect. "I am glad I never quoted a price in pesos, though," he adds.

- *Have you made your online notes, brochure, catalog, and sales letters understandable to people whose grasp of your language may be shaky?* In particular, watch out for:

  - Obscure slang ("scam artists")

  - Jargon too recent to be in foreign dictionaries ("outsourcing")

  - Nonuniversal measurements (inches, without centimeter equivalent)

- – Noninternational acronyms (I.R.S.; V.A.T.)

- – Convoluted syntax (sentences only a lawyer would understand)

- – Relative terms ("domestic" and "foreign," e.g., would be understood differently in every country)

- – National terms ("the Dow Jones average" rather than "stock exchange index")

- – Large numbers in words (in Britain, a billion is a million million, while in the United States it's a thousand million)

- – Humor (rarely travels well)

In most cases, when you make your materials understandable internationally, you improve their readability for natives of your own country too.

According to Irene Agnew, president of Agnew Tech-II, a translation company in Westlake Village, California, companies based in the English-speaking world should give serious thought to making their materials available in other languages. "Consider what it would do for your outreach to post a one-page profile of your company in, say, five languages—Spanish, French, German, Chinese, and Japanese," suggests Agnew. (See Figure 16.1.) "Companies are missing opportunities by not providing information in target languages. If you're going to export at all, you'll go further against the competition by doing that. Microsoft, for example, was the first to translate its software for Europe, and it has the bulk of the market there."

Suzan Nolan, president of Paris-based BlueSky International Marketing (see Figure 16.2), argues that retooling a Web site for patrons in other countries should go beyond translation. She cites a Swedish company called Boxman, which became Europe's top online CD merchant by mounting sites in eight countries and languages—the United Kingdom, France, Germany, Holland, Norway, Finland, Denmark, and, of course,

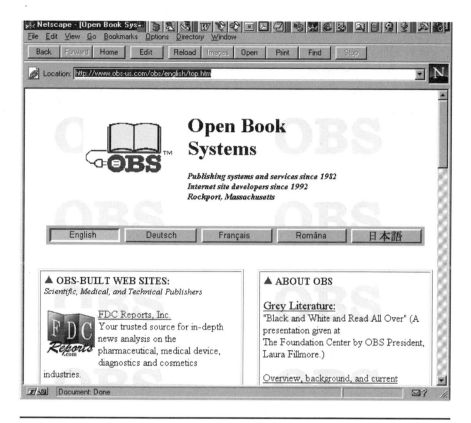

Figure 16.1. Open Book Systems offers content in five languages.

Sweden. "What's impressive about Boxman," she says, "is not only that they managed to translate their site eight times, but they also localize the content and products—their Top Ten hits in France are not the same Top Ten for Germany nor Spain." While you may not be able to afford such localization on $500/ year, it's something to consider as your online operation grows.

- *Have you made sure you're permitted to do business with customers abroad?* The United States Government classifies software that produces so-called "strong encryption"—encoding so secure that even supercomputers can't crack it—as munitions and prohibits its export. The U.S. Customs Service began a campaign of harassment when it learned that Phil Zimmerman

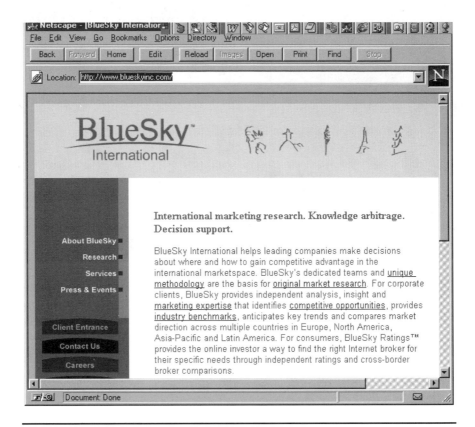

Figure 16.2. BlueSky International consults on international marketing.

had posted his PGP, or Pretty Good Privacy, encryption program on the Internet, where it could be downloaded and, in effect, electronically exported.

Similarly, in 1995 computer consultant Charlie Gallie told me that he was working on bringing the Democratic Party online but facing the problem that federal law prohibits collecting money from foreign nationals. "How are we supposed to prevent this? We're waiting for a ruling from the Federal Elections Commission on applying laws and FEC regulations to this new medium. The problem doesn't occur only on the Internet, but we don't send mail solicitations outside of the country, and borders don't exist on the World Wide Web."

FAST FACTS

What about Computerized Translation?

A free online utility at *http://www.babelfish.altavista.com* will translate your copy into French, German, Spanish, Italian, or Portuguese. Cost: $0.

In this case, however, the value is $0. Don't do this! Ralph Wilson, creator of Wilson Web, used Babelfish to translate part of his site, then asked Europeans' opinions of the results. Native speakers of French, German, Spanish, Italian, and Portuguese all agreed that the translations made little sense.

More recently, the exact opposite dilemma presented headaches for Rob Emerick, director of marketing for iWorldLottery.com, an online lottery that cannot sell to residents of the United States, Canada, or Sweden, among other countries. "Online gaming halls will become a commodity of the Internet once we figure out how to be certain who lives where," he says.

Be Sensitive and Flexible

For those who provide business services, it's probably even more important than for those selling products to keep your radar tuned for intercultural static that may impede your attempt to build a relationship with someone you've encountered online. Don't assume that the buildup to a deal with someone from another culture will look or feel the same as with someone from the same background as you. Alan Weiss, president of the Summit Consulting Group in East Greenwich, Rhode Island, and a consultant for numerous multinational companies, says that the decision-making process differs in different parts of the world. "Americans prefer to make relatively quick decisions, and except for the Germans, Swiss, and Dutch, most other cultures have a much slower process," Weiss says. "You have to be patient and understand that even if the other party isn't ready to act immediately, that doesn't mean they're not interested."

You may also have to adjust your style of communication, Weiss says. "Americans are likely to put a subject on the table and say, look, this is a difficulty, we need to discuss it. That could be suicide with other cultures. For example, in Latin America, people can say 'yes, yes, yes' to you forever and not mean it for one minute. It's not that they're dishonest, it's that culturally they don't confront issues that directly. So I would think that online, you need to be very circumspect in how you present things. Instead of asking, 'Do you like this or not?' it might be better to ask, 'What questions do you have about what I've just told you?'"

Several people, both British and German, told me that Europeans are in awe of American marketing savvy, but this has several consequences that may not be obvious. A straightforward chase after business may make some otherwise promising prospects from other countries skitter for cover. Stephan Uhrenbacher, a marketing strategist in Hamburg, Germany, put it this way: "Although I have quite a lot of experience with American marketing, I am still often amazed by the kind of hype that is created by some people online. We here in Europe very often prefer a more low-key approach to new contacts, even when selling our products. On the other hand, sometimes I have found that even when I was seriously interested in an offer, my relatively low-key reaction ('please send more information') led my partners abroad to believe that after all we were not too convinced of their product."

Similarly, although Peter Wherritt, a technology consultant based near Oxford, England, was wary of overgeneralizing, he said, "In the United Kingdom there is not usually the open sharing of personal and company objectives as seems to happen in the United States, and many American methodologies seem a bit too 'pushy' or even 'embarrassing' for the typical Englishman. I must stress it's only an initial reaction because people are good at accommodating that kind of thing when meeting face to face."

According to Wherritt, these cultural differences very much complicate international e-mail business communication. "E-mail makes it difficult to accommodate these differences. Because e-mail can be so impersonal, the individuals never get a chance to become comfortable with each other. People in the United Kingdom often need to get to know you, your values, how you work, and only then will they start thinking about how you may be able to help them. When you add the cultural differences to the impersonal aspects of e-mail, it gets quite interesting. On the other hand, I have noticed a tendency for U.K. correspondents to open up more via e-mail, so that possibly it gives them a means of 'escaping' from their more restrained normal environment and explore opportunities that they wouldn't otherwise seek out."

Another area of potential international friction in business relationships concerns the attitude toward rules, agreements and contracts. From what I can observe, the United States may be the most legalistic country in the world. "Americans love rules and are very rigid about them," says Edna Aphek, a professor of educational psychology in Jerusalem, Israel. Englishman Tim Bourne agrees: "The legal side of running a business seems to be very important to Americans, but is largely nonexistent in Europe—I've never consulted a lawyer in ten years of running my business. I have an agent in Germany who sells my products there. The deal is good for both of us, so we both want it to succeed. What good could a lawyer do?" Someone who routinely asks all his or her business contacts to sign a formal agreement needs to know that in many other countries, doing so may not carry the same meaning or effect.

I've only scratched the surface with respect to cross-cultural difficulties that might crop up in your international dealings, which are probably as various as the countless combinations of backgrounds of parties engaged in global business. Some general guidelines worth keeping in mind include:

- Remember that your assumptions about how to carry on business might be considered bizarre, obnoxious, or even unethical in another part of the world.

- Whenever possible, seek out information about the culture of the other countries from which your clients and customers hail.

- Avoid remarks that cast you as the superior or as the party who has to educate the other side. Humility works better. Hoo Shao Pin, cofounder of Asia Online, an online service business in Singapore, told me that he was getting e-mails from Americans telling him that his Internet name, Online Coolie, was derogatory. "But I was raised in the vicinity of Singapore River, where coolies would load and unload sacks of goods on and off the bumboats. When I got to know some of the coolies personally, they seemed like friendly folks to me and although they had a hard life, seemed contented with it. Since then, I have always associated the word 'coolie' with the positive meaning of hard work and earning an honest living. Hence I called myself Online Coolie, first to signify my late nights building the server, and secondly because it contains 'cool' if you read it. People need to recognize the cultural diversity on the Net and realize that I am free to call myself whatever name means something to me."

- Actively display your awareness of the international environment. According to Jay Linden, an Internet presence provider in Toronto, Ontario, non-Americans almost always name their country in their Internet signature, while Americans rarely do. "Also, no Canadian, Latin American, European, Asian, or Australian would dream of describing part of his country's political process without also naming the country and explaining anything which might be vague to 'foreigners'. Yet Americans on the Net are constantly talking about First Amendment issues and other facts of American life whose effects on the rest of the Net community will be indirect at most." Pause before pressing the Send button to think about how your message will come across in the wider world community.

- Let your foreign business prospects know you are open to learning what you can do to make them more comfortable doing business with you. As you build up mutual trust, this kind of feedback becomes more likely. You might learn not to send faxes or expect an e-mail reply on a certain day of the week— or that a phrase you considered innocuous has a salacious connotation somewhere else.

Most of all, don't let the possibility of knots keep you from tossing out international ropes. I'm happy to follow the advice of Meinrad Mueller, owner of an innovative recycling business in Munich-Grafath, Germany, who urged me, "Encourage your readers to take advantage of the new highway tools to reach out to the entire world!"

17

E-mail Etiquette

Normally I'm a pleasant person, but I've been known to scold telemarketers who interrupt my work with awkward pitches I've heard before. When I can figure out who's selling my name and address, I may call to get myself taken off the lists. I even gave the county sheriff a talking-to when he showed up at my door for the third time trying to serve a summons on a previous occupant. Obviously I don't appreciate intrusions—and I'm not alone. Mass unsolicited e-mail is particularly intrusive. Michael Strangelove, author of *How To Advertise on the Internet*, calls it "...bad PR. Stealing both time and money from the recipient, it is in direct violation of the most emotionally charged community norm in cyberspace—do not put unwanted information in my mailbox." Strangelove also notes that people regularly lose their Internet and online service accounts for disregarding this norm. In the last few years, some jurisdictions have even made it illegal.

Nevertheless, certain kinds of e-mail to people who are not expecting to hear from you are hardly intrusive or risky at all. In all of your e-mail communications, follow some simple rules that keep your exchanges polite and productive.

You Were Asking About...

Mike Bayer, head sysop of CompuServe's PR and Marketing forum, explains the well-mannered method of snagging clients online with the example of a coffee dealer who serviced professional offices and showed up in the forum asking about a mass mailing he was working on. "About five or six of us asked questions and offered advice. Some-one suggested that he hire someone to write the piece, and he shot back, 'Do you know someone?' I sent him an e-mail saying that I could help and then sent my electronic brochure when he asked for it. A day later I sent him another message, and three days after that he called me. He said I'd been one of five or six who had contacted him, and he picked me because I'd done a lot of work with his target audience—doctors and attorneys." Note that Bayer didn't send his complete canned information until the prospect asked for it, a policy Bayer follows "because I don't like it when people promote them-selves aggressively to me."

Bayer's procedure is practically guaranteed to keep you in the good graces of its recipient because (1) the offer of help is brief, infor-mal, and related to a need the prospect publicly expressed, and (2) after offering help, it puts the prospect in the driver's seat. The farther you stray from those two guidelines, the greater your risk of annoying a prospect and inviting complaints that, if repeated, could lead to losing your online access. This effect occurs not because of arbitrary rules but because of the way communications come across in cyberspace.

Someone who asks for help or information does not experience a courteous offer of paid help as intrusive. This holds as true for e-mail as it does in the antipromotional atmosphere of an Internet newsgroup, about which Bryan Pfaffenberger told me, "If I had a company and saw someone ask if anyone knew where to get a certain kind of prod-uct, no one would get upset if I posted a response about my product and said where you could find free files about it. Ninety-nine percent of participants would see that as a positive contribution to the dis-cussion, not an ad."

When in doubt, compare appropriate behavior at a social gather-ing. If someone at a dinner party said, "By the way, everyone, I'm looking for a portrait photographer. Can anyone recommend some-one?" would you whip out your briefcase right then and there for a show-and-tell of every item in your portfolio? You'd do far better to pass your business card quietly to that person and say, "Give me a call and I'll be glad to show you my portfolio." In e-mail as well, avoid overwhelming the person. I once publicly asked for some information in a forum and found an enormous file in my e-mail the next day from a consultant with qualification after qualification, credential after credential, testimonial after testimonial. What irritated me in this case was the amount of information, not the consultant getting in touch with me per se. Had the very same file arrived at a later stage of my decision-making process, I might have welcomed it and read it carefully, but too much too soon gave me the impression that this fellow was self-centered and overbearing.

Now rewind to the person mentioning at the dinner party that she's looking for a photographer. Would you take that as a cue to stand up and perform a loud television-type commercial message to her? I hope not! It's just as bad to send a "Three for the price of one! Special offer expires December 31st!" ad to someone's mailbox when they have indicated a need. Your offer of help needs to be low-key, conversational, and person to person, not worded like an ad or a promotion. Frederic Wilf, an intellectual property and business law attorney in Media, Pennsylvania, mutes the promotional aspect of an e-mail response by providing an answer to the seeker's question—or as much of an answer as he reasonably can. "Since I am a lawyer and am asked legal questions, I can't provide detailed legal advice without first getting all the information (and without first getting a retainer to cover my services). However, I can respond to a request for legal information by providing general background information and pointing the person to resources for more information. This way, the person who asked the question has received helpful information and knows that I am available to provide legal services. Enough of these contacts do mature into paying clients to make the process worthwhile for me."

Some of the people I interviewed who get business by approaching potential clients through e-mail do not wait until a person explicitly asks, "Does anyone know a...?" Instead, they humbly and politely introduce themselves and state how they might be of help with respect to something that person was discussing in public. Computer consultant Gary Ellenbogen, for instance, relies on his intuition to tell him when someone wrestling with a technical problem in a forum might be open to hiring him. "When it's clear that someone is looking for something that they're not getting and that I could help with, I might pop them a note. Usually I get a reply saying, 'You couldn't have done this at a better time. I'm so grateful'." Numerous unsolicited offers of this sort go unanswered, but Ellenbogen has never received a complaint.

Naturally you don't have to wait until someone expresses a need to get in touch electronically. You can get the ball rolling with friendly, to-the-point correspondence. If the person you're e-mailing won't recognize your name, make sure both the subject line and your opening sentence or two will capture the interest of your reader without coming across as a mass mailing or as a blatant sales message.

E-mail Etiquette

While we're discussing e-mail communication, let's review some do's and don'ts that apply to any electronic business messages you may send. If you're instinctively considerate on paper, on the telephone, and in person, most of these guidelines will appear obvious, since they have to do with respect for those you communicate with. Don't worry, however, if some take you by surprise. Mannerliness can always improve when you put your mind to it.

* *Do use your name in all correspondence.* If your e-mail address does not indicate your name, write your name before you sign off so that your recipient has a human being to reply to, rather than a mask, a pen name, a disguise, a nickname, or just a company identity. I've seen couples sharing

FAST FACTS

Free Directory Assistance Online

Instead of spending up to $1.00 each time to find a phone number far away from you, consult these sites first. They're not quite as up-to-date as the telephone company's directory assistance, but they're free.

* *http://www.people.yahoo.com*
* *http://www.switchboard.com*

e-mail by having both names on the account, or by one spouse signing her name on e-mails although the other spouse's name heads it. In a business context, both forms of sharing feel disconcerting and confusing to respondents. Because of my widely dispersed FAQ files, I get a lot of questions from beginning writers, some of which arrive unsigned and with no real name in the header. That feels rude to me, but it became downright scary when the e-mail address was something like *terrorist5401@hotmail.com*. He really expected me to reply to that?!

- *Don't pester people.* Sending e-mail seems so easy that some people overdo it, says Susan RoAne, author of *The Secrets of Savvy Networking*. "If you call someone who's not your friend every three days, that's encumbering, and the same goes for e-mail. Use some decorum; honor people's time. Don't use the technology to excess just because it doesn't take any brains to press 'Reply'."

- *Do, when continuing a correspondence, repeat the context.* For someone who gets a lot of e-mail, it's aggravating to receive an e-mail like this: "Yes, go ahead with idea number two." Which idea was number two? This kind of reply necessitates either another exchange or a search back through past messages to find the earlier message. Learn how to cut and paste in your e-mail program so that you can quote the most important part of the previous message within your reply. Or restate the context concisely in your own words: "Yes, go ahead with idea number two, the one having to do with national radio ads."

- *Don't burden business colleagues with your taste in jokes, political causes, chain letters, or computer-danger alerts.* Too many people receive something they enjoy reading and send it on to everyone in their address book without stopping to consider what a waste of time it may be for people who rely on e-mail to keep their business up and running. Moreover, all too often the petitions or warnings are outdated or inaccurate. Chain letters that invite people to send money to the first person on the list are as illegal on the Internet, by the way, as when they travel through the mail.

FAST FACTS

How to "Copy In" When Replying

If your e-mail software doesn't do this automatically, use the following generally accepted technique to indicate quoted material.

Original message:

> Are you going to the BOHSUZI conference this year? Are you bringing Ned?

How to quote it in your reply:

> Kathy, I'm not sure what you meant here.
>
> >>Are you going to the BOHSUZI conference this year?
> >>Are you bringing Ned?
>
> What's BOHSUZI? And which Ned did you mean?

Or like this:

> Kathy, I'm not sure what you meant here.
>
> >>Are you going to the BOHSUZI conference this year? Are you bringing Ned?<<
>
> What's BOHSUZI? And which Ned did you mean?

- *Do use an informative and inviting subject line.* Suppose you're e-mailing a business owner you read about in the newspaper with an idea for joining forces. "Hello" is too vague; "YOU CAN MAKE $60,000 NEXT MONTH" sounds overhyped and impersonal, like a mass solicitation; "Ingrid, maybe we can collaborate" strikes an appropriately personal tone and would be more likely to be read by the recipient.

- *Don't be devious.* A bestselling novelist told me that someone had tracked him down through an e-mail account held by his wife. "This person had quizzed anyone and everyone, randomly firing off inquiries until she found my wife. I don't recommend this tactic. It felt like an invasion. And with that kind of sneaky stuff at work, it doesn't give me a good impression of someone who would do that."

- *Do cushion canned messages.* Instead of sending an impersonal informational file to someone who wants to know more about what you do, either add a customized introduction or send a personal "here's what's coming" message first. "I usually either send a canned message enclosed in my reply or I say that the following e-mail contains information about my firm or about a particular topic," says attorney Frederic Wilf. "The recipient knows that the information is canned but the accompanying personalized message takes the edge off."

- *Don't overburden your recipient.* "I call to get permission before I send a ten-page fax," says Susan RoAne. "You should do the same with e-mail." Anything longer than 20,000 bytes (seven or eight single-spaced pages) may clog up someone's e-mail gateway, according to Michael Strangelove. E-mail that goes on and on is tiring to read on the computer screen and taxing on the attention span.

- *Do write in a businesslike way.* Use complete sentences, look back over your spelling, capitalize in the standard way, make sure you've explained yourself clearly, and don't use profanity or slang.

- *Don't send attached files without prior agreement.* Many people don't have the faintest idea what to do with a nontext file—a program, program-specific file, or specially compressed file—that turns up in their e-mail. Even if they know how to unpack and read it, that's a lot of trouble to expect someone to go to, particularly for something like your resumé rather than the software patch that's going to allow them to meet a pressing deadline, and that they've requested. If they don't know you, they could fear that a malicious virus lurks in your attachment. It's better not to provoke suspicions.

- *Do use discretion with multiple addressees.* Someone who doesn't reveal his or her e-mail address to every Dick, Jane, and Sally may get incensed to see you listing it visibly when you send one message to many recipients at once. It's also annoying to have to page down through a long list of addresses to get to the real message. (See Figure 17.1.) Most e-mail systems have separate procedures for "carbon copies," where the list of recipients appears along with the message and "blind carbon copies," where the list is nowhere to be seen. Bother to send the "blind" kind of message to a list, especially where those on the list really deserve to remain anonymous to each other.

- *Don't discuss confidential, raunchy, or illegal matters by e-mail.* It takes only a slip of the finger for your e-mail buddy to broadcast your confidential message to everyone in his or her electronic address book. Did you know that if you are using an employer's computers or network to communicate, download, or store files, that employer can legally snoop on you and dismiss you upon finding something unpalatable? Discretion should rule in e-mail as in cellular phone conversations. Someone may be listening in!

Figure 17.1. When you use "cc" instead of "bcc," e-mail looks cluttered.

18

Handling Hotheads

As for your snotty little remarks—I'm not as petty, small, and vindictive as you. You're a vicious and pathetic person who twists the words of others for their own small ego. And, I'll tell you this, your attitudes, your snide posts, your egregious smugness and superciliousness disgust me.

Name Withheld

Well, I'll tell you this: It's no fun finding words like these on one's computer screen first thing in the morning. I hope it never happens to you, because getting "flamed," as abusive computer messaging is known, can be a scorching experience. I had not received such a burst of venom since I was 14 years old. It wreaked no lasting damage, but it helped me appreciate how important it is to be prepared for a phenomenon that can go far beyond ritual blade-to-blade combat with verbal swords. Certain factors in the process of communicating via computers seem to prod some people into emotional overtilt. Since engaging in flaming, even its tamer forms, can broil your business image, I'll explain why flaming occurs, how to handle flare-ups directed at you, and how to disengage yourself from provocations so that you don't ignite or fuel a searing exchange of insults.

Hotheadness in Cyberspace

In its mildest form, flaming involves an exchange of emotional remarks in stronger language than most of us normally use in everyday life. Yishai Almog, an Israeli-American psychologist and management consultant, points to four reasons flaming easily gets going online. First, because there's no nonverbal context for someone's words, it's easy for the recipient to misunderstand a message and read into it a very different meaning than what was intended. "In face-to-face communication, when someone says 'Thanks a lot' you know from their tone inflection or facial expression whether that means 'I really appreciated that' or 'I hate your guts'. Online, you lose those multiple levels of communication."

Second, emotions may get too intense for ordinary civil exchanges of words. As Almog puts it, "People communicate online in ways that are very intimate with respect to content, or very charged, so that the level of content is high and a lot gets across substantively, but the channel of communication is too narrow to contain and convey all of what they're feeling." So arguments quickly escalate. When I asked sysops what were the perennial flame topics in their forums, I got answers like these: for a desktop publishing forum, the "Macintosh versus IBM" debate and whether or not one should ever work on speculation; for a PR forum, the ethics of doing public relations for a tobacco company such as Philip Morris. These are issues where logical methods of persuasion rarely change anyone's mind, so frustrations run high.

Third, says Yishai Almog, the asynchronous or time-delayed nature of message boards allows misunderstandings to set in without correction. "You don't have an immediate chance to check out what the other person meant the way you do on the telephone or in person, where you can ask, 'Wait a minute, are you saying...?' and the person can respond, 'No, no, no! That's not what I meant'. If somebody sends you something that rubs you the wrong way, whatever starts getting stirred in you stays there. That built-in communication break can cause trouble, especially on a bulletin board, where one person responds to what they thought someone else meant, and then a whole series of people piggyback on that. Before you know it you have a free-for-all, with people interpreting an interpretation of an interpretation."

And fourth, says Almog, the online world lacks clear expectations, limits, and sanctions against extreme behavior. "The medium encourages people to act out their psychological agendas in ways that are ordinarily curbed by social norms. On the Internet, there's no framework to contain the behavior, so that things can escalate freely. Other than the desirability of open and free expression, there is no agreed-upon set of norms."

Barb Tomlin, formerly a Board Leader on Prodigy and now president of Westward Connections in Albuquerque, New Mexico (see Figure 18.1), also suggests that many of the more offensive messages that get sent through cyberspace aren't really meant as communication. "We all have thoughts going around in our head that we wouldn't normally put on paper. But on the computer, it's like you're talking to yourself. Something in the little fuzzy ions around the characters releases thoughts that are actually self-talk." Almog calls it "dump-

Figure 18.1. Westward Connections Web site.

ing"—an attempt to vent and have an emotional impact. What I compare it with is those times when you are in a bad mood, someone cuts you off in traffic, and you let loose a stream of belligerent slurs about his or her driving (and perhaps parentage). Such venting may look and sound like communication, but it serves a very different purpose.

On the Internet, flaming can also serve as a means of vigilantism. Since no one owns or officially governs the network, morally self-righteous folks sometimes take on a policing role and use whatever weapons they have available. These include threats, complaints to the offender's service provider, "mail bombs"—the sending of dictionary-sized files repeatedly to an e-mail address—and invective that would send chills down the spine of a serial killer. The frontispiece of Michael Strangelove's book, *How to Advertise on the Internet*, features messages from three such characters promising to retaliate if they receive any unsolicited e-mail advertisements. "I'll mount a personal campaign to flood the mailbox of the person who sent it," one wrote. Retaliatory sabotage really can wreak havoc on your online marketing plans. Some well-known personages who have rubbed people the wrong way have become the victims of skilled imposters putting up odious messages under their name. An organization called the Mail Abuse Prevention System, or MAPS, maintains a "Realtime Blackhole List" of spam-friendly domains that numerous Internet service providers use to filter e-mail (see Figure 18.2). If you've landed on the MAPS list, people who get their e-mail through ISPs that use the MAPS service will not be able to receive e-mail from you—even if they've requested it or paid for you to contact them. Other blacklisters post personal names, phone and fax numbers, e-mail and postal addresses, and other details about spammers so that those outraged by the violators can take action.

Among the younger set, flaming appears to have developed into a competitive sport. Several Internet newsgroups, such as alt.flame, provide a playing field for top-notch word sluggers to enjoy bashing matches for fun. But when a grown adult with professional standing wallops you with industrial-strength vilification, as happened to me and to *The New Yorker* writer John Seabrook from a technology columnist for a major newspaper, something besides adolescent horseplay may be going on. "Unfortunately, not everyone who is chronologically an adult is also psychologically mature," says Yishai Almog. "A certain percentage of the population may appear to be adults but really are not. For example, an individual with a reputation to maintain who would

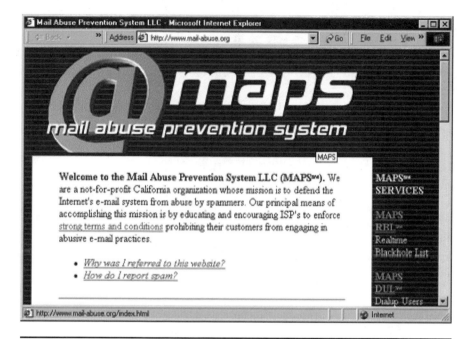

Figure 18.2. The Mail Abuse Prevention System runs the Realtime Blackhole List, something you definitely do not want to be on.

send that kind of extreme message clearly has difficulty containing his emotions. As we know from phenomena like driveby shootings, some people out there are volcanoes waiting to erupt."

What To Do When It Happens to You

It's hard not to get shocked and troubled when vicious language meant for you shows up on your computer screen. Early in 1994 Seabrook, who had profiled Microsoft chairman Bill Gates for *The New Yorker*, received an e-mail flame much too obscene for me to comfortably quote in this book. "The flame seemed to put a chill in the center of my chest which I could feel spreading slowly outward," he later wrote. "My shoulders began to shake. I got up and walked quickly to the soda machines for no good reason, then hurried back to my desk."

Not only were the words still on the screen, Seabrook couldn't wipe the nasty message out of his brain. He spent most of that day composing equally vile replies that he held back from transmitting and instead sent a subdued attempt at polite irony. In return came another fierce insult.

"When you happen to trigger the minefield, the last thing you should do is take it personally," advises Almog. "It's pointless to respond." Janet Attard, who administers numerous forums, agrees. "The smartest—and the hardest—thing to do is simply to ignore a provocation," she says. "When someone attacks you, your natural impulse is to defend yourself. But the more you say, the longer the episode goes on, and flaming back will make you look unprofessional. On a bulletin board, often other users will come along and defend you, and if they don't, just one or two messages will get quickly forgotten. But if you respond in kind, it turns into something like rubbernecking on the highway—everyone comes along to see who's going to say what next to whom."

Angela Gunn, editor of *Web Week*, remembers one particularly regrettable instance in which she jumped impetuously onto the field of combat with both dukes up. "In the Comics forum on CompuServe, someone said something about copyright that I replied to with a thoughtful post detailing both sides of the issue. Thinking that everyone knew who I was, which was stupid, I signed it, 'A.G., former 'zine publisher'. He came back on and started ranting at me as if I was some 17-year-old, and I wrote, 'Look, Buckwheat'—that's New York City slang, I hear it a lot—'you want a standdown? Here's my resume'. Then he really let loose. 'How dare you, you racist bitch...'. He forgot that I couldn't see him on my monitor. How was I supposed to know he was African-American? It was an unfortunate choice of words on my part, and he overreacted."

I have seen apologies work wonders when it looked like things were going to heat up into that vehement an exchange. Once, having decided to buy a new dictionary, I listed my criteria and asked other writers which one they would recommend. I mentioned that I wanted it to include new American expressions but without giving a green light to what I considered overly permissive usage, like saying that "all right" could also be spelled "alright." Many writers offered useful information, but one took me to task for expecting dictionaries to dictate usage. Her use of the phrase, "You should know better than anyone..." set me off, and I replied, "Please! Surely I have the right

---

FAST FACTS

Reminders for Avoiding Flame Wars

- *Don't* publicly express opinions on unresolvable, emotionally charged issues.

- *Don't* belittle or insult someone you disagree with.

- *Don't* jump to the worst possible conclusion about what someone meant.

- *Don't* respond in kind if someone insults you.

- *Do* wait a few hours or overnight before pressing the Send button.

- *Do* remind yourself that a hotheaded response harms your business image.

- *Do* respect someone's complaint and try to respond constructively.

- *Do* apologize if you've flown off the handle.

---

to buy whatever kind of dictionary I want." Someone whose name I didn't recognize posted a message that read, "Uh-oh, flame war coming :-) Be kind, everyone :-)," and just while I was thinking that perhaps I should have known better than to speak so sharply, I saw that the next message was an apology from the woman who had admonished me. The entire affair ended there.

What you most need in order to avoid fanning the flames is a method of disengaging yourself from provocative messages on the screen or of allowing yourself to sound off but keeping your finger far away from the Send button. Chances are that if you wait to reply until the next time you go online, you'll be in a better position to decide how to do so in a way consistent with your professional image. Ask yourself, Is your pride worth the mayhem you'll cause? One time I was so concerned about what I saw as a deceptive offer that had been posted publicly that I could prevent myself from getting involved only by telling myself dozens of times, "It's none of your business. It's none of your business."

When "flames" arrive from people who've tried to place an order at your Web site, or who are unhappy about delivery of your goods, it's especially crucial to sit back and not react in kind. On the discussion list I-Sales, a video merchant asked for advice on dealing with irate customer e-mails, like this one:

> *BOB,*
>
> *I HAVE TRYED [sic] MORE THAN ONE HOUR TO ORDER ON YOUR STORE...*
>
> *I WILL REPORT YOUR STORE FOR STEALLING [sic] CREDIT CARDS FROM CUSTOMERS*

The consensus of other electronic merchants was that no one could prevent customers from fuming like this, probably out of frustration. Regardless of how wrong or dumb one believed the customer was, the merchant should apologize for the trouble and suggest a resolution of the problem, others advised. Above all, don't pooh-pooh the customer's complaint. I can remember steam practically coming out of my ears when I e-mailed someone to let them know that their site wasn't functioning as advertised and being told in reply that it actually worked fine. "The very first statement must take the customer out of attack mode," wrote Kent Krueger of Extraordinary Dog Supplies. "We've had customers write or call after they've received our response to apologize for their communication."

Prevention Tactics

A few communication techniques will help you avoid triggering or becoming a target of overly emotional messages online. Some are variations of advice your parents probably taught you; others pertain particularly to the online environment.

- *Stay out of no-win arguments.* On certain topics, such as whether or not all lawyers are scumbags, the chances of you swaying opinions are just about nil. Save your energy for issues where people are more likely to be interested in what you have to say. If you know what makes the other person wrong, try explaining it point by point rather than simply disagreeing. "This tactic is not for the faint at heart," warns Angela Gunn. "You might have to go back and defend yourself."

- *Don't make personal remarks.* Call someone a jerk, an idiot, an ignoramus, or a hick, and it's safe to assume he or she will take offense. Take issue with the substance of what he or she said, on the other hand, and constructive dialogue can ensue.

- *Notice what triggers misunderstandings or misplaced outrage.* "People seem to have a hard time understanding the dry humor typical of Vermonters," says computer consultant Gary Ellenbogen of Winooski, Vermont. "I've learned to be careful about that." Don't rely on symbolic grins or smileys to take the edge off disrespectful remarks. I know one person who makes gratuitously nasty comments and then adds a "<g>," as if that would sweeten the thought. It doesn't.

- *Always begin by assuming you've misunderstood.* "Actively assume that you've put a more negative interpretation on a remark than was intended," says Yishai Almog. "Restate it in your own words and ask the person who said it for a clarification." This policy saves face for both you and your respondent and helps prevent the creation of unnecessary enemies. Simi-

FAST FACTS

Your Payoff from Good Customer Service

According to customer service expert Terry Vavra, only 1 in 27 dissatisfied customers will ever complain to the vendor. The others simply take their business elsewhere. However, of those who do complain, if the complaint is handled satisfactorily, 90 percent of the time the complainer becomes a repeat customer. Therefore, an explicit complaint represents an opportunity—a chance to create a loyal customer. Your out-of-pocket cost to respond courteously to complaints with a let's-solve-this attitude: $0.

larly, if someone flames you, tell yourself it has nothing to do with you personally and it reflects more on them than on you. "It's equivalent to you bumping someone and them yelling very loudly," Almog says.

- *Sandwich a negative message between positive comments.* I learned this from communication consultant Laurie Schloff, with whom I wrote *Smart Speaking* and *He & She Talk.* Instead of flying off the handle with "You sexist pig!" try: "You made some valid points, but did you realize the phrase 'executives and their wives' falsely assumes all executives are male? Acknowledging the accomplishments of women lets people know you're aware of what's happening in today's business world."

- *When appropriate, express criticism privately.* The old saying, "If you can't say anything nice, don't say anything at all" is as appropriate for the business world as it is for the playground. Writer Lary Crews follows this policy, he says. "When I have anything negative to say, I say it by e-mail. If I put it up on America Online, it's going to stay there for a long time."

- *Add self-effacing apologies in advance.* If you're going to promote yourself in Internet newsgroups, avoid flames by doing it in a humble, self-deprecating way that excuses itself, advises Bryan Pfaffenberger, author of *The Usenet Book.* For instance, "Is it OK if I also mention my own book, *Guide for Tiddlywinks Tournamenters?* It includes a section on competitive strategies that people say has been helpful to them."

- *Apologize afterward when appropriate.* If you provoke a mess with one of your messages, undo as much damage as you can with a sincere apology. I forgot to use the sandwich technique when I e-mailed an author of a book on online marketing about a mistake I'd noticed in his book. He replied grumpily and defensively, and I apologized, acknowledging that I should have written, "I'm looking forward to reading your book. I couldn't help noticing, however, that you referred to X as a Y when she is a Z. If it's not too late to correct this, it will help your book's reception." The other author not only accepted my apology, but also took on part of the blame for the rift that had almost occurred.

- *Never pretend to know more than you do.* Whether it's the black market in Bulgaria or the medical causes of "the bends" that you've ignorantly sounded off publicly about, chances are that someone will correct you, and not always in a face-saving way. Get your fingers busy doing something else when you're tempted to butt in with "facts" for which you have no basis.

- *Do your homework.* Avoid antagonizing the regulars in an online area by "lurking" and listening for a while before asking one of the questions that they're tired of answering. Most newsgroups have a "FAQ"—Frequently Asked Questions (with answers)—file available that gets newcomers up to speed for constructive, welcomed participation. (See Figure 18.3.)

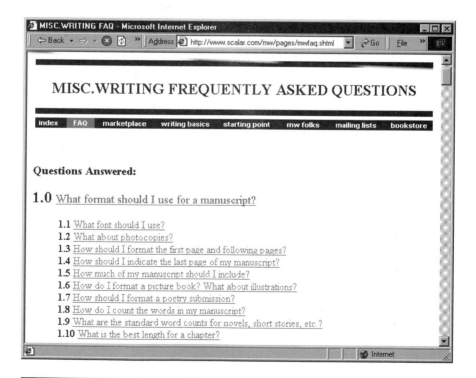

Figure 18.3. Frequently Asked Questions file for the newsgroup misc.writing.

Other Psychological Hazards Online

Practically any psychological dynamic that occurs in our three-dimensional world can get going online as well, with similar consequences. Novelist Neal Shusterman of Irvine, California, encountered the troublemaker-come-to-town syndrome when he went looking around Prodigy for other writers with whom he could discuss serious professional issues. "Barb Tomlin, Board Leader of the Office Board, asked me to become a Member Representative and suggested I recruit people for professional discussions there. Like an idiot I posted a note on the Books Board that we were opening a new area on publishing over on the Office Board, and I got the bashing of my life." Shusterman hadn't considered the possibility that his well-meant invitation would be perceived as a threat to a cohesive online community. "About ten people riled up the others in thinking that I was trying to 'steal' people from their board, and no matter what I said, some people believed that I was Satan's second cousin. I had no idea that there was a sense of territoriality on the different boards because I was thinking in terms of interesting conversations. In my mind I was just an individual sitting at my computer and no threat to anyone."

Jealousies, rivalries, cliques, crushes, transference, and projection in viewing forum leaders as parental figures—if it happens anywhere it can occur in cyberspace. Shusterman also experienced online stalking when he irritated someone who had been posting off-topic notes. "He started chasing me around the boards, leaving nasty notes wherever I went. Several people came to my defense, which made him more vicious. It was scary because he knew where I lived in California." I've both witnessed and experienced heckling—being badgered with disparaging questions, insinuations, and labels no matter what the topic. In one community, a guy kept disrupting discussions with irrelevant jibes at direct marketer Sheila Danzig. Elsewhere one particularly exasperating individual kept referring to me in his messages to others as "the brat."

There's no magic remedy for such situations. When you are lucky, eventually hecklers and harassers go away. See Chapter 20 for cases in which unlucky folks experienced online threats becoming real offline, in what Barb Tomlin calls "geospace."

Occasionally an initially unpleasant episode has a happy ending. "I got into a flame war with a guy named Bill Beam," Angela Gunn recalls. "We took it into e-mail, and after going back and forth for a while, we got tired of it." Beam mentioned something about *PC Magazine*, where Gunn was then working, and the conversation shifted to a professional level. "He gave me a lead about a publisher looking for writers, and that led to my first published book, *Plug-N-Play Mosaic for Windows*."

19

Staying Out of Trouble

To hear some people talk, cyberspace is everywhere and nowhere, an intangible and thus legally untouchable world apart from nations, governments, and the earth that we inhabit. When you and I meet online, this line of thinking goes, we don't go head to head on your computer or on mine, or on some master monster mainframe in Virginia or Ohio, but in the realm of the imagination. We may need silicon, plastic, and metal devices to communicate electronically, but computer bytes themselves have no weight, no taste, no color, no physical size, and no geographical location. We meet in the ether, which no one owns or governs, and which therefore is invulnerable to national laws and traditional customs. We may be subject to the frontier justice meted out by self-appointed vigilantes but otherwise anything goes, including ordinarily outlawed crimes and cons.

Sorry—that's a dream.

Physicists proved long ago that there is no ether, once thought of as an all-pervasive massless medium through which electromagnetic waves traveled. Similarly, legal authorities familiar with online communication assure us that a realm invulnerable to human laws does not exist. Take heed! If you want a thriving business with repeat customers and clients who sing your praises, you'd better cotton up to prevalent ethical expectations too.

The Reach of the Law

"A lot of people have the misconception that cyberspace is somehow different from anyplace else, and it's really not," says Hilary Miller, a Greenwich, Connecticut, attorney who specializes in publishing law. "All the same rules about copyright infringement and defamation, for example, apply in exactly the same way for electronic communication as for newspapers, magazines, letters, paintings, or any other medium of expression." Because laws don't become null when you're using a modem to communicate, online you should be at least as careful as anywhere else not to violate others' legal rights and to prudently safeguard your own.

According to Montclair, New Jersey, attorney Lance Rose, author of *Netlaw: Your Rights in the Online World*, online jurisdiction has less to do with exactly where a breach occurs than with whether a governmental court system has power over the parties involved. For example, if I, who live in Boston, posted material on a server in Sweden that violated some other Bostonian's rights, I could have to answer for it in a Massachusetts court, Rose says. This would be so even if online messages did drift around in space without the aid of land-based computers and telephone lines. In this discussion I'm referring specifically to U.S. law, although many of the principles hold in other countries as well. Consult a knowledgeable lawyer for advice on any specific legal situation you face, but here's a general orientation to issues you should know about.

1. *Intellectual ownership.* Anytime someone creates a work and fixes it in tangible form, it's instantaneously covered by copyright law, which, with a few exceptions, gives the creator the exclusive right to distribute the work, copy it, perform it publicly, or authorize others to do so. This is true whether or not the work carries a copyright notice, whether the tangible expression involves marks on paper or digital codes on a disk, and whether you happen upon it in print, in the airwaves, or on the Web. In other words, almost all the words and pictures you encounter in cyberspace legally belong to someone else, and you must gain permission to publish, transmit, or otherwise reproduce the work.

One exception, known as "fair use," allows you to quote brief portions of someone else's work—not the whole work—for purposes of commentary. You're usually free to make a complete copy for your own private use as well. When someone explicitly grants readers the right to upload and distribute the work elsewhere, you are of course free to do so. I should also note that when someone creates a work in the course of his or her regular employment, the copyright generally belongs to the employer, not the employee.

These concepts of ownership apply to software programs you might encounter online, text files, graphics and photos at Web sites, e-mail messages, newsgroup or forum postings, mailing list items, newspaper articles available in electronic form, and so on. Because of rampant infringements in the wired world, I know this will strike some of you as shocking or even unbelievable news. But neither "everyone else does it" nor "I didn't know" excuse you from responsibility for respecting others' property rights. So let me restate the legal situation as simply as possible: You must seek permission from the copyright holder before you can legally republish on paper or distribute to other online arenas any significant proportion of a program, uploaded article, e-mail message, forum thread, picture, graphic, and so on, that you encounter online. You also may not upload other people's material to the Internet or online services without their

FAST FACTS

Copyright Resources

- U.S. Copyright Office: *http://www.loc.gov/copyright*
- Canadian Copyright Information: *http://stauffer.queensu.ca/copyright/index.html*
- Australian Copyright Council: *http://www.copyright.org.au*
- Electronic Frontier Foundation Archives: *http://www.eff.org/intellectual_property*

permission. Copyright laws have bite. *Playboy* once collected $500,000 from a bulletin board that was distributing images from the magazine without authorization.

The membership agreement or terms of service you accept when you sign on for online access (see Figure 19.1) may contain additional rules about copyright. For instance, CompuServe members agree that "neither member nor its designated users may reproduce, redistribute, retransmit, publish or otherwise transfer, or commercially exploit, any information, software or other content which they receive through the Service." A violator gets one warning and upon repeating the misdeed, can get cut off from CompuServe and face legal action. Similarly, your Internet service provider's terms of service may include the right to terminate your account if you violate someone's copyright.

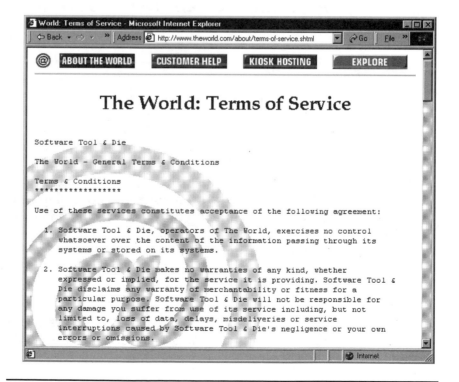

Figure 19.1. Terms of Service for my Internet service provider.

When it comes to your own work that you wish to protect, the prudent thing to do is to insert a copyright notice that lets people know that they should understand that what they're reading or looking at is your property. A copyright notice should take the following form:

Copyright 20xx Jane Author.

You can abbreviate "copyright" to "copr.," says Hilary Miller, or replace it with the letter C within a circle (©), but a C within parentheses, (C), is not legally recognized as equivalent. If you do wish to authorize or even encourage certain kinds of distribution and reuse of your work, specify what you do and do not permit. For instance, my Freelance Writing FAQ contains the following notice:

This FAQ is a primer on freelance writing. All comments welcome. Copyright 1995, 1999 Marcia Yudkin. Electronic redistribution allowed so long as you make no changes in the file. Please address questions and comments to Marcia Yudkin at marcia@yudkin.com.

To ensure that you'll be able to collect attorney's fees from the other side if you should ever sue for copyright infringement, you can register your copyright with the Library of Congress. Currently registration costs only $20, and the form is easy to fill out. (Write to the Library of Congress, Washington DC 20559 and request Circular R1 and Form TX.) Note that neither a copyright declaration nor registration can truly *prevent* unauthorized exploitation of your work. "No one should post anything in a public place today, whether a Usenet newsgroup or the Web or a public mailing list, with the thought that they're going to be able at a practical level to tightly control its distribution, unless they're a huge company like Paramount that's able to run after every violator and threaten to sue them," says Lance Rose. "In the future, artists' and creators' rights groups may be able to obtain similar enforcement for individuals and small businesses."

2. *Libel*. Despite the prevalence of insults online, you shouldn't get the impression that all's fair and safe in a war of words. The doctrine of defamation defines certain kinds of pronouncements as legally actionable. "The most harmful thing you can say is something that injures someone in their business or profession. For instance, if you call someone a crook whose reputation particularly depends on probity, like a banker—as opposed to, say, a ditch digger—that could be libel," says Hilary Miller. According to Edward Cavazos and Gavino Morin, authors of *Cyberspace and the Law*, libel involves written language that has a tendency to harm a specific person or company's reputation by attacking his, her, or its honesty, integrity, or sanity. A libelous message must be disseminated to someone else besides the one attacked, so private e-mail can't fall into the category. There must also be factual content, not merely general insults or a statement of opinion. Finally, libelous statements are necessarily false.

"Declaring that 'Joe is a con artist' when, in fact, Joe has been found guilty of fraudulent activities, will not get you into trouble," write Cavazos and Morin. Nor will saying, "Watch out—I sent XYZ a certified check for $350.00 and he never sent the merchandise or refunded the money," if in fact that happened. But beware of writing, "XYZ is running the biggest scam on the Internet, cheating buyers right and left" if they cheated only you or if you're only furious for some reason with XYZ.

The degree of harm done may have to do with the size of the audience receiving the message as well as the contents of the message, so it might seem like common sense to take a careful look at any broadsides you send off into cyberspace. Journalist Brock Meeks found himself facing a legal bill of $30,000 when he was sued for libel by an entrepreneur whose business practices he criticized in his widely disseminated online column, CyberWire Dispatch. Nevertheless, according to Mike Godwin, legal services counsel for the Electronic Frontier Foundation (see Figure 19.2), relatively few people, online or off, get sued for libel. "For one thing, it's expensive, which means you ei-

Figure 19.2. The Electronic Frontier Foundation Web site.

ther have to be rich or you have to have such a convincing case that you can persuade a lawyer to take your case on a contingency-fee basis. For another, the long, drawn-out process of suing someone for damage to your reputation is almost always wearying and very rarely satisfying."

On the other hand, Lance Rose warns against extreme self-censorship. "If people are going to veer away from saying things that are controversial, even if they might not turn out to be libelous, then we're watching a demonstration of the 'chilling effect'," he says. "The Supreme Court has said that defamation laws are limited so that people can speak freely. Keep in mind too that when someone is a public figure, a statement about him or her has to be not only false to be libel, but also said maliciously, with an intent to hurt the person, or with a reckless disregard for the truth. There's a strong First Amendment value in being able to discuss famous people and companies."

What should you do if someone is spreading negative, untrue rumors online about you or your company? "First," advises Hilary Miller, "find out who is doing it. Second, ask the person responsible to change their ways. And third, if that doesn't work, consult with an attorney. It's no different from any other medium."

3. *Free expression.* With our civics lessons a foggy memory, many Americans have the idea that our First Amendment gives us a near-absolute right to free speech. Sorry, that's another misconception. The First Amendment to the U.S. Constitution prevents the *government* from interfering with our freedom of expression. Government cannot swoop down and stop you from expressing your opinions or disseminating pictures online, except where obscenity, child pornography, and a few other categories like threats against the President are concerned. Yet an online service or Internet service provider can legally censor messages or deny access to U.S. citizens, as Lance Rose puts it, "for any reason, or for no reason at all."

   Thus an online gatekeeper can "kill" messages containing any of a given set of prohibited words, forbid certain kinds of discussions, or terminate your membership if you make a verbal nuisance of yourself—without you necessarily having any legal recourse. The key is the rules set out in the service agreement you were asked to agree to when you signed up with the service. Because of our general belief in the value of fairness and a cultural/political bias against unreasonable censorship, it may help you to cry "unfair!" when you think an online system is trying to shut you up, but you won't be entitled to help from First Amendment watchdog groups.

4. *Privacy.* Thanks to the 1986 Electronic Communications Privacy Act, you have a right to expect that your private e-mail remains for your eyes only. Exceptions include your employer in many circumstances having the right to inspect private mes-

sages within a company e-mail system, law enforcement officials sifting through e-mail and transmissions pursuant to court orders, and an online system specifying in its user agreement that no messages are truly private on the system. According to the Identity, Privacy and Anonymity on the Internet Frequently Asked Questions file, however, you should not expect much privacy from your system administrator, who usually has a variety of monitoring procedures in place to detect unauthorized use of the system, which can also reveal your patterns of usage and even recover your deleted messages. Still, if a system administrator were to reveal to another person private messages not addressed to him or her, you might have a basis for a lawsuit. The rules are complicated, so if an issue like this arises, consult a lawyer.

5. *Online agreements*. Is a deal arranged and concluded through electronic communication legally valid? Yet another common misconception operates here, says Hilary Miller. "Most business in the world transpires without any written agreement, and in most cases the writing is merely evidence of the agreement rather than the deal itself," he says. "Very, very rarely are disputes about the formation of a contract—usually they're about the *performance* of the contract. And in those cases, whether there's a manual signature on a letter or just an electronic message containing the terms doesn't matter." Miller says that his retainer agreement for clients, which he asks them to hand sign, includes a clause saying that an electronic communication between them is valid—"and I think that's enforceable."

6. *Commercial misrepresentation*. All the laws forbidding false or misleading advertising apply in the online environment, as do most other kinds of governmental regulations over commerce. In 1994 the Federal Trade Commission brought to heel a company advertising a purportedly "100 percent legal and 200 percent guaranteed" credit repair program that the agency found to be advocating illegal methods of credit repair. The same year, Missouri securities regulators caught up with a man who praised to the skies on Prodigy the stock of a public company without disclosing that he was the public relations manager of the company and the son of its president. Outside of

the securities field, competitors of a company making believe that its messages about itself were posted by disinterested bystanders might be able to sue for unfair competition, says Lance Rose. See "Ethics in Cyberspace" later in this chapter for opinions on such practices from an ethical point of view.

7. *And*....This doesn't exhaust all the possible legal concerns. Consult *Netlaw* or *Cyberspace and the Law* (see Appendix B) if your business ventures might involve sexually oriented material, incitement to break laws, hacking, killer-for-hire ads, use of celebrity names or images, or dissemination of others' trade secrets.

Ethics in Cyberspace

Most of the ethical issues I have encountered in my online travels have to do with the withholding or distortion of information. Skimping on honest, frank disclosure can open you up to moral condemnation that may ultimately prove far more destructive to your business than even a barrage of flaming. If you don't see anything wrong with the practices described here, you need to recognize that many of your online and offline prospects do. Never assume you're clever enough to escape detection! Instead, where your own moral sensors don't sound an alarm, sift questionable tactics with the question, "Would I feel completely comfortable having everyone online understand what I'm doing?"

Online veteran Marty Winston told me about running

FAST FACTS

Free FTC Information

The Federal Trade Commission has a number of highly readable educational documents at its Web site describing the danger zones and forbidden zones when it comes to advertising and marketing. Particularly recommended:

- Advertising and Marketing on the Internet: The Rules of the Road

- Frequently Asked Advertising Questions: A Guide for Small Business

See *http://www.ftc.gov/bcp/guides/guides.htm.*

across a message along the lines of "Hey, I found this great thing, you've got to call so-and-so and ask for such-and-such" in a forum he was helping to run. Winston's nose alerted him, and he called the telephone number posted in the message and asked for the person named as the one offering this seemingly disinterested hot tip. "She's on the phone right now," came the answer, corroborating his suspicion. Winston then asked for the company president, read him the posted message and told him that selling under disguise was not allowed in the forum and it had better not happen again. Winston did not "out" the company by letting other forum members know what its employee had done, but that might be the logical recourse where no moderator, host, or sysop is in charge.

Indeed, someone as prominent as *New York* magazine editor Kurt Anderson became the object of negative publicity in several print publications after he went on the Internet and praised a forthcoming cover story of his magazine. He signed his plug "Kurt Anderson" but failed to mention that he held any position at the magazine. Alert cybernauts who did make the connection scolded him roundly for the ploy. The operative expectation is that if you have any sort of financial interest in a product, service, or company you mention, you should say so, to let readers know how to take your comments.

A related kind of hooha broke out when a new employee of Microsoft named John Callan applied to join a high-tech-journalists-only mailing list with the mystifying affiliation, "MSN News Service." Several journalists blasted Callan for trying to trick his way onto the list as a sort of spy for Microsoft (the "M" in "MSN"), and Callan exacerbated the situation when he acknowledged that of course he would forward relevant messages from the members-only list up his corporate ladder. Because people disdain deception so much, it's worth bending over backward with disclosures and disclaimers when you really do lack any underhanded intent. If you wait until someone challenges you, you'll rarely be able to defuse the suspicions.

Probably the most ethically dubious practice I heard about was a scheme where a company gets accounts under different names from several different Internet providers and uses them to drum up discussion about their product without appearing to be advertising. As I explained in the chapters on schmoozing, if you answer someone else's question, you're not soliciting. Why wait for questions and positive interest to get a thread going, the reasoning runs, when you can stage the process yourself? Usenet expert Bryan Pfaffenberger called this "a very risky strategy. If word got around—as, for example, through a disgruntled employee—man oh man would you find yourself on the wrong end of flames!" Paul Edwards, system administrator of the Working from Home forum on CompuServe, condemned the subterfuge even more strongly. "Normally we have a 'two-strikes-and-you're-out' policy, but that's a one-strike offense. Anyone who did that on our forum would be permanently locked out. It's highly unethical." He likened it to "shilling," an old carnival ruse where an accomplice encourages gambling or buying by posing as an enthusiastic or successful customer.

Edwards also tsk-tsked about two other cases I described involving misleading publicity on bulletin boards. In one case a person was telling people who had expressed interest in the World Wide Web about the opportunity to get a home page for just $10 a month, consistently failing to mention that this was part of a multilevel marketing scheme. In another case someone was offering publication and royalties for a certain kind of business material, yet failed to mention in the initial message that authors would have to pay a significant fee to participate. "To me, anything where an important fact is concealed that when revealed would cause an individual to turn off is not good business ethics. You need to present the salient information up front. There's a strategy called 'the curiosity method,' where you describe the benefits of a business, get people to a meeting, and then tell them the name of the company, which makes people feel deceived. We cut that off at the knees whenever we see it."

Other ethical principles to remember include respecting clients' and correspondents' requests for confidentiality and being careful not to spread misinformation. Anne Stuart, senior writer for *Inc.* magazine, told me that some publications have a rule that every bit of information coming from the Internet has to be independently verified. "Someone had apparently doctored the text of the Bible at one site, and in lots of places information online is out of date," she warns. Stuart also proceeds with caution when it comes to assuming that people really are who they say they are electronically. "When I initiate e-mail contact to the address on someone's stationery or business card, I feel pretty confident about their identity, but in other cases identity can be tricky, and I think it's better to call and check the situation out. Once I saw a post asking for contributions to a racist textbook, and it turned out that while the professor was on vacation, a student was using his I.D. and sneaking into his electronic mailbox." Stuart sensed that that situation was fishy, but where you intend to blast someone's conduct far and wide it might be fair to do a little checking first.

FAST FACTS

A Free Course in Fact Checking

It Says So on the Internet:

http://www.conknet.com/hhs/library/sezwho.html

Pause to think before you repeat information you found on the Net. This document offers five simple guidelines to separate probably reliable information from probably unreliable.

In addition, if you wish to check a particular fact, spelling, or statistic, call the reference desk of your largest local library. Most will look up one fact for you, absolutely free.

20

Keeping Trouble Away From You

In the classic story *The Wizard of Oz*, Dorothy discovered that where she landed after the storm, strange and wonderful things were possible that would have been fantasy back home in Kansas. Some surprises, like the welcoming Munchkins, were pleasant; others, like flying monkeys and witches on broomsticks, were utterly horrible. Similarly, it's important to recognize that in the brave new world of cyberspace, not everyone honors values like honesty and respect. Unsavory characters, mischief, and outright crimes can spoil your online journeys. To a great extent, however, you can minimize the dangers by taking some simple precautions.

Personal Risks

The scariest stories I heard came from two women who experienced personal threats to their safety from people who learned of their existence online. When a woman I'll call Wendy happened to mention in a forum message that she lived in Chicago, another woman from Chicago posted a message expressing similar interests and suggesting that they get together. "We exchanged e-mail, and she sounded sane and interesting, so I gave her a call," recalls Wendy. "It was the most bizarre conversation. The one and only time I'd experienced anything like it was in a locked psychiatric unit. She expressed a lot of anger at certain people in the forum, and she sounded truly dangerous. I didn't want her showing up at my door." Wendy made some calls to mental health contacts and discovered that sure enough, this woman had been hospitalized for psychiatric problems. She also learned that several sysops of the forum had been receiving middle-of-the-night phone calls from the woman. "I called and begged CompuServe to delete an e-mail I had already sent her with my telephone number, but they said they couldn't do that except with a court order. Then the woman disappeared." Relieved, Wendy decided to proceed more cautiously in making offline contacts with online people. "Looking back, I think that if I'd carried on a little longer in e-mail she wouldn't have seemed so normal."

The other woman, whom I'll call Brenda, began receiving unwelcome sexual comments from a man by e-mail and then by telephone. "I was shocked and alarmed," Brenda says. "I have a publicly listed phone number, and at that time my address was listed too." The problem escalated. Although he lived in another state, the man told Brenda he was sending someone to her house to let her know he was for real. "He vandalized my car. I contacted the online service where this had all started, but when things happen offline, they can't help you." Brenda decided she wasn't going to be victimized by this jerk and hired a private detective in another state to let *him* know that she knew where he was and to warn him to stop communicating with her. That worked. "It cost me about $300, and the damage he had already done was much greater than that. Now I have Caller I.D. service, no listed address, and an immediate call-back capability as deterrents."

Although these two incidents happened to women, men can experience genuine threats as well. Neal Shusterman (see Chapter 18) was harassed online by another man who knew his home city, and a male attorney told me he had been threatened with bodily harm by someone he'd encountered online who hated lawyers. Both Wendy and Brenda say that the best tactics for preventing real-world harassment are caution in giving out one's home telephone number and address, and arranging with the telephone company for one's home address to be omitted from directory information. Those who have a home-based business and want prospective customers and clients to be able to get in touch can insert a layer or two of security by giving out a post office box address, making it difficult for people to find your street address, and acting as if you run a big company out of a conventional office. That way, you can have credibility and accessibility without sacrificing personal security.

If you're a small or home-based business, you might also want to avoid posting your address, fax, and phone numbers publicly when you're just asking for information. Send your contact information privately instead—unless you don't mind getting onto the lists of folks who will flood your mailbox and fax with silly money-making offers. One fellow told me, quite erroneously, that if you post a fax number online you are telling people it's fine to fax advertising to you. On the contrary, in the United States you can owe a $500 federal fine if you fax solicitations to folks with whom you do not already have a business relationship.

Computer-related Risks

"Security is the number one concern expressed by people interested in doing business on the Internet," says Dan Janal, a publicist for high-tech companies and author of *Risky Business*. If you're worried that going online will expose your business to theft, sabotage, or elec-

FAST FACTS

How to Protect Your Privacy

- To opt out of Web sites collecting your personal information: *http://opt-out.cdt.org/online*

- To learn more about, and if you wish, to stop the collection of data about you through "cookies": *http://www.cookiecentral.com*

- To find out about technical tools that protect your privacy online: *http://www.epic.org/privacy/tools.html*

- To get tips on protecting yourself against actual or potential stalkers: *http://www.privacyrights.org/FS/fs14b-stalking.htm*

tronic mayhem, you are not alone. Yet according to the experts I consulted, most of the fears you might have in this area are groundless if you're an individual or small firm connecting to the outside world via a personal computer. Here's why.

Even before the mass implementation of elaborate security systems that we're told are in the works, the risk of credit card thievery online is minimal, says Rich Roth, an Internet connectivity consultant and the founder of On the Net in Georgetown, Connecticut. "It's the same level of risk as using a credit card at a restaurant. As at the restaurant, an e-mail with a credit card number could be misappropriated by someone working for your own service provider or the one at the other end," Roth says.

In addition, Internet e-mail passes through a number of gateways, at any one of which it might get bottlenecked. While waiting to be sent across an ocean via satellite, for example, data might sit in a queue for several minutes, where someone might be tempted to rifle through it. We could compare this to credit card data passing through a procession of restaurants amid a flood of bills, personal notes, and business data, increasing the chances of interception but only by an extraordinarily patient or clever snooper. According to Roth, "Smaller providers are more likely not to have proper safeguards in place, but any provider is vulnerable to human mistakes or misdeeds. You can build a maximum security system and if a guard leaves a door open...."

On the World Wide Web, Roth continues, whatever slight transmission delay you see when you submit your credit card data is the actual length of time—seconds—the information is most vulnerable to snatching. "The risk of someone hanging around a site that takes orders waiting for a buyer to show up is very low. And when there is fraud, banks usually charge it back to the vendor. In fact, there's a bigger risk of a vendor selling to a bad card than of a buyer getting their credit card information stolen and used." Although the widespread fears may be overblown, it's essential to recognize security trepidations and to provide alternative ways of taking payment besides e-mail or direct Web orders. Fax and phone orders feel much more secure to many Internet shoppers, so be sure to explain those options at your site.

Another common fear, fueled by highly publicized incidents, is of having one's computer broken into and private data stolen or the system damaged. Here reality is even more divergent from perception if you're a small organization. Chances are you go online with a personal computer, a single machine not otherwise linked to any computer network.

"There's no risk at all—none—if you dial onto the Internet in those circumstances," explains Rich Roth. "Your individual computer probably isn't even capable of letting in an incoming call when you're dialing out. With a direct connection of your individual machine to the Internet, there is a slight security

FAST FACTS

Credit Card Fraud Affects Merchants

If someone orders goods from you using a credit card that's not theirs, you the merchant almost always get stuck. Learn the telltale warning signs of possible credit card fraud:

- Different billing and shipping addresses
- Much larger order than normal
- Free e-mail account used to place the order
- Incomplete address, no phone number

With any of these, investigate further before filling the order. For more information, go to *http://www.scambusters.org/reports/walker.html*

risk, but it's pretty low." The real risk, experts concur, occurs with a corporate network that offers information to the outside world as an Internet server or "host." You're also vulnerable if you have cable modem access, which remains connected all the time, regardless of whether or not you're using the Internet connection. In those cases you do need sophisticated security protections that set up various kinds of technical barriers, particularly "firewalls," which are beyond the scope of this book.

According to Christian Crumlish, author of *A Guided Tour of the Internet*, if you access the Internet by dialing up to a service and using their software, your vulnerability has nothing to do with your own computer but rather with your account on the service. Someone who knew your password there could not only spy on your e-mail but also use your identity to place messages or run up a bill. The best security tactic in that case, Crumlish says, is changing your password frequently. Since a hacker can break into your account by automatically trying all the words in the dictionary, a secure password is not an official word, but equally should not be your birthday, the name of your beloved or your pet, or some cute but guessable phrase like "letmein" or "knockknock."

An electronic bandit can also learn your password by watching you type it. This rascal can also wreak mischief if you leave the machine unattended to, say, go to the bathroom while you're signed on. Or, when you have set up a script for an automatic sign-on, the scoundrel merely has to run the access program on your computer when you aren't around. A crook could also steal into your account by tricking you into revealing your password, so never give it out verbally for any reason. To further tax your memory or organization skills, experts recommend that you not use the same password for all of your accounts, so that someone who broke into one wouldn't be able to get into them all. Whew! Have you resolved to safeguard your passwords and computer yet?

Then there are "viruses"—rogue programs that vandalize your computer from within. You cannot catch a computer virus by receiving and reading e-mail text or downloading and reading a text file—only by running a software program or receiving a program file—such as a Microsoft Word or Excel file. A virus cannot take up residence within straight text, but it can within almost any kind of program or program file. Take care especially, then, when downloading programs from the Web, opening program files attached to e-mail, or installing programs from floppy disks or CD-ROMs. Even commercial software from large companies has occasionally been shipped containing infections. Inexpensive or free virus-scanning programs that help you practice "safe computing"—if you remember to use them—are available widely online or at computer stores. (See Figure 20.1.)

Finally, you face the risk of valuable, time-sensitive e-mail getting delayed or lost. Computer columnist John Dvorak reports that using MCI mail, he sent a series of three e-mail messages to one correspondent who received the third first, 10 hours after it was sent, the first 24 hours after it was sent, and the second 39 hours later. Another time, when messages seemed to be getting lost, not delayed, he called the MCI help desk and learned that a server had crashed during that time and many messages were indeed lost, with no notification of regular users. "Even one lost message is one too many" where important business is concerned, Dvorak complains.

Similarly, Cliff Stoll, author of the true-life cyberspace thriller *The Cuckoo's Egg*, performed an experiment comparing the reliability of snail-mail postcards and e-mail. Of two months of daily post-

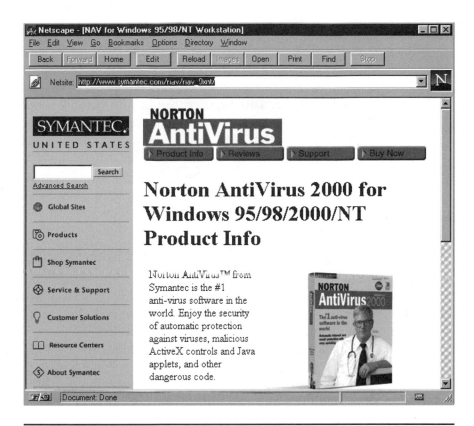

Figure 20.1. One popular virus protection program.

cards from Buffalo, New York to Oakland, California, half arrived in two days, many in three, and one took as long as eight days. Whereas all the postal mail arrived, of the e-mail he sent to himself from five different accounts, "most letters arrived within two hours; some took up to two days," he reports. "Average delivery time: twelve minutes. But I discovered that five messages never made it. Three of them bounced, due to network problems or crashed computers along the way. The other two? Swallowed by the electronic abyss." It seems wise, then, to use the telephone, fax, or postal mail as a backup when you don't receive an e-mail reply you're expecting—or not to depend on e-mail at all when something has to get there positively, absolutely this afternoon.

Business Risks

The old IBM slogan, "Think!" serves as a good guideline to follow before rushing ahead to put your company online. According to Dallas investment banker Fred Richards, more businesspeople should carefully consider the consequences of posting information publicly about their company, given that they won't be able to control exactly who will be accessing it and with what motive. "We use the Internet primarily when we're looking into a field that's completely new to us," Richards says. "And lo and behold, we recently discovered just how amazingly stupid people can be. One company in England had its entire pricing schedule and distribution technique out there for anyone to see. He had contract offers up there too—35 inquiries from customers all over the world. If you wanted to compete with them you'd have everything right there that you needed—without them knowing you had seen it. I showed this to six different bankers as well as the guy trying to raise money and they were all incredulous. Maybe a marketing or sales person did it without the CEO knowing."

I kept this issue in mind in the early stages of researching this book, when it was important not to let competing writers, editors, and publishers know precisely what I was working on. Whenever I publicly asked for input on a topic, I avoided describing the angle of the book, although I did brief those I interviewed. Through the grapevine effect the news could still have reached someone in a position to "scoop" me, but at least I minimized the odds.

Besides unwittingly giving away your secrets, make sure you understand that by doing practically anything besides e-mail online you are opening up your business for public scrutiny. Fail to satisfy your online customers and they have an effortless way to spread their discontent. Put out an announcement that provokes skepticism and, fairly or not, questions will pop up. I once looked in on a thread where a company president was getting roasted for talking about his company's service in terms that professional marketers would not accept. "The guy was talking about going on the Internet and creating editorial interest with a 'proprietary' method," said forum leader Marty Winston months later. "My suspicions were raised, and I said, 'If this isn't what you're doing you'd better tell us, and if it is what you're doing, you'd better not do it'. It was like saying you had a miracle cure for cancer that worked through exposure to dangerous levels of radiation." In response to merciless challenges from Winston and others, the company president offered unconvincing stalls like "I need the permission of my board to tell you anything about that." Verbally it was the equivalent of five schoolyard tough guys piling onto one poor schnook, and I wasn't surprised to learn from Winston that the man didn't show up there again.

Note that the public, interactive nature of the online world makes this risk much more acute than in any other marketing medium. If you use direct mail to deliver a pitch that some recipients find fishy, rarely will any one of them be able to discuss it with more than one other prospect at a time. If they don't like it, they'll probably just toss it out. With ads or press publicity, half a dozen people sitting around a lunch room might share opinions, but this doesn't begin to compare with thousands or tens of thousands being able to pose objections and debate something fundamental about your business, such as your price, product, or ethics.

A final business risk is falling prey to overpriced promoters, consultants, and providers. I have seen seminars that offer less than the information in this book being hawked at thousands of dollars a head and companies being told that they need to budget $50,000 plus a new full-time employee for the most minimal sort of Internet presence—which the entrepreneur down the road already has up and running for $50 a month. The best way to locate value in this frontier area is to go online, find arenas where people know more than you do, and ask, ask, ask. Exercise skepticism when it comes to offers that sound irresistible or that try to terrorize you into acting right away. For example, I've seen come-ons like these:

- "How to reach over a million ripe, virgin prospects for less than a penny a day!" (A chance to pay $100 for an eight-week classified ad online—and my calendar says that eight weeks is 56 days, for $1.79 a day, not "less than a penny.")

- "What will you do when your business is banned from the Internet?" (The context implies that if you don't obtain your own registered Internet domain name right away for $297—a price that's way inflated—you won't be able to get onto the Internet. Completely false.)

Caution, friends. Calm down and forget about the "gold rush" mentality. Unless you really don't mind spending eight times more than you have to, separate the rackets from the services that fairly help you onto the Net in a way that makes sense for your business.

21

Don't Overdo It

A $200-an-hour executive management skills coach confessed that after he received online access as a gift, he became "completely fascinated" with the work dilemmas people were describing online, spending an hour or two every day reading and commenting on messages. "One Friday afternoon I signed on when I had a report for an existing client that I had to get out that day, and the next thing I knew three and a half hours had gone by! I wasn't procrastinating, I'd just gotten totally sucked in to these discussions that I didn't often run across offline. I barely got my report finished, and that scared me. I quit and haven't used my modem since."

"I'm happy to help out with your book—just one request," replied another person I contacted." *Please* don't tell anyone to contact me by e-mail, for my sake and the sake of my family. I don't want to be flooded. E-mail has consumed my life (100–150 messages a day). :-)"

As with almost any human activity, too much of a fun or useful thing holds a potential for trouble. You can fall victim to your own fascination with the byways of this incredible new world or people's eagerness to seek you out for business. Your involvement spins out of control, and either in volume or intensity, you get overwhelmed. "I expect there to be a 12-step online addicts group forming soon," jokes Susan RoAne, author of *The Secrets of Savvy Networking*. "I just hope they don't have their meetings online."

Help for the Obsessed

If you check your e-mail box twenty times a day, find yourself dreaming about disputes among people you've met online, or aimlessly surf the Web for hours every day, it might be time to wonder if you have a problem. Control *is* a problem for some people, says long-time forum host Janet Attard, and out-of-control bills don't force a solution the way they used to. "When I first went online, in the eighties, I used a service that cost $35 an hour during the daytime. To send manuscripts I was working on, it was still cheaper and faster than overnight mail, though, so I used it as a substitute fax machine. Now that the hourly rates have tumbled, people don't always cut back when they should. Because the online medium is interactive, you can get really tied up in it, but you can learn to control your usage the same way you learn not to watch TV all the time. You need to treat going online the same way you would treat any other kind of outreach to customers."

Self-help for online "addiction" begins with figuring out what exactly is happening that makes your cyberspace involvement a problem. Are you losing track of time and missing deadlines? Is it really someone else who's complaining about your time spent online? Do you have great fun at it but don't have any time for other activities you enjoy as well? Is there a compulsiveness about your online entanglements? Have you been getting emotionally overinvolved with the conflicts and connections that come to life through your computer screen? Is it the bills that pose the problem? Once you've isolated the difficulties, remedies should be easier to come by.

Anne Stuart, a senior writer for *Inc.* magazine, told me that she sometimes spends so many hours at a time online that her vision begins to go double and she finally looks away

---

FAST FACTS

Are You Addicted?

Take a self-rated quiz to find out:

http://www.addictions.org/internet.htm

http://www.virtual-addiction.com/appraisal.htm

This site has special information for and about compulsive online gamblers, online auction users, and online traders:

http://www.netaddiction.com/net_compulsions.htm

at a window and gets shocked to see that it has gotten dark outside. "My husband is into it almost as much as I am, and we can be wrestling for control of our one telephone line," she says. Still, she doesn't see her involvement with numerous electronic penpals and participation on four work-related mailing lists as a problem. "I lose myself in it the way other people get absorbed in gardening or other hobbies. It's all related to my work as a writer, and I'm not on 24 hours a day or anything like that."

When she used to subscribe to close to a dozen mailing lists, however, she did feel overwhelmed and out of control. "Sometimes I'd turn my computer on and there'd be 200 messages, and I didn't feel able to delete any of them without reading them. I've learned how to do that, though. I also cut back on the mailing list subscriptions even though I felt I was learning a lot, because it felt like I was working all the time." Stuart turns one particular subscription on and off according to whether or not she's drowning in e-mail.

So, what's the real problem you're concerned about?

- *You lose track of time.* If overabsorption creates difficulties for you, rig up a system to remind you of the passage of time. Put an alarm clock near your computer and set it before you boot up. If you have two phone lines and a ringing telephone gets your attention more than an alarm, phone a friend before you go online and ask him to call you in exactly one hour. Entrepreneurs and inventors, how about a product that automatically logs you off after a preset length of time?

- *You're in conflict with others.* Discuss the problem with the other person or people. Negotiate. Describe the pleasure and educational benefits you derive from being online, and the money you're making. Give in a little to keep the peace.

- *You're simply overdoing it.* Set priorities, advises Anne Stuart. Realize that you don't have to respond to every item or contribute to every debate. Separate the indispensable forums and business matters from the optional ones and wean yourself from the latter when necessary.

- *You can't stop signing on.* If you're spending more time online than off or your world of online relationships exceeds your other involvements in number and intensity, you might need professional counseling, says psychologist/consultant Yishai Almog. For less extreme compulsiveness, try rewarding yourself for checking your e-mail only five times a day, or three or two.

- *You're overinvolved emotionally.* Take a vacation, leaving your laptop at home. One married man who had developed quite a roster of online girlfriends told me that he quit cold turkey. Hiking through high desert for two weeks, he was relieved to discover that he got along fine without his daily hours of "online sex."

Sometimes just putting your attention on the problem leads to a change. When I asked to hear from online addicts, electronic publisher Jim Migneco of Vernon, Connecticut, wrote to me, in part: "Online, each time you open a door, you are entering a hallway with more doors and are tempted into opening another portal to yet another wondrous place—all without going outside! But 'going out' is exactly what is missing from cruising through cyberspace. Years ago, I never missed an opportunity to walk along the beach on a blustery, frigid January day or to hike through the woods with the smell of pines and burbling sound of a thousand-year-old brook. Now I spend entire Sundays in my swivel-rocker office chair in a virtual world where the only exercise I get is moving my right index finger on a mouse key. Sitting in front of a PC in a heated and air-conditioned condo, it doesn't matter much whether it's sunny or cloudy outside, winter or summer. Have I gotten too wrapped up in cyberspace? Yes! Writing about this has helped me realize that I must make the effort to step outside again and venture into cyberspace in moderation."

Liberation from E-mail Slavery

The wired business folks I spoke with differed greatly in the volume of e-mail they found unmanageable. One handled 100 messages a day fine while another found 30 to 40 a week totally burdensome. Syndicated columnist and business owner Alice Bredin said she knew the cure and couldn't wait to hire an assistant to speed up the process. "I used to have an assistant who could provide my answers to commonly asked questions and then call me and ask about the rest. It's a huge investment of time to train someone to do that for you, because it takes about three months before they're efficient, but in the long run it will let you concentrate on more important things. All the business people that I have interviewed who make tons of money know how to delegate."

Bredin admits, though, that delegation holds pitfalls. "You have to tell the assistant to check with you if they're not 150 percent certain of how they should respond. Once someone I used to work with got in touch, and my assistant sent back an ordinary reply instead of the 'Hi, how are you doing, how's Bill?' I would have written."

Brian Kilgore, a communications consultant from Toronto, argues that e-mail is no different from any other in-basket in an office. "If you're never going to get e-mail you don't want your assistant to see, and if you have someone smart enough to do it well, then delegating your e-mail handling is fine, just as with conventional mail. And when you travel without an electronic connection, wouldn't it be good to have someone pull the messages out of the machine back at the office and call you if anything important is there?" But Peter

---

FAST FACTS

Is a Virtual Assistant the Answer?

"I get between 300 and 500 e-mails per day," says Stacy Brice, president of AssistU, which trains virtual assistants. "Fortunately, I have an assistant who brilliantly handles two thirds of them. I'm in Baltimore, and she's on the Upper Peninsula of Michigan. For me, it's been a lifesaver.

"On an easy day, with 300 e-mail messages, Marie gets about 200 of them, and, of those, I only see about 6. Of the 100 I would get, I usually off-load about 20 to 30 percent of them to her or shoot back standard replies. I use both the Stationary feature in Eudora Pro and a sweet program that throws macros for me, called My Function Keys."

To find out more about what would be involved in using a virtual assistant, go to

http://www.assistu.com/client/client_faq.shtml

Lloyd, a creativity consultant based in Newport, Kentucky, says he's noticed telltale signs that his addressee isn't handling his or her own e-mail: "People who have others reading their e-mail for them answer less faithfully—or not at all. The worst is people who do not answer polite, businesslike e-mail messages which call for a response. It's as rude as not giving the time of day. Another dead giveaway is talking to the person on the phone and finding out they know nothing about something you e-mailed them. Even worse: They call and ask about something you've already e-mailed."

Chris White, a speaker and writer from Sacramento, California, says that when she receives the exact same reply two or three times, or when she gets a reply beginning "Dear Mr. White," she suspects someone else is typing the message. White expresses skepticism that e-mail assistants can do an adequate job. "Queen bees like to talk to other queens! If you're a worker, never been queen, and never will, how can you know what's a queenly matter and what isn't?" I'll let Lloyd have the last word on this controversy: "If Microsoft mogul Bill Gates can read his own mail, no one has an excuse." Indeed, Gates has said that while almost nobody has his home telephone number, he lets his e-mail address be widely known and reads everything that lands there himself.

Before you decide to foist all your e-mail on someone else, consider these other solutions:

- *Separate e-mail accounts.* Of several accounts used by direct-mail whiz Sheila Danzig, one is her "private" account that her customers learn of only after they buy something from her, or if they meet her online. "I answer all of the mail in my private account myself," she says. "A high school girl, Ali Davis, takes care of 150 e-mails in the other account in about an hour and a half, answering the phone at the same time! It frees Ric, my director of operations, to take care of more pressing matters, and in turn, Ric frees me to do only the creative and trouble-shooting ends of the business."

- *Divided responsibilities.* Janet Attard of Centereach, New York, who hosts numerous forums, has an assistant who answers all the questions that fall within one particular topic and leaves the rest for her.

- *Macros (scripts) for repeated situations.* Save time by developing explanations or other responses in files that you can call up and customize with your respondent's name and some other appropriate introductory comment before sending them. Make sure these canned responses sound natural, as if you really did write them on the fly.

- *Priorities.* I'm told that you can program e-mail management software to follow any rules you can formulate for what should come to your attention first, later, and last. For instance, you might want to read messages from your boyfriend, sister, editor, and best friend first; then your top clients with pending projects; then others; finally stuff from mailing lists you subscribe to; with anything from that jerk in Portland who keeps on writing you getting automatically deleted. Other software can save you time by collecting your e-mail from different accounts automatically and presenting it to you all in one batch.

- *Escapism.* Who says you have to respond to every message, argues Chris White. Or that you have to respond right away? Napoleon, it's said, opened his mail only once every three weeks. Much of it concerned problems that had already been solved in the meantime.

- *Brevity.* Adopt the habit of writing only what needs to be said and no more. Yes. Tuesday at five. See you!

- *Thoughtful scheduling.* "I used to answer e-mail at the end of the day when I was tired, but it requires a lot of energy to do it well," says Alice Bredin. "Now I do it whenever I have 20 minutes free, as a break or a filler." I enjoy turning my computer on in the morning and seeing who sent me messages overnight. It warms up my mind to reply while my mug of coffee is waking up my body.

- *The Dave Barry solution.* I sent humorist Dave Barry an e-mail asking how he felt about being listed in Seth Godin's little book, *E-mail Addresses of the Rich and Famous.* Within minutes I received the answer: The account had been disconnected.

But Don't Over Control

You might suppose that a good way to keep your online activities manageable is to determine which tasks regularly produce results and to drop the others. In the next chapter, however, you'll learn why in the long run that might not be helpful. Of the following four kinds of online business tasks, all contribute to a thriving business:

1. Incoming business such as orders and requests for information

2. Research—receiving or gathering data, ideas, news, and perspectives that you can put to work in your business

3. Outgoing public marketing messages designed to attract business

4. Opportunity scouting

Ignoring #1 would be near-suicidal. Forgetting about #2 would mean falling out of date. Overlooking #3 would soon cause inquiries and sales to dry up. Yet neglecting #4, which seems the most remote category, might mean missing the biggest payoffs of all. To understand the importance of online exploration, read on.

22

Open Mind, Thriving Business

If you've ever run across conventional career counselors, you know that among their bag of tricks are questionnaires that ask you to fill in rows of spots with your number 2 pencil: Would you rather do A or B? Eventually you receive an assessment that explains why you, a lawyer, hate your profession. Your responses indicate that your most congenial careers, tied for first place, are: (1) hairdresser and (2) cleaning lady.

I have no such predictions in store for you, but I did notice numerous themes running through my interviews with people benefiting on a regular basis from their online activities. Apart from the techniques I have described in previous chapters, these people tended to share certain attitudes and leanings. The common threads weren't personality characteristics or abilities so much as basic operating assumptions, long-settled habits, and even philosophical approaches to life. If you find yourself fundamentally at odds with these assumptions, you'll have a harder time catching on and may conclude that getting business online isn't for you. But if you recognize yourself in this profile or are willing to try these attitudes on and put them into practice, you're likely to benefit more than others from your rambles through cyberspace.

Open Mind, Fluid Boundaries

Do you expect the unexpected? Not one person I spoke with mentioned specific goals, plans, quotas, or hopes governing their online participation. Instead of any fixed preconception of a payback from their time and money spent online, my successes talked of surprises, discoveries, and connections that zigzagged into an unanticipated type of deal. For example, when Robert Savage, an information broker specializing in international trade based in Woodstock, Vermont, joined an Italian forum, he sent an introduction to all three of the sysops thinking that perhaps he'd make a book of his about Italy available in the forum library. One of the sysops, a British publisher specializing in Italian themes, suggested putting the material into his magazine. Upon hearing about the magazine, Savage proposed becoming its distributor for the United States. And upon hearing more about the sysop's publishing company, Savage mentioned an unpublished novel he had written about Italy, which the publisher asked to review. "One thing leads to another," Savage told me with a smile in his voice.

The way in which people look for and find opportunities online resembles scouting more than hunting, browsing more than searching, and cruising more than driving. They have a relaxed, fuzzy focus rather than a sharply defined intention, and they're equally prepared to come out with nothing or with a coup worth celebrating. "It's an open-ended thing—maybe something good will come out of it, maybe not," Savage says. "You wait and see how things progress. There are a lot of dead ends—and a lot of deadbeats out there—but if only a few leads work out, you're ahead." Compare this with the pleas I've seen from marketing managers for hard-and-fast numbers they can use to bolster proposals to take their company online.

Are you curious? An inquiring mind can take you through some pretty interesting twists and turns. Robert Savage once saw a message about a well-known multilevel marketing company, planning expansion into Europe. Instead of going on to the next message with his reflexive recoil from multilevel marketing, he took the opportunity to ask what it was all about. "They put me in touch with someone higher up in the organization, to whom I happened to mention my CD-ROM project. A trip to Florida ensued to discuss it, and he's now scrambling around trying to find investors for it."

Similarly, Robert Bixby, an international marketing consultant based in Santa Cruz, California, told me about his delight at learning about a free source of international trade leads. "I did the download and worked the leads for quite a while, with no success," he says. "There was a little note, however, about a Chamber of Commerce in Russia newly online. I contacted them, we traded mail back and forth, and I ended up doing a research project for them. There hasn't been any work since, but Yuri and I stay in touch. I think it's mainly a matter of keeping your eyes open."

Do you trust your intuition? After his weekly chat session for professional speakers had run for a year, Wally Bock was unable to point to hard evidence that it was bringing in more subscribers to his newsletter, "Cyberpower Alert!," or paying off in some other concrete way. Yet he had no plans to discontinue the schmooze sessions. "My gut says it works—it's part of how I establish expertise," Bock says. "My invitation list has grown from 12 to 140 people, but there's really no way to quantify your relationships with people. That's what reputation is." When I mentioned to consultant Jeff Senné that the word "intuition" kept coming up in my interviews, he commented, "Intuitive people can take in the future and the past, and aren't stuck with the five senses or the way things are now. So it wouldn't surprise me if a great many of the people excited about the online world are intuitive." In a realm where A leads to Q and Q to C-squared, instincts may be a more reliable guide than logic.

Where will today's interactions lead you? If you're truly an Internet pioneer, you don't have the faintest idea.

Can you spot and act on opportunities? Here too entrepreneurs and professionals out on their own have an edge over employees who need layers of approval for each move. More than self-employment comes into play here. You could be "just" a solo accountant serving clients or an accountant who also publishes, becomes a partner in a software venture, and advises Hong Kong entrepreneurs on how to set up a Canadian branch office. I encountered many more of the latter type than the former during my research. It's less a matter of being multitalented than of having a flexible conception of business activities appropriate for you. Paulette Ensign doesn't see many of her colleagues in professional organizing getting as much out of being online as she does, some because they don't create products, others because "they spend untold hours giving advice and never toss out a lasso." If you have or would contemplate multiple income streams, the online world offers very promising fishing.

Are you willing to blaze a trail? So many marketing strategies for the online environment remain untried that you may need to go forward with the spirit of a pioneer. In 1993 Laura Fillmore acquired first serial rights to a story from Stephen King's new book, *Nightmares and Dreamscapes*, and offered it for sale on the Internet. The idea generated "a vast amount of smoke, a tremendous marketing boost for the printed book, lots of noise, but not enough in per-copy sales to pay for the phone bills for setting up the deal." Nevertheless, Fillmore regards the venture as a valuable learning experience that demonstrated a way to do things for which conditions weren't yet ripe. (In 2000, Stephen King again served as a publishing pioneer, offering a new story for sale in e-book formats, provoking half a million downloads in the first 48 hours.) "Who wants to be a sheep?" Fillmore adds. "The Internet is a meritocracy of the mind, where you can get recognition for your ideas and for doing something different. A company can spend millions there and get nothing back, but someone else can spend almost nothing and the word about it spreads everywhere."

FAST FACTS

The Value of Listening

"Good products and services are co-created," says Kevin Kelly, author of *New Rules for the New Economy.* "The desires of customers grow out of what is possible, and what is possible is made real by companies following new customer desires."

Two of my own services grew out of vague customer requests: "I want to learn how to do what you do so well," one woman told me, and I created a marketing training program for her that proved successful, and with continual modifications, for others too.

When I announced seminars in the Boston area in my weekly Marketing Minute, several subscribers asked, "Isn't there some way you can present the seminar virtually?" Thus emerged a series of teleclasses—telephone seminars.

Do you value accessibility? A perennial query in the business forums concerns Jay Abraham, a marketing consultant who runs $5,000 to $20,000 seminars and charges $3,000 an hour for private advice. Is he worth it or is he not worth it—opinions fly back and forth so regularly that I began to wish Abraham himself would show up to give the masses a taste of his caviar-class talent. But when I thought about it more, it became clear to me that staying out of reach bolstered his ability to remain one of the world's most highly paid consultants. The same goes for those who pride themselves on being a well-kept secret. If you like or depend on working behind closed doors, electronic schmoozing—or online anything—probably isn't worth your time.

Can you accept the reality of intangibles? Plenty of people steadily cash in on good will, reputation, and word of mouth, without knowing exactly which former client's praise, which publicity appearance, which third-hand mention influenced someone new to buy. Chris Brandlon, who formerly worked with Jay Abraham, disagreed with my reasoning in the previous paragraph, giving another reason certain people reject online schmoozing. "Since there's no way of quantifying the net impact on one's business of a typical talk show appearance, media release, or online forum participation, there is no basis for asserting that this is a productive way to build a business. It's not that Jay Abraham is trying to maintain a 'Man Behind the Curtain' facade, it's that 'getting his name out' is a 'soft, fuzzy' concept that cannot be tallied and costed on a per- basis, giving him a clear picture as to whether a piece of programming in question is working." (See Figure 22.1.) Well, the means may not be quantifiable, but the greenbacks earned by the people I've quoted in this book were real enough!

Do you subscribe to the motto, "Nothing ventured, nothing gained"? Or to "It never hurts to ask"? Many of my sources showed a definite tendency to reach for the long shot. Stamps journalist/entrepreneur Dick Sine once described an idea online very roughly and almost tongue-in-check said he'd like to find some investors. The next day he received a private message from a man who said he might indeed want to invest $10,000 in the project. Likewise, consultant/ speaker Nikki Sweet sometimes searches online directories for CEOs whose names she has encountered in her reading. When she couldn't get through to one of these CEOs by phone, she e-mailed him and

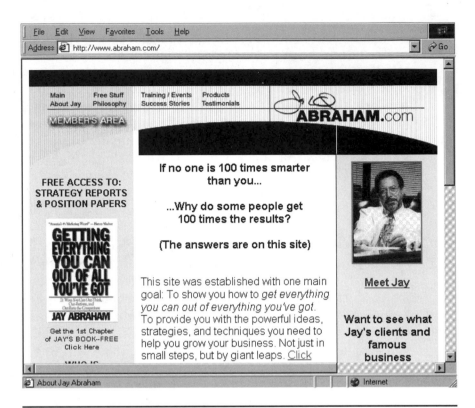

Figure 22.1. Jay Abraham does have a Web site after all.

received a reply the next day along the lines of "Wow, isn't this e-mail a great invention? The answer to your question is, please feel free to call me any time, here's my private telephone number."

Do you proceed in a spirit of contribution and reward? Lary Crews, for instance (see Chapter 7), focused on making a contribution above cashing in. Reasonably enough, however, he wasn't willing to subsidize his volunteering indefinitely, and a fairer arrangement came his way because the nature of his contribution became so clear. In a myriad of ways, the interactive spirit of the online world rewards givers, not takers.

Are you patient? Copywriter Al Bredenberg of Cornwall, Connecticut, says that business sometimes develops more slowly on the Internet than in the traditional business world. "People contacting me online want help with concepts and may not have a specific project in mind. It takes a lot more discussion before we get something definite going. In contrast, when someone calls in response to one of my ads in an industry journal or directory, that usually leads to immediate work. On the Net, inquiries are also more likely to come from out in left field, like a guy asking me if I can help him sell king salmon on the Net. I kind of like that."

Do you get a kick out of trying new things? Computer consultant Lawrence Seldin of East Patchogue, New York, decided to use his vacation to master the procedure of posting to Internet newsgroups. "The very first night, I got 20 book orders from the Internet," he told me, still amazed months later. "I couldn't quite understand what was happening, but my mailbox was filling up with orders for my book, *Power Tips for the Apple Newton*." He had just as much fun posting to forums where he happened to be interested in the topic, such as journalism, and having people ask him upon seeing his signature line if he did consulting. "I got several clients that way, from hanging around places I enjoy," Seldin says. This is decidedly different from the attitude, "I'd better find three new paying clients this month—or else!" A relaxed approach not only fosters success in online marketing, I believe, but also makes it likelier that you'll stick with it.

FAST FACTS

"Give, Then Take"

John Audette, moderator of the invaluable I-Sales discussion list, counts the principle "Give, then take" as one of 16 key factors in his financial success.

In the early days of the Web, Audette had created a list of the Top 100 places to register a site, which his company implemented for clients for $295. One day someone said he couldn't afford the fee, and could he have the list to perform the registrations himself?

Audette took a deep breath and made the list publicly available. Traffic skyrocketed, and the number of clients wanting to pay his company to register their sites for him also exploded.

"The concept of `give, then take' is pretty well known now. But we felt pretty brave using it in those early wild and woolly Internet days," Audette says.

Planning for Success

I don't want to leave the impression that online marketing is all haphazard serendipity. Despite the unpredictability, you need a focused plan of action. A good way to begin developing such a plan would be to reread this book, notebook in hand, listing tactics and approaches that might make sense for your business. Keeping your overall marketing goals in mind, translate those possibilities into a series of action steps. For instance, after noodling around on the Internet for several months, copywriter Al Bredenberg formulated a plan that in part read like this:

Goals

- To increase client base through new Internet marketing efforts.

- To develop a new service as a writer of Internet marketing messages.

- To serve business and industry by providing information in my areas of expertise.

Ongoing Activities

- Participate in forums and discussion groups, as a way to provide information, make contacts, and promote my services.

- Set up an affordable World Wide Web page and e-mail capabilities to disseminate my marketing presence.

- Prepare a series of free reports as a service and as a soft-sell marketing effort. Find ways to distribute these reports and make them available online.

- Regularly initiate discussions and dialogue that increase exposure by raising questions, conducting surveys, participating in discussions, etc.

- Develop organized methods to follow up leads, respond to inquiries, keep site information up to date, etc.

- Evaluate and test the success of the efforts.

If you haven't yet gone online at all, here is one way to proceed step by step toward a successful online marketing program.

1. Sign up for a trial membership with a service that's friendly to newcomers, such as America Online.

2. Learn how to send and receive e-mail, read bulletin board messages, post messages, download files, and surf the Web.

3. Formulate your online marketing goals, including the occupations, interests, age groups, geographical groups, and so on of prospects you wish to reach. After reviewing this book, list possible ways of achieving those goals.

4. Prepare and refine any materials you'll need for your marketing efforts, such as Web copy, a signature file, articles to distribute, or an electronic sales letter or follow-up piece, and make any necessary technical arrangements, such as with an Internet provider or Web hosting service.

5. Implement your plan, and give it at least four months before evaluating results.

Although I can't give you help on technical questions, I can coach you on strategy and help you develop online lures that work. I can also help you achieve publicity in paper or broadcast media for your online programs. If you became intrigued by the creative marketing perspectives I've expressed throughout this book, you'll enjoy my free weekly e-mail newsletter, "The Marketing Minute." To sign up, send an e-mail to *majordomo@world.std.com* with the message: *subscribe marketing* (the subject line doesn't matter). Or just send me a personal e-mail asking me to sign you up.

Remember, please visit the Web site exclusively for readers of this book at *http://www.maxpress.com* for regularly updated additional resources and to find out more about the $500 A Year Club and its publicity opportunities.

Here's how to find out more about my coaching services, seminars, audiotapes, books, and other offerings. I'd also love to hear about how you implemented the ideas in this book.

By mail: *Marcia Yudkin*
P.O. Box 1310
Boston, MA 02117

By phone: *(617) 266-1613*

By e-mail: *marcia@yudkin.com*

Web: *http://www.yudkin.com/marketing.htm*

Courage, and good luck!

Appendix A: Glossary

@ Pronounced "at," this symbol appears in e-mail addresses to separate someone's log-in name from the name of his or her Internet service provider or his or her domain name.

acronyms, online Any unfamiliar group of capital letters you encounter online might be one of these. For instance, BTW means "by the way," PMJI means "pardon me for jumping in," and TIA "thanks in advance." Unless you deliberately want to make "newbies" feel unwelcome, don't use these yourself.

AOL Common abbreviation for America Online, a popular online service especially friendly to Internet newcomers.

article What Internet newsgroups call a posted message.

ASCII Pronounced "askee," this stands for American Standard Code for Information Interchange and denotes a standard set of 128 characters that can be recognized and displayed by any computer, whether a Macintosh, IBM-compatible, or mainframe. Pure ASCII text includes only the letters and numbers on a standard computer keyboard and a few more generic symbols and commands, but no special codes used only by a specific program.

autoresponder Also called a mailbot, this signifies an e-mail address programmed to automatically return a fixed marketing message to anyone who corresponds with it. Convenient—but make sure you have a "live" e-mail address too where you personally respond to questions or requests.

banner ad Rectangular graphical ad designed to lure Web site visitors from one site to another.

baud rate Usually used interchangeably (wrongly so, the experts say) with bps, this indicates the sending and receiving speed of a modem. 9600 baud is much faster than 300 baud. Some online services have different telephone access numbers for different baud rates.

BBS The universal nickname for Bulletin Board System, a small-scale and often noncommercial version of the commercial online services, frequently operated as a hobby or home business. Most offer users files, message boards, and live chat. BBSs are almost obsolete, overshadowed by the Internet.

binary files   In contrast to ASCII files, binary files include graphics, programs, or codes specific to a particular program, such as WordPerfect or Lotus 1-2-3. If you attempt to read a binary file in your word processor, it will look like a bunch of nonsense. Avoid e-mailing or posting binary files unless you're sure your recipient or target audience knows what to do with them.

bit   Short for "binary digit," this is the 0 or 1, or on/off electrical state, that comprises the basic unit of information for computers. Eight bits make up a byte.

bps   Bits per second. A measurement that shows how many bits a modem can transfer in a second. In 2001, 56,000 bps is considered fast for a phone-line connection, 14,400 bps slow, and 2400 bps painfully slow for file transfers, although 2400 bps is plenty fast for real-time online conversation.

browser   A program such as Netscape, Internet Explorer, or lynx that allows you to visit sites and read information on the World Wide Web.

bulletin board   This can mean either a special-interest discussion group on a commercial service, as on Prodigy, or a standalone electronic bulletin board system.

byte   Eight bits, or the number of basic units of computer information that convey an alphabetical letter (01000001 equals "a," for instance). Larger units of information are measured in kilobytes (a thousand bytes), megabytes (a million bytes), and so on.

cancelbot   A program used by cyberspace vigilantes to delete messages throughout Usenet from posters deemed to be abusing their Internet privileges.

chat   Interacting online with at least one other party who is also logged in and typing away at that time. Also called live conferencing.

client   In the computer world, this may not mean a person or company you provide services for but a computer that connects to a remote computer somewhere else (a server or host), which contains files and programs that the first computer can then use. The person working at the client computer can then perform functions as if that remote computer were sitting on his or her desk.

compressed files   As the word suggests, computer files can be squished so that they take up less storage space. To use them, though, you then have to unsquish them, with a program such as PKUNZIP or Uncompress.

conference Either a live group chat session online or, as with the Great Britain–based CIX service, a special-interest message board or forum.

cyberspace A term coined by science fiction writer William Gibson that denotes the nonphysical universe in which those networked by computers and modems feel they are interacting.

content Computer jargon for articles or other text.

dialup account An account that gives you inexpensive access to the Internet by means of the much larger computer of your Internet service provider.

directory A free service providing a topical index of Web sites searchable by subject. The most popular Web directory is Yahoo!.

domain name The part of an Internet e-mail address that specifies the organization of a user. For instance, in nightly@nbc.com, "nbc.com" is the domain name for the National Broadcasting Company; ".com" shows that it is a commercial organization. If you hanker for your own domain name, apply for one through your Internet service provider.

DOS Disk Operating System, or the set of commands designed to perform basic functions on older IBM-compatible computers. If a software program is DOS-based, you'll probably start it from a screen prompt that looks something like C:\>.

downloading In contrast to uploading, downloading involves transferring files from a remote computer to your own.

e-commerce Buying and selling directly on the Internet.

e-mail Electronic mail—private messages sent almost instantaneously from one computer user to another. They are easy to reply to, forward, or save.

e-mail newsletter Messages sent out on a regular basis via e-mail to a group of subscribers.

electronic book A collection of information organized attractively on a disk or for download in an Adobe Acrobat file. Sometimes abbreviated as e-book.

emoticon Combinations of traditional typewriter symbols used to convey emotions, such as ;-) for winking or :-O for surprise (turn your head sideways and you'll get it). Some businesspeople (like me) consider these hokey and clichéd.

encryption   Computerized coding of a message to conceal its meaning so that only authorized recipients can read it. Currently the U.S. government considers some digital encryption tools "munitions" and controls their export.

e-zine   A magazine or newsletter delivered periodically by e-mail.

FAQ   Frequently Asked Questions—a digest of common questions and their answers. Usenet "newbies" are supposed to retrieve and read these to prevent wasting the time and taxing the patience of the regulars. You can write one yourself on any subject and allow it to propagate throughout the Internet.

firewall   A security system for organizational computer networks designed to control the ability of outsiders to access proprietary information or perform other mischief in the system from afar.

flaming   Internet jargon for electronically hurling insults and verbal abuse at people deemed idiotic, obtuse, annoying, or depraved. When lots of people get into the act, it becomes a "flame fest."

forum   An online special-interest group with message boards, libraries of information, and conference facilities.

frames   Devices that display multiple documents simultaneously on the user's screen.

Freenet   A no-charge public gateway to the Internet.

freeware   Software or electronic text packets that can be downloaded, distributed, and used for free. Contrasts with shareware, which is free for trial purposes only.

FTP   Acronym for file transfer protocol. A command-based system for fetching files from remote locations on the Internet.

Gopher   A menu-based system for reading or fetching text files from anywhere on the Internet. Much easier to use than FTP, but largely rendered obsolete by the World Wide Web.

handle   Virtually all chat systems, most Internet providers, and some commercial online services allow you to select a nickname by which you'll be known. Your real name may or may not be available for discovery.

home page   An electronic set of text and graphics that you can post about your business via the World Wide Web and link to others' home pages anywhere on the Internet. At a large Web site, this term denotes the page most people would visit first.

hosting service   See *Web hosting service*.

hotspot   A link on the World Wide Web that when clicked, sends the user to another site.

HTML Hypertext markup language, the coding system that produces World Wide Web pages.

hypertext A nonlinear system of nesting information that allows you to find out more about certain items if and only if you're interested. On the World Wide Web, hypertext links can transport you with just a mouse click from one site to another.

interface The visual and functional façade with which you interact via your computer screen. When a service has "improved its interface," that means they have made it more attractive on screen and easier to use.

Internet The international network of computer networks that links organizations and individuals on every continent, including Antarctica. Although the United States Department of Defense created much of its initial infrastructure and procedures, no one now owns or governs the Internet.

Internet Explorer A browser created by Microsoft.

Internet Service Provider, or ISP A company providing access to the Internet for its subscribers, usually in exchange for a monthly fee.

link A function that takes a user with just one click from one page on the World Wide Web to another that may be based in a computer system ten thousand miles away.

log on, log in To start a session on a computer service by entering your account number and password. When you're finished, you log off, of course.

lurker Someone who reads messages regularly without actively participating.

lynx A program available through many older Internet providers that allows you to browse text on the World Wide Web. In the place of pictures you'll see something like [IMAGE].

mailbot An electronic mailbox programmed to do something automatically with all incoming messages, such as sending back a canned set of information or forwarding the mail to another address. Also called an autoresponder.

mailing list On the Internet, a system for exchanging ideas on a given topic by sending discussion notes to a central location for e-mail distribution to subscribers to the list. Some mailing lists have a moderator who screens contributions; others are unmoderated. It's best to "lurk" in a mailing list first before participating.

merchant credit card account An arrangement that enables you to accept credit cards for payment.

meta-tag   Special information encoded into a Web page so that it is properly classified and indexed by search engines.

modem   Short for modulator–demodulator, this is a telecommunications device that is either installed within your computer or attached outside it and that connects your computer to others via telephone or cable lines.

moderated   A newsgroup or mailing list where contributions are screened for relevance and informational (versus promotional) content.

navigation   The process of getting around from one part of a World Wide Web site to another.

Net   The affectionate nickname for the Internet.

Netiquette   Desirable and acceptable behavior on the Internet.

Netscape   A popular browser that enables you to view images and text on the World Wide Web.

newbies   A not-so-affectionate nickname for newcomers to the Internet.

newsgroup   A special-interest message area on the section of the Internet known as Usenet, similar to a forum or bulletin board.

newsreader   A program that allows you to sort through, choose for reading, reply to, and forward messages in Internet newsgroups.

offline reader   A program, often created by a third party, that saves you online time and money by enabling you to log on, grab your messages, and log off for you to read them at your leisure.

online service   A subscription-based service that you can connect with via modem for news, games, information, forums, and more. Usually you pay a monthly access fee and extra for the hours you spend online.

page   Words and images placed on the World Wide Web that can be viewed from top to bottom by visitors without clicking on any links.

plug-in   Any file that a visitor to a Web site needs in addition to a browser in order to properly view or experience a site.

post   To send a message for public viewing to a newsgroup, forum, or mailing list (each defined above).

protocol   A specific set of rules with which two computers can communicate.

real time   Pronounced with emphasis on "real." The mode in which events such as online conversation actually occur, as opposed to the delayed communication of e-mail or message boards.

roundtable Another word for an online special-interest group.

scroll What text does when it moves up and then off the computer screen. On CompuServe, scroll rate is the rate at which new messages force old ones off the board.

search engine A site that gives you access to much of the material on the World Wide Web (and sometimes Usenet as well) by typing in subject words or proper names.

server A "master computer" that provides information services to other computers called clients that dial into it.

service provider An organization that, usually for a fee, connects you to the Internet. Many service providers offer additional services such as getting you a domain name, setting up mailbots, and providing storage space for your World Wide Web pages.

shareware "Try-before-you-pay" software, much of which equals in quality better-financed "pay-first" commercial software.

signature Standard sign-off you create to use as boilerplate for the close of your Usenet, mailing list, or forum postings. Affectionately called a "sig file."

site An area on the World Wide Web maintained by an individual or a company, comprising one or hundreds or even thousands of pages.

smiley A picture composed of punctuation marks to be read sideways (e.g., :-(), which many people use online to perform the function of tone of voice or facial expression.

snail mail Postal, paper-and-envelope-type mail.

spamming The widely despised practice of mass posting an advertisement in irrelevant newsgroups on the Internet. Also, the sending of commercial e-mail to masses of people who have not requested it. The term originated in a Monty Python comedy skit before Big Business discovered the Internet—but the flaming you'll get if you try it won't be funny.

sysop Short for system operator, a person in charge of an online area, either a forum or a section of a forum.

telnet A service program that allows users to log onto the Internet by modem or use a remote computer site on the Net. Also called remote log-in.

thread In newsgroups and forums (both above), a series of replies to an initial post, organized in chronological order in isolation from other threads.

UNIX The user-unfriendly operating system of most Internet server computers.

upload   The opposite operation to downloading, uploading involves transferring files from your own computer to a remote computer system, usually to make them available for others to read and/or use.

URL   Universal Resource Locator—an "address" on the World Wide Web that begins with *http://*.

Usenet   The anarchic collection of special-interest newsgroups on the Internet.

virtual   Not physical in nature. A virtual bank has an e-mail address instead of walk-up tellers; a virtual corporation provides services to clients without physical interaction among its members.

virus   A mischievous or malicious program embedded within another one that wreaks mild to catastrophic damage on your computer after you "catch" it (download and use it).

Web   Nickname for the World Wide Web.

Web hosting service   A company that houses Web sites for a fee on its servers.

Web ring   A group of Web sites on a particular topic that offer links to one another in a circular fashion.

Windows   The mouse-based Microsoft operating system for IBM-compatible personal computers.

World Wide Web   The multimedia section of the Internet, through which you can navigate without learning special commands. Since 1994, it has been exploding in popularity.

Appendix B: Resources

Note: In addition to the following resources, please visit the special Web site created exclusively for readers of this book, at *http://www.maxpress.com*, where I will post updated recommended resources and where you can join and learn from other members of the $500 A Year Club.

Getting Started on the Internet

- Crumlish, Christian, *The Internet for Busy People*. New York, Osborne Publishing, 1999. Don't be fooled by the full-color graphics: This is a well-organized, breezy tutorial on all the major Internet functions, chock-full of solid tips. Highly recommended for beginners.

- Lewart, Cass R., *The Ultimate Modem Handbook: Your Guide to Selection, Installation, Troubleshooting & Optimization*. Englewood Cliffs, NJ, Prentice Hall, 1997. Stumped about how to choose a modem or get yours back up and running? Includes compatibility and troubleshooting tips and pros and cons of cable, cellular, and wireless modems.

- Pfaffenberger, Bryan, *The Usenet Book: Finding, Using and Surviving Newsgroups on the Internet*. Reading, MA, Addison-Wesley, 1995. If you're interested in exploring the still-lively backwaters of Usenet, this book can save you a lot of frustration. Most valuable features: exactly how to master newsreader programs; list of newsgroups with archived info available; eye-opening reviews of more than 300 specific newsgroups—but only one focused on business.

- *Yahoo! Internet Life*. General-interest, nontechnical magazine that can help you understand and appreciate what's available online. For subscription info: 303-665-8930; *http://www.yil.com*.

On Internet Marketing and Sales

- *Business 2.0.* Magazine with nontechnical features on what companies (mostly well-financed, larger operations) are doing on the Web to make money. Articles on trends and online marketing challenges as well. For subscription info: 800-234-0804; *http://www.business2.com.*

- Easton, Jaclyn, *StrikingItRich.com: Profiles of 23 Incredibly Successful Websites You've Probably Never Heard Of.* New York, McGraw-Hill, 1999. Highly readable case histories of Web businesses in a range of industries, complete with amounts of investment and return.

- Helmstetter, Greg, *Increasing Hits and Selling More on Your Web Site.* New York, John Wiley & Sons, 1997. Sound strategies for making your Web site a success. Covers submitting to search engines, soliciting links, buying and selling ads, using e-mail effectively for promotion, and more.

- *Industry Standard, The.* My favorite print magazine, focused on Internet companies and trends. A good read. Subscription information: 800-395-1977; *http://www.thestandard.com.*

- Janal, Daniel S., *Dan Janal's Guide to Marketing on the Internet: Getting People to Visit, Buy and Become Customers for Life.* New York, John Wiley & Sons, 2000. Step by step, how to put your company online. Emphasizes product sales and serving shoppers. Strong on World Wide Web marketing and public relations possibilities.

- Kelly, Kevin, *New Rules for the New Economy.* New York, Penguin USA, 1999. From the editor of *Wired* magazine, ten generalizations and examples of how the Internet economy works. Highly recommended.

- Kinnard, Shannon, *Marketing With E-Mail.* Gulf Breeze, FL, Maximum Press, 2000. A spam-free guide to increasing sales and awareness while building customer loyalty. Topics include e-mail newsletters, on-line networking, signature files, and e-mail promotions.

- Pirillo, Chris, *Poor Richard's E-mail Publishing: Creating Newsletters, Bulletins, Discussion Groups, and Other Powerful Communication Tools*. Lakewood, CO, Top Floor Publishing, 1999. Eye-opening case studies and resources for running your own e-zine, e-mail newsletter, or discussion list. Technical and strategic tips, too. Highly recommended.

- Silverstein, Barry, *Business-to-Business Internet Marketing*. Gulf Breeze, FL, Maximum Press, 2000. Excellent, in-depth treatment of how to generate leads, sell online, and serve customers through a Web site and e-mail.

- Sweeney, Susan, C. A., *101 Ways to Promote Your Web Site*. Gulf Breeze, FL, Maximum Press, 2000. Filled with proven Internet marketing tips, tools, techniques, and resources to increase your Web site traffic.

- Zimmerman, Jan, *Marketing on the Internet*. Gulf Breeze, FL, Maximum Press, 2000. A seven-step plan for selling your products, services, and image to millions over the information superhighway.

On Marketing in General

- Caples, John, *Tested Advertising Methods*, fourth edition. Englewood Cliffs, NJ, Prentice Hall Trade, 1998. Dated examples, but timeless and deliciously specific advice on copywriting that gets results.

- Ott, Richard, *Creating Demand: Move the Masses to Buy Your Product, Service, or Idea*. Burr Ridge, IL, Symmetric Systems Inc, 1999. Whether you're selling online or traditionally, read this book to understand the psychological underpinnings of buying behavior.

- RoAne, Susan, *The Secrets of Savvy Networking*. New York, Warner, 1993. Highly readable, humorous, and sensible guide to making business connections face to face. Much of RoAne's advice applies online as well.

- Yudkin, Marcia, *Six Steps to Free Publicity—And Dozens of Other Ways to Win Free Media Attention for You or Your Business*. New York, Plume/Penguin, 1994. Practical tips for making your business newsworthy and getting print or broadcast publicity without spending a bundle. Learn how to write and send news releases and deal effectively with reporters.

Web Design Guides

- Flanders, Vincent, and Michael Willis, *Web Pages that Suck: Learn Good Design by Looking at Bad Design*. Alameda, CA, Sybex, 1998. Entertaining, educational course in the do's of Web design by highlighting the don'ts. Abundant full-color screen shots drive the lessons home.

- Kent, Peter, *Poor Richard's Web Site: Geek-Free, Commonsense Advice on Building a Low-Cost Web Site,* Second Edition. Lakewood, CO, Top Floor Productions, 2000. Massive resources for building a Web site on your own, from someone who understands the technical challenges involved and explains everything step by step. Lots of free programs and services listed that do the job of commercial counterparts costing thousands of dollars.

- Morris, Mary E. S. and Randy J. Hinrichs, *Web Page Design*. Mountain View, CA, Prentice Hall, 1996. Excellent discussion of Web site structure, with lots of planning aids for useful navigation and content.

- Nielsen, Jakob, *Designing Web Usability*. Indianapolis, IN, New Riders Publishing, 2000. Brilliant, eye-opening Web design guidelines and commentary from a world-famous usability guru. A smart educational investment!

- Parker, Roger, *Guide to Web Content and Design*. Foster City, CA, Hungry Minds, 1997. Accessible, helpful overview of principles of Web design for nondesigners. The color shots of Web sites are especially illuminating.

- Williams, Robin, and John Tollett, *The Non-Designer's Web Book*, Second Edition. Berkeley, CA, Peachpit Press, 2000. Read this book not for the technical instructions (which it has in abundance) but for the unusually clear, persuasive explanations of what makes for visually pleasing Web sites.

Online Law

- Bick, Jonathan, *101 Things You Need to Know about Internet Law*. New York, Three Rivers Press, 2000. Nuanced, readable answers from an attorney to questions about Internet contracts, online privacy, domain names, digital signatures, linking, and more.

- Cavazos, Edward A., and Gavino Morin, *Cyberspace and the Law: Your Rights and Duties in the On-Line World*. Cambridge, MA, MIT Press, 1994. Compact, readable summaries of American legal issues concerning contracts, copyright, libel, obscenity, and crimes involving computer networks. Contains the full text of the U.S. Electronic Communications Privacy Act and other federal and state laws covering computer rights and crimes.

- Rose, Lance, *Netlaw: Your Rights in the Online World*. Berkeley, CA, Osborne/McGraw-Hill, 1995. Illuminating, in-depth window on the culture and legal controversies of cyberspace. Essential reading if you host a forum or moderate any online area; highly recommended for others.

General Reflections on Cyberspace

- Heim, Michael, *The Metaphysics of Virtual Reality*. New York, Oxford University Press, 1993. I don't know where else you'll find Heidegger (twentieth-century German philosopher) and hypertext on the same page. Philosophical reflections on the way we experience computer technology.

- Kroker, Arthur, and Michael A. Weinstein, *Data Trash: The Theory of the Virtual Class*. New York, St. Martin's Press, 1994. "In the beginning was the Word, but in the end there is only the data byte." A hip exploration of digital life, but don't venture in unless you enjoy portentous combinations of five-syllable words.

- Levine, Rick, Christopher Locke, Doc Searls, and David Weinberger, *The Cluetrain Manifesto: The End of Business As Usual*. Cambridge, MA, Perseus Books, 2000. "Markets are conversations," say these four experienced Internet observers, who explain how business as conversation turns Big Business as usual upside down. Provocative.

- Stoll, Clifford, *Silicon Snake Oil: Second Thoughts on the Information Highway*. New York, Anchor, 1996. From an Internetter of 15 years, reflections on cyberspace as an illusory nonplace and on the addictive glut of unnecessary online information. "Life in the real world is far more interesting, far more important, far richer than anything you'll ever find on a computer screen."

- *Wired*. The relentlessly neon color scheme of this monthly magazine fooled me for years. Not until I encountered back issues archived online did I realize it carries seminal articles about the legal, social, and economic implications of technology. For subscription info: 800-769-4733; *http://www.hotwired.com*.

Internet Marketing Discussion Lists

- I-Advertising. Discussion of online advertising: *http://www.internetadvertising.org*

- I-Content. Discussion of creating, selling, buying, and distributing content online: *http://www.adventive.com/lists/icontent/*

- I-PR. Discussion of online and offline public relations: *http://www.adventive.com/lists/ipr/*

- I-Sales. Discussion of online sales and marketing techniques and philosophy: *http://www.adventive.com/lists/isales/*

- Online Ads. Discussion of online advertising: *http://www.o-a.com*

Service Providers

- America Online. Toll free in the United States and Canada: 800-827-6364; phone: 703-448-8700; *http://www.aol.com.*

- CompuServe Information Service. Toll free in the United States and Canada: 800-848-8990; phone: 614-529-1340; fax: 614-529-1610; toll free in United Kingdom: 0800-289-458; *http://www.compuserve.com.*

- Prodigy Service. Toll free in the United States and Canada: 800-776-3449; *http://www.prodigy.com.*

- Directory of 9000+ Internet service providers: *http://thelist.iworld.com.*

- Directories of Web hosting services:

    http://www.budgetweb.com/budgetweb/

    http://www.hostsearch.com

    http://www.tophosts.com

    http://www.webhostdir.com

Online Tools and Resources

- Top search engines and directories:

    http://www.altavista.com

    http://www.dmoz.org

    http://www.excite.com

    http://www.go.com

    http://www.hotbot.com

    http://www.looksmart.com

    http://www.lycos.com

    http://www.webcrawler.com

    http://www.yahoo.com

- Master list of other search engines and directories:

    http://www.searchenginecolossus.com

    http://www.searchpower.com

- Information on search engine rankings:

    http://www.searchenginetalk.com

    http://www.searchenginewatch.com

- Internet marketing educational resources:

    http://www.clickz.com

    http://www.emarketer.com

http://www.wilsonweb.com

- Directories of Web rings:

    http://www.webring.yahoo.com

    http://www.ringsurf.com

- Autoresponder services:

    http://www.fastreply.com

    http://www.getresponse.com

    http://www.realreply.com

- Web design and marketing tips:

    http://www.mydesktop.com

    http://www.sitepoint.com

    http://www.webmonkey.com

    http://www.webdeveloper.com

- Merchant credit card services:

    http://www.charge.com

    http://www.acceptcreditcards.com

- Information for vendors on online fraud:

    http://www.scambusters.org

    http://www.fraud.org/ifw.htm

- Mailing list/discussion list/e-mail newsletter services:

  http://www.ecircle-uk.com

  http://groups.yahoo.com

  http://www.listbot.com

  http://www.sparklist.com

- Access to newsgroups' current and past postings:

  http://groups.google.com

- Directories of Internet mailing lists:

  http://catalog.com/vivian/interest-group-search.html

  http://paml.alastra.com

  http://tile.net/lists

  http://www.topica.com

- Directories of FAQs (Frequently Asked Questions):

  http://www.faqs.org

- Online publicity tools:

  http://www.ereleases.com

  http://www.imediafax.com

  http://www.newsbureau.com

  http://www.pressbox.co.uk

http://www.pressreleasenetwork.com

http://www.prweb.com

- Free goodies for your Web site:

    http://www.conferenceroom.com/backpack.shtml

    http://www.coolboard.com/index.cfm

    http://www.everyone.net/main/html/community_tour.html

    http://www.freesticky.com

    http://www.isyndicate.com

    http://www.moreover.com

    http://www.picosearch.com

About the Author

Author, consultant, and seminar leader Marcia Yudkin helps business owners around the world gain attention for their businesses and themselves creatively and cost-effectively.

Through her initiative, her book *Marketing Online* became the first book published by Penguin USA to have a Web site and became a featured book at the 1995 Frankfort Book Fair, the publishing industry's annual international exhibition.

Her nine other books include *Six Steps to Free Publicity, Persuading on Paper*, and *Freelance Writing for Magazines & Newspapers*. She writes a syndicated column, "Marketing Matters," distributed by Paradigm News, serves as the moderator of the I-Content discussion list, and delivers occasional commentaries on WBUR, the National Public Radio station in Boston.

Despite online marketing prowess that has brought her bucketloads of clients and opportunities, Marcia Yudkin does not love computers. She says she'd rather read an old-fashioned book any day than learn to use new software.

If you would like to contact the author, you can reach her at the following:

E-mail address: *marcia@yudkin.com*

Web site: *http://www.yudkin.com/marketing.htm*

Mail: *Marcia Yudkin*
Creative Ways
P.O. Box 1310
Boston MA 02117
USA

Index

Reader Feedback Sheet

Your comments and suggestions are very important in shaping future publications. Please email us at *moreinfo@maxpress.com* or photocopy this page, jot down your thoughts, and fax it to (850) 934-9981 or mail it to:

Maximum Press

Attn: Jim Hoskins

605 Silverthorn Road

Gulf Breeze, FL 32561

_____

_____

_____

_____

_____

_____

_____

_____

_____

_____

_____

_____

_____

_____

_____

_____

_____

_____

_____

*101 Ways to Promote
Your Web Site,
Second Edition*
by Susan Sweeney, C.A.
552 pages
$29.95
ISBN: 1-885068-45-X

*Marketing
With E-Mail,
Second Edition*
by Shannon Kinnard
352 pages
$29.95
ISBN: 1-885068-51-4

*Business-to-Business
Internet Marketing,
Third Edition*
by Barry Silverstein
528 pages
$29.95
ISBN: 1-885068-50-6

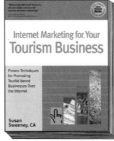

*Marketing on
the Internet,
Fifth Edition*
by Jan Zimmerman
512 pages
$34.95
ISBN: 1-885068-49-2

*Internet Marketing
for Information
Technology
Companies*
by Barry Silverstein
464 pages
$39.95
ISBN: 1-885068-46-8

*Internet Marketing
for Your Tourism
Business*
by Susan Sweeney, C.A.
592 pages
$39.95
ISBN: 1-885068-47-6

*Building Intranets
with Lotus Notes &
Domino 5.0,
Third Edition*
by Steve Krantz
320 pages
$39.95
ISBN: 1-885068-41-7

*Internet Marketing for
Less Than $500/Year*
by Marcia Yudkin
334 pages
$29.95
ISBN: 1-885068-52-2

To purchase a Maximum Press book, visit your local bookstore
or call 1-800-989-6733 (US) or 1-850-934-4583 (International)
online ordering available at *www.maxpress.com*

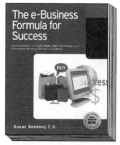

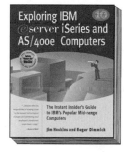